# The Swordfish Hunters

# THE SWORDFISH HUNTERS

*The History and Ecology of an Ancient American Sea People*

BRUCE BOURQUE

BUNKER HILL PUBLISHING

*for Diane Chase*

www.bunkerhillpublishing.com
by Bunker Hill Publishing Inc.
285 River Road, Piermont
New Hampshire 03779, USA

10 9 8 7 6 5 4 3 2 1


Library of Congress Control Number: 2012937196

ISBN 9781593730383

Designed by Joe Lops
Printed in China

# Contents

# List of Figures

# Acknowledgments

THE PROBLEMS DISCUSSED here have perplexed Northeastern archaeologists for five generations. Many of us have had pet theories. I set mine forth in this book. Most of our theories have not been in even partial agreement, and yet, I do not recall many instances where those of us who have studied this population let our different theories become unkind words directed against each other. Rather, I sense that we have made common cause in the struggle for understanding. Better, we have benefited greatly from our many conversations, in person and in print, about the Red Paint People.

To a significant extent, this book seeks to overcome a museological challenge. Pulling together the far-flung, often forgotten elements that made it possible required the help of many people. It began when Stephen Williams, my graduate advisor and mentor, arranged for a slate bayonet from one of C. C. Willoughby's early excavations to be transferred from Harvard's Peabody Museum to the new Maine State Museum in 1980. It accelerated during the 1980s, when Mike Gramly took on the challenge of gathering the necessary collections for the museum's archaeology exhibit hall, Twelve Thousand Years in Maine, which opened in 1991. Brian Robinson's diligent search for lost collections, which became an important part of his dissertation completed in 2001, and his close attention to radiocarbon dating and stone tool typology changed my perception of the Red Paint People. All these moving parts were ably coordinated by my laboratory and collections manager, Bob Lewis, who also supplied much of the photography that appears here.

But none of these efforts would have come to fruition without the encouragement of Ib Bellew and Carole Kitchell of Bunker Hill Publishing, who several years ago asked me to write this book. Also critical was the support of state archivist David Cheever, who gave me access to the Odiorne Fund, which supports archaeological archiving and publication, and to Maine State Archives photographer Peter Mallow, who provided excellent imaging services.

To all, I owe thanks for a book that has been building in me for four decades.

# Preface

IN 1700, SIGISMOND HERTEL, Sieur de Cournoyer and governor of Three Rivers, Quebec, made a most unusual donation to the Ursuline convent of the College Marie de l'Incarnation—a collection of prehistoric stone artifacts. This is certainly the first archaeological collection in Canada and probably in all of North America.[1] Among the artifacts were three long, beautiful lance tips ground from slate. We don't know why the governor chose to donate the collection to the Ursulines, but they had opened the college only three years earlier, and their convent was probably the most established institution in the community, the closest thing to a safe repository, a function now served by museums. The Ursulines still carefully curate the collection today. This donation is remarkable because, judging from available historic accounts, it was made in an era when people seem to have been completely uninterested in aboriginal prehistory, and yet someone thought these strange relics of the past worth preserving.

Fast-forward to 1881, when Augustus C. Hamlin, a prominent physician and naturalist from Bangor, Maine, found several virtually identical ground slate lance tips buried in patches of a bright red powder called ocher in nearby Bucksport.[2] As an amateur naturalist and a lover of gemstones,[3] Hamlin was curious about things that come out of the ground, and he gave a paper about his discoveries at the 1882 meeting of the American Association for the Advancement of Science. Unfortunately, the text of Hamlin's paper has been lost, but it caught the attention of one person in the audience, Frederick Ward Putnam of Harvard's Peabody Museum of American Archaeology and Ethnology. Arguably America's first professional archaeologist, Putnam found Hamlin's paper interesting enough that he dispatched an assistant, Charles C. Willoughby, to explore Hamlin's site along with other similar sites in the area.

These two events show us the fascination many people have found in these beautiful objects of ground slate that are found scattered over a wide area between the eastern Great Lakes and New Brunswick but greatly concentrated in several sites on and near the Maine coast that Hamlin was the first to explore. They are shaped with great precision and ground almost to a polish on all surfaces. Many are made of colorful banded slate, and some are so delicate that they could not have functioned well as actual weapons. They reflect the highest level of attention to design that goes well beyond that seen in other stone artifacts. They are now generally called bayonets (figure 1).

**FIGURE 1.** Slate bayonets in the collection of the Ursuline convent of the College Marie de l'Incarnation, Three Rivers, Quebec. The longest specimen is 6.5 inches (16.5 cm) long.

After Hamlin's discovery, it rapidly became clear that the sites where bayonets had been found were not at all like other archaeological sites along the Maine coast, the hundreds of deposits of mollusk shell refuse called shell middens. The sites that produced slate bayonets, on the other hand, were clusters of pits dug into sand and gravel in which bayonets and a great many other kinds of artifacts had been placed, all covered with red ocher. Early archaeologists accurately interpreted them as cemeteries, even though human bones were almost universally absent from them. So many had been found by 1913, that archaeologist Warren K. Moorehead dubbed their makers the Red Paint People.[4] Prehistoric cemeteries are not common, particularly in northeastern North America. Because of this scarcity, Moorehead felt compelled to make a forceful case for their special nature. He commented:

> We are accustomed to regard the South, the Mississippi valley, and the Southwest as sections in which one expects to be confronted by archaeological problems; but it is in the most easterly portion of the United States that we have now found indications of a culture different from that existing anywhere else in this country.[5]

After Moorehead published his research on the Red Paint People in 1922, archaeology in the Northeast declined, as many American archaeologists shifted their attention away from home to more exotic foreign regions. And so the Red Paint People remained, for a half century, mysterious, poorly understood, and clearly unlike other prehistoric cultures in the region.

Northeastern archaeology began to revive in the late 1960s, and that is when I picked up the story left by Hamlin, Putnam, Willoughby, and Moorehead. Together with a few other researchers, I began to reexamine old collections and to seek out new sites to excavate. Both these efforts were aided by new research tools not available to the earlier pioneers, such as radiocarbon dating and geological identification of stone artifacts from far-off places. Since then, I've devoted much of my professional energy to reconstructing a picture of these fascinating ancient people, continuing to examine older collections and to excavate newly discovered sites, trying to better define this unusual culture and to understand how and why it appeared and how it was related to other groups throughout the Northeast. In this book, I share stories of that quest and relate some of the surprising discoveries I've made along the way.

In 1782, the French philosopher Étienne Bonnot de Condillac wrote of jargon that "[e]very science requires a special language because every science has its own ideas." That certainly applies to archaeology. The problem with jargon is that it hampers communication with nonspecialists, and I've attempted in this book to keep its use to a bare minimum. Nevertheless, there are cases where the technical term seemed to me the best way to make my point, but I've also provided a brief glossary of these terms in the back matter.

# 1

# THE RED PAINT PEOPLE, ARCHAEOLOGY, AND ME

THERE ARE THREE stories interwoven in this book. The first is about the Red Paint People themselves. It explores what their lives were like and why that lifestyle was so unusual compared to other prehistoric people of the Northeast. The second is about archaeology's attempts to deal with this anomalous culture. Scientists struggle with unique cases such as this, and there has long been a debate between those, including me, who proclaim the unique features of the Moorehead phase and those who wish to deemphasize its uniqueness in order to fit it into the larger spatial and temporal schemes of northeastern prehistory. The third story is about the dominant role this culture has played in my research career.

The Moorehead phase is a little-known prehistoric culture of the Maine coast that has puzzled archaeologists for well over a century. In many ways, it remains an enigma today. Archaeologists refer to such discrete prehistoric cultures as phases, and I've labeled it the Moorehead phase in honor of Warren K. Moorehead, who devoted so much of his field research to it.[1] The term *phase* is not a comfortable fit in this case, though, because a phase suggests that something comparable both preceded and succeeded it. The culture of the Red Paint People, however, arrived without warning, flourished for a few centuries, and then disappeared without a trace. These qualities suggest that a better term for it might be the Moorehead event. The popular term for this culture, introduced by Moorehead in 1913, is Red Paint People, which I happen to like, and so I will use it interchangeably with Moorehead phase.

## A Stone Age Culture

Like all prehistoric North American cultures, it was a Stone Age culture, meaning metals were never smelted. That term implies primitiveness, but actually Stone Age people were sophisticated judges of the raw materials they used to make tools. Smaller edged tools like spear tips and knives were flaked from hard, fine-grained, silica-rich rocks that fracture in a predictable way when struck by a skilled stone worker. The typical production sequence begins with a hard blow from a handheld stone hammer, or hammerstone, to a block of suitable raw material, called a core. After a few more shaping blows with the hammerstone, a large chunk of antler—sometimes wood—was used to remove several smaller flakes. At some point, a small antler tine was used to press off the final series of small flakes. People of the Moorehead phase often chose a compact gray to green volcanic rock called felsic rhyolite, which has been made less glassy over time by metamorphism (exposure to geological heat and pressure). A major source of rhyolite is found in the Moosehead Lake area of north central Maine, but during the last ice age, large volumes of this rhyolite were torn from bedrock and transported by glaciers in a southeasterly direction toward the area where the Red Paint People lived.

Other tools, like larger woodworking adzes and stone weights called plummets, were made in a very different way from very different raw materials, called mafic rocks, which have a lot of silica plus manganese and iron. They are softer and less brittle than those used for flaking and are thus less likely to break during use. Mafic rocks are common and generally locally available. Those used by the Red Paint People come mainly from the Ellsworth Formation, which occurs along the same portion of the central and eastern Maine coast where their sites are most common.[2] These tools were shaped from suitably sized chunks of mafic rocks by thousands of gentle taps with a hammerstone, each tap pulverizing a bit of rock as the toolmaker achieved the desired shape. The cutting bits of woodworking tools were ground to a sharp edge with a whetstone, while a groove was ground around the top of the plummets to secure a fishing line.

The famous bayonets of the Red Paint People are made of slate, another kind of metamorphic rock that fractures naturally into thin flat slabs. Slate artifacts were apparently neither flaked nor pecked, certainly not in their final stages of manufacture, which involved careful grinding and polishing to achieve their precise forms and faceted surfaces. Some stone tools used by the Red Paint People were not made by them and so are helpful in revealing their external contacts and trade networks. Some projectile points from the cemeteries, for example, are clearly imports because not only are they are made of specific raw materials that do not occur in the Maine region but they are also of shapes typical of their areas of origin.

## Discovering and Rediscovering the Red Paint People

Soon after their initial discovery in the 1880s, the Red Paint cemeteries began to attract a great deal of attention, but before much could be learned about them, American archaeologists became interested in exploring far-off places, and interest to local prehistory American prehistory waned for several decades. This trend can be seen in a television show from the early 1950s that first got me interested in archaeology. Titled *What in the World*, it featured prominent anthropologists who, during each show, tried to identify mysterious objects from the collection of the University of Pennsylvania Museum of Archaeology and Ethnography. These artifacts came from around the world, but very few were from North America. (You can watch episodes of the show on YouTube.)

As the Red Paint site discoveries tailed off, the lingering view of the Red Paint People was of an inexplicably odd culture that stood apart from that of "regular" prehistoric Indians. Many artifacts from the cemeteries were too beautifully made and too extreme in design to be functional, meaning that they must have been made for special, ceremonial purposes, which included, but may not have been limited to, placement with the dead. Ideas about who these people might have been and to whom they might have been related were vague and speculative and little better than folktales recalling the golden days when excavations by national figures the likes of Putnam, Willoughby, and Moorehead were attracting national attention.

This was the situation when I came on the scene as a graduate student in the late 1960s. Early archaeologists were preoccupied with prehistoric cemeteries and the unusual stone artifacts found in them, but by the time I began working in archaeology, the profession had shifted its focus from studying artifacts per se to more anthropologically based questions about how their makers had lived and why they had made the artifacts they did. The anemic literature about the Red Paint People that existed in 1969 was frustrating, as was the fragmented and disorganized state of their artifact collections. Everyone involved in the early cemetery excavations sensed that they had gotten into something very interesting, but they had no way to get beyond their own idiosyncratic speculations about what it all meant. Archaeology is difficult because data are scarce, and no archaeologists ever feels that the existing sample is adequate for the cultures they study, but for this culture, the problem was especially acute. There seemed to be so much to consider in its technology and ritual behavior, and yet so few detailed reports on its sites or readily available examples of its artifacts to examine. It was a case of insufficient iteration, the process by which scientists repeat an operation or an observation often enough to establish that it is part of a pattern. The first observation, or iteration, will raise interesting possibilities, but repeated iterations are required to accurately define and explain it; something that, in 1969, was impossible for any aspect of this culture. As a result, I decided to initiate a program to amplify the record. Understanding how the Red Paint People lived became the main focus of my research in the early 1970s. That focus led me in two directions: first excavating a very unusual archaeological site that contained a lot of evidence about how they lived and second building a collection at the Maine State Museum, where I've curated archaeological collections since 1972.

The excavation came first. It took me to North Haven, an island in

Penobscot Bay, and specifically to the Turner Farm site, where I found a 4,000-year-old village of the Red Paint People. Between 1972 and 1980, I led teams that recovered more information on this culture than had ever been found before. Then, in 1980, our emphasis shifted to analysis, which culminated in a monograph published in 1995, laying out much of what I'd learned from this remarkable site.

A second way to learn about the Red Paint People was to gather together collections of their artifacts in one place. Several excavators, working for various institutions or operating privately, had separately built discrete collections, which had been in so many different places and under such variable conditions that getting a general understanding of the Red Paint People's artifacts was nearly impossible. Until then, I had seen only a few of the culture's most interesting artifacts at a time, but I could now examine many, consider the styles they exhibited, seek out their geologic origins, and determine which ones had been buried together. What I learned in the process constitutes a significant portion of the story told in this book.

By the late 1980s, the Maine State Museum's Red Paint collection had grown into one of the largest in existence. My collecting activity also had an ulterior motive: to construct an exhibit space. The Maine State Museum moved to a new facility in the early 1970s, and during the 1980s, we were in full exhibit-construction mode. We needed artifacts for an exhibit titled "Twelve Thousand Years in Maine," which opened in 1991.

By the time we built the exhibit, most archaeologists knew that the Moorehead phase existed around 4,000 years ago, during a long period of prehistory archaeologists call the Archaic. The Archaic had been preceded by the first humans to enter North America, called Paleo-Indians, who arrived in the Northeast around 10,500 years ago. We can't be sure of the precise date because, for reasons we don't understand, their sites produced little datable charcoal. The Paleo-Indians did not stay long in the Northeast, probably because the rapidly changing environment of the time soon became unsuitable for their wide-ranging hunter-gatherer lifestyle. By hunter-gatherer, I mean a lifestyle without domestic plants or animals. The most prominent environmental change was the emergence of forests not too different from those that persist in the region today, and they were increasingly inhabited by forest-dwelling Archaic immigrants from the Southeast who began to arrive around 8,500 years ago.

Archaic people were hunter-gatherers, too. The name *Archaic* was coined by William A. Ritchie to describe "an early level of culture based on hunting, fishing and gathering of wild foods."[3] In order to organize this long span of time, archaeologists typically divide it into more manageable segments. Details of the division vary from region to region. In the East, the Late Archaic, which began around 5,000 years ago, saw a rapid population increase, or perhaps merely a tighter clustering of populations, which seems to have caused widespread changes in prehistoric cultures throughout eastern North America, as a few earlier, vaguely defined, widespread patterns of thinly distributed artifact styles began to give way to more definable, concretely regional cultures evident at a great many sites.[4]

It is not clear what caused this apparent population increase. Some archaeologists have suggested that it came in response to the northward expansion of forests with many broadleaf, nut-producing tree species that provided food for deer and other large mammals. Others suspect sea-level rise played a role, forcing human populations off coastal lowlands and onto less hospitable higher ground, or perhaps stabilizing sea levels made coastal zones more productive. Some are not sure there actually was an overall population increase and suggest instead that some climatic or other factor created conditions favoring larger, more tightly integrated communities. Whatever the cause, it seems that human populations began to form regionally based and culturally distinct communities. Some threshold seems to have been reached that suddenly created what scientists call a scalar change in the region's cultural environment.[5] Before it, archaeological cultures throughout the Northeast and beyond were quite similar, almost indistinguishable from area to area. After the change, they divided into two broad patterns: one called the Laurentian tradition focused on the St. Lawrence Valley, and the other, which we shall refer to as the Small Stemmed Point tradition, was farther to the south.[6] Over time, both the Laurentian and Small Stemmed Point traditions tended to develop smaller regional cultures, though the details of these divisions are still debated.

This scalar change is especially apparent in northeastern North America, but even here, while interesting and deserving of explanation, nothing really remarkable occurred at the regional level. Artifact styles were still quite uniform over large areas and included only a few forms with aesthetic merit. Archaeological sites generally remained small, temporary encampments. Burials were apparently infrequent and, with a few interesting exceptions, were not clustered in cemeteries.[7] The one exception to this pattern was the emergence sometime before 4,500 years ago of a highly distinctive culture that occupied a clearly defined territory on and near the present coastline of the Gulf of Maine.

## An Archaeological Puzzle

The spatial discreteness of the Moorehead phase is highly unusual for any prehistoric group, particularly for one occupying a long region of coastline and not bounded by obvious environmental constraints. One could,

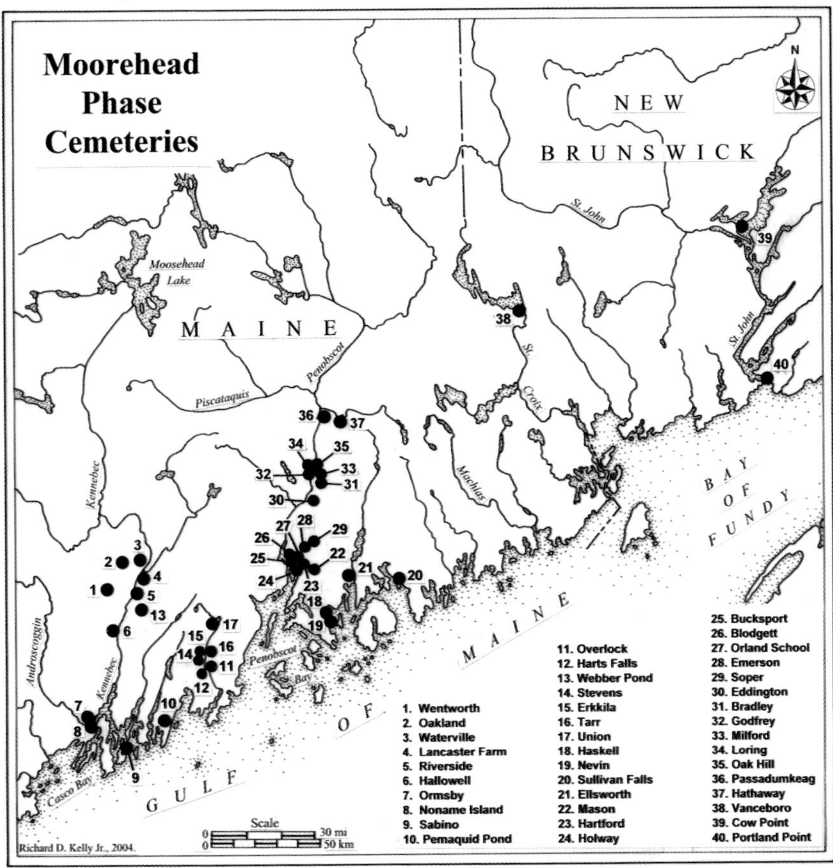


**FIGURE 2.** Distribution of Red Paint cemeteries.

for example, imagine Moorehead phase people leading successful lives in Casco Bay to the west, or across the narrow Bay of Fundy in Nova Scotia, both of which have produced evidence of the ancestral Small Stemmed Point tradition. Yet only the merest traces of the Moorehead phase have been found in these areas. Moreover, since 1948, its known territory has remained centered between the Kennebec and Penobscot rivers, its geographic range expanded only slightly westward to include Merrymeeting Bay and eastward to the lower St. John River drainage.[8] Perhaps the most significant new information about Moorehead phase territory is the discovery that both the Small Stemmed Point tradition and the Moorehead phase extended their range across the Bay of Fundy to southernmost Nova Scotia. But this new information only underscores the absence of any evidence of the Moorehead phase east of the Portland Point and Cow Point cemeteries in New Brunswick (figure 2).

The Moorehead phase was a strange beast, with a complex technology and ceremonial dimension that were strikingly different from anything that preceded or succeeded it and very unlike any of its contemporaneous neighbors. A sense of its existence began to emerge in the 1890s with discoveries of remarkable ceremonial sites found in the course of farming, gravel quarrying, or construction activities. By that time, many people were aware of prehistoric artifacts found along the shores of many Maine waterways and also of the shell middens that dot Maine's coastline. The latter were correctly understood to be the remains of villages left by the Indians who were probably ancestral to the region's historic tribes, but these ceremonial sites were so different from the shell middens in both in their form and contents that there seemed no way to link the two and thus to put the cemeteries into some kind of historical context. No one in the 1890s was equipped with the theoretical perspectives that anthropology has since developed, but they intuitively understood that Maine's prehistoric people lived mainly by hunting, fishing, and gathering wild foods—that is, hunter-gatherers.

Moorehead's 1916 suggestion that the Red Paint People presented a significant "archaeological problem" because they were "different from that existing anywhere else in this country" was met with stiff resistance. The archaeological establishment wasn't having it.[9] David I. Bushnell of the University of Virginia, for example, pointed out that humans buried with red ocher had been found in Florida and Illinois, so the Maine graves were not unique. He also pointed out that the pilgrims of Plymouth had opened a human grave containing a fine red powder along with European artifacts, concluding that the use of red ocher may have continued until the beginning of colonization in New England.[10] In fact, that red powder was probably another European product, vermillion, which, though toxic, was eagerly sought by North American Indians during the colonial era because it was even more vividly red than ocher.

Moorehead countered that, having excavated 197 Red Paint graves, the "Red-paint culture is all I have claimed for it." He also cited Willoughby's 1898 report on the Orland and Ellsworth cemeteries, stating that its conclusions "are entirely true."[11] Bushnell sanctimoniously fired back, stating that Moorehead's graves were "not a veiled mystery as he is striving to have all believe" and implied that Moorehead was among those "seeking the weird and mysterious."[12] In this round, Bushnell was joined by an equally sanctimonious Clarence B. Moore, who suggested that Moorehead had "accorded himself overmuch praise" and criticized him for daring to choose the name Red Paint People when other previously reported groups had also used ocher in their burials.[13] Finally, the mild-mannered Willoughby calmed the debate when he pointed out, in Moorehead's defense, that many unusual artifacts had accompanied red ocher in the Maine cemeteries, clearly setting them apart from other ocher-laden cemeteries.[14]

What animated these attacks on Moorehead? Reading between the lines of Bushnell's and Moore's attacks, I see an unwillingness to acknowledge Moorehead's (and Willoughby's) claims for the great age and uniqueness of the Maine cemeteries. Prehistoric hunter-gatherers just weren't supposed to create elaborate mortuary ritual sites. And yet, there they were, first a few in Bucksport, Orland, and Ellsworth, and then they kept turning up in other places between the Androscoggin River in Maine and the St. John River in southwest New Brunswick, signaling something truly unusual on a larger scale. It was most confusing.

Before the first traces of the Red Paint People were being discovered in the 1880s, Maine people must have encountered strange-looking objects such as those deposited with the Ursulines of Three Rivers, yet there seems to be no surviving record. The reason for this silence must be that in the 1880s few understood the true antiquity of our species, *Homo sapiens*, much less of American Indians. Any recognizable stone artifacts were probably regarded as the traces of local tribes just before the arrival of Europeans. In fact, at least some evidence for "deep history," as anthropologist Ben Anderson calls it, had been building for decades.[15] But Darwin's radical *On the Origin of Species* had only been published in 1859, and the scientific establishment was still firmly in favor of a short chronology based on Genesis and dated by James Ussher, the Anglican bishop of Ireland, who put the time of creation at 4004 B.C. Some clever minds had begun to suspect that humans had been around in the Old World for a very long time, and not unreasonably, some, including Putnam, argued that this might be true in the New World as well, but prevailing opinion there strongly favored the short chronology.

The idea of very early human arrivals in the New World eventually lost out because no human skulls resembling the Neanderthals of Europe were found in the New World. The preponderance of opinion was that modern humans had arrived in North America only in the last 3,000 to 4,000 years. Thus, archaeological artifacts were usually regarded as the products of some historic Indian tribe or their immediate ancestors. In the case of the Red Paint People, the extensive use of red ocher was especially puzzling, because there was no historic record of New England Indians making much use of the pigment. Seeking some linkage between the cemeteries and a historic ocher-using culture, Putnam turned to the Beothuks of Newfoundland, a defunct culture also known as the Red Indians because of their fondness for red ocher.[16] Moorehead resisted this idea, still arguing that the Red Paint People were unique. In 1922, he stated that "the Red Indians of Newfoundland" were not descendants of the Red Paint People of Maine and that "the Red Paint People did not merge with any other known culture to the east, the west, the north, or the south; that they were absolutely distinct and very ancient," though he admitted "no one is able to set even approximate dates."[17] Moorehead, it has since turned out, was pretty close to the mark.

With Moorehead's pronouncement, professional exploration of the Red Paint People ceased for over four decades as American archaeologists began to focus on more exotic regions. Unfortunately, so little understanding of the culture had been achieved at that point that it was difficult even to discuss in the archaeological literature. The situation was aggravated by the absence of any general scheme for the spatial or temporal classification for northeastern prehistoric cultures. As Douglas Byers put it, the Red Paint People represented "the most widely known and at the same time most striking expression of Archaic culture in the Northeast."[18] In fact, it was the only such expression, and archaeologists like Byers were grasping at similarities among artifacts from as far away as Virginia and Kentucky, trying to make sense of the scattered, poorly documented Moorehead phase collections available at the time.

Confusion also stemmed from the fact that stratigraphic excavation, the removal of soil layers successively from top to bottom, was slow to emerge in North America. Stratigraphic excavation only makes sense if one accepts the possibility that a prehistoric site might extend back far enough to preserve evidence for cultural change over time. Europeans had understood its importance since the middle of the nineteenth century, but in North America, it wasn't until 1919 that archaeologists in New Mexico found stratified sites deep enough that they bothered to excavate them stratigraphically. Archaeologists in the Northeast did not quickly adopt the technique because there was a general belief that stratified sites were rare in the region. The first attempt was in the 1930s, when Byers and his colleagues excavated at the Nevin shell midden at Blue Hill Falls, a site whose importance is hard to overestimate because it contained both a Moorehead phase shell midden and a Red Paint cemetery. Although Byers's team intended their excavation as a model of stratigraphic excavation, in the end they were defeated by disturbances of the midden's layers—its strata—caused by erosion and other factors, and their analyses thus combined artifacts we now know to be from different periods. This confusion caused Byers to resist publishing the results of his work for decades. When, shortly before his death in 1978, he finally did write a brief report on the Nevin burials, he remained noncommittal about their age and cultural affiliation. Even then, however, the situation might have been rectified by radiocarbon-dating the bone artifacts found in the burials if Byers had not contaminated them with organic resins in an unwise attempt to stabilize them.

## Shell Middens

How prehistoric peoples made a living is key to understanding a great deal about the rest of their culture, and by the time Byers wrote his brief report on the Nevin site burials, archaeologists had come to realize what a rich source of information on prehistoric lifestyles lay in shell middens. In temperate climates like that of Maine, buried bones quickly dissolve in acid soils. In shell middens, however, they are preserved by the calcium carbonate of the mollusk shells that make up most of the midden.

The first archaeological excavations of shell middens occurred in Denmark in the 1840s. The excavators' goal was simply to determine whether these sometimes massive deposits were the result of human activity or some ancient natural process. The middens' bone and artifact contents proved their human origin, but inquiries about what those objects might tell us about the people who discarded them was not appreciated at first.[19] Shell midden archaeology was first attempted in the Northeast in the 1880s, but disagreement regarding appropriate methodology persisted until the 1960s, when New York State archaeologist William Ritchie, frustrated by the apparent absence of excavations throughout the Northeast, received funding from the National Science Foundation to explore shell middens on Martha's Vineyard, Massachusetts, and in the Deer Isle area of Maine. During this research, Ritchie developed a series of strategies for excavating shell middens that has since become standard.

I was fortunate to be among the graduate students who worked with Ritchie on Martha's Vineyard. The project represented a revival of professional archaeological research in coastal New England, and we all benefited from Ritchie's decades of fieldwork experience. When Ritchie later shifted the project's focus to Maine in 1967, I became his crew chief at three shell midden excavations on and near Deer Isle. That summer, I applied and refined lessons learned on Martha's Vineyard, and that gave me the confidence to tackle the deep, complex Turner Farm midden. Equally helpful was the fact that Ritchie saw so many differences between the midden contents from Martha's Vineyard and those from Maine that he thought the two data sets would require entirely separate interpretive projects. One striking difference, for example, was that on Martha's Vineyard, a variety of species contributed shell to the midden, including quagog, oyster, bay scallop, clam, and blue mussel, whereas the softshell clam *Mya arenaria* predominates in nearly all the middens of midcoast Maine. Ritchie graciously offered me the whole body of Maine material as a contribution to my thesis research. This allowed me to complete our excavations and then carry on seamlessly through the process of analysis and report writing for my dissertation.[20]

A major innovation introduced by Ritchie was the systematic collection of faunal remains during excavation. It seems hard to believe today, but as recently as Byers's excavations at the Nevin site in the 1930s, only the best-preserved bones were saved, thus hopelessly skewing any later attempt to reconstruct the patterns of animal exploitation there. Ritchie was explicitly intent on countering this methodological inadequacy, hiring Villanova biologist Joseph Waters to identify the species of each bone, where possible. The data were reported in Ritchie's monograph on his Martha's Vineyard work and, for the Maine sites, in my dissertation. This was the first systematic interpretation of archaeological faunal remains—now called zooarchaeology—ever published in the Northeast.

Pioneering though Ritchie's attention to faunal remains was, his methods were crude by modern standards of zooarchaeology. When I asked to borrow the Maine bone samples for further analysis a few years later, I was horrified to learn that they had been thrown out! Waters's, and I suppose Ritchie's, opinion was that once the taxonomic group of a bone was identified, what more was it good for? We'll answer that question in greater detail below, but the short answer is: a great deal.

One fact that instantly jumped out from the Maine faunal remains compared to those from Martha's Vineyard is the greater importance of marine resources in Maine. But those sites dated back no more than 3,000 years. When we began to examine bones from the much older strata at the Turner Farm site, we understood that, if anything, marine resources were even more important to the people of the Moorehead phase than in later times. Mollusks were the most obviously marine resource, but fish were even more important, and this observation is supported by recent isotopic analysis of human bone that we will consider below.

Our claims that heavy reliance on marine resources was key to understanding the Red Paint People were resisted by some archaeologists and natural scientists, at first because there are few remaining coastal sites to provide evidence of it. I argued that this scarcity reflects not prehistoric inattention to marine resources but rather the fact that the archaeological record of humans living along the seacoasts has often been destroyed by erosion. This is certainly the case for the Gulf of Maine coast, which, we learned in the 1970s, is slowly being submerged.

Archaeologists can do little to counter the impact of coastal erosion because the process of submersion is not gentle and passive. It is storm driven and dynamic, and the materials that compose a shell midden are not merely rearranged by storm waves but are washed down onto the beach and tumbled in the beach gravel until all the bone and shell disappears and even the stone artifacts are battered beyond recognition.

In only a few rare instances have fishermen or divers encountered what appear to be intact sites on the near-shore sea bottom. One such case lies near Deer Isle, Maine. Here, scallop draggers and archaeologists have recovered large oyster shells and artifacts that appear fresh and unabraded by storms, probably all that remains of a 5,000-year-old site located in a calm estuary that protected it from storm action.[21]

Resistance to the importance of marine resources also stems from the common assumption that the modern Gulf of Maine is an accurate model for prehistoric times. This turns out to be highly questionable. Today, it is common knowledge that the gulf's fisheries are badly depleted by overfishing, but that depletion is perceived in comparison to an abundance thought to have persisted until the 1950s, when, in fact, the depletion probably began over three centuries ago and, as we shall see, perhaps much earlier. Nevertheless, the marine resources available to the Red Paint People were staggering in comparison to recent times.

The complexity of Moorehead phase ritual ceremonialism is likewise viewed uneasily by some. There have been many attempts, beginning with Byers's 1959 paper for example, to fit them into some geographically larger or temporally longer construct, rather than presenting them as outstanding and unusual. This unease comes from the conventional wisdom that hunter-gatherers could not have achieved such ceremonial complexity. This opinion, though, rests on what archaeologists call ethnographic analogy, the drawing of helpful parallels found in recent hunter-gatherer societies that can stand as well-documented examples of prehistoric cases. And indeed, most hunter-gatherer societies that might provide ethnographic analogies do lack this degree of ceremonial complexity.

But the sample available is twice biased. First, ethnographic hunter-gatherers can only survive where the larger societies that surround them choose not to displace them. Thus, they now occupy marginal regions, not the prime territories available to prehistoric hunter-gatherers. Second, there are not many coastal hunter-gatherer societies to choose from any more because European colonial expansion around the world generally first impacted coastal zones, introducing disease and other alien influences that drastically altered the indigenous cultures of coastal peoples. As a result, they were often driven into the interior or became extinct. The Beothuks of Newfoundland are a well-known example of a coastal culture that became extinct under colonial pressure.[22]

These ethnographic biases have contributed to the widely held assumption in anthropology that human cultures find recourse in marine resources only after all terrestrial resources have been exploited.[23] Textbooks used in college-level archaeology courses, for example, will turn up very few references to shell middens or other evidence of prehistoric maritime exploitation. Moreover, this assumption carries through to archaeological theorizing about what kinds of social organization are possible among prehistoric hunter-gatherers. In fact, it turns out that prehistoric and ethnographic maritime hunter-gatherers sometimes developed patterns of cultural complexity that anthropological theorists have traditionally reserved for farmers and herders, whereas terrestrial hunter-gatherers rarely did so. We will take a look at a few examples of coastal hunter-gatherers whose traditional patterns of marine fishing and hunting survived long enough to be recorded by travelers and anthropologists in order to suggest that the patterns that shaped them are similar to those operating on the Red Paint People with similar result.

The immediate lesson of the Turner Farm site was that the Moorehead phase was something that could be clearly defined not only by its cemeteries but by its whole lifestyle, which clearly set it off from other cultural entities in the region. I've not been alone in trying to tell cogent stories about this strange culture, and in constructing my own, I've had to consider others' versions as well. Most of them I've found wanting in one way or another because most were constructed with reference to conventional, twentieth-century archaeological thinking, using some concepts and habits of thought that I find distorting or unhelpful for other reasons. I've become most critical of two paradigms that have served as "explanations," which they are not. The first let's call the historic continuity paradigm and the second, the regional continuity paradigm. Here, I'll tell you where these ideas have led us astray. Later, we'll return to them, and I'll offer what I suspect will be better alternatives.

## Continuity Models and Adaptionalist Thinking

Until the twentieth century, indeed even until the advent of radiocarbon dating circa 1950, the prevailing view of prehistory might be called the historic discontinuity paradigm. It saw changes in the archaeological record as indicative of the comings and goings of different groups. It was basically a short chronology paradigm because the alternative possibility, that over deep time one group might change its behavior in a way that changed its archaeological record, was much less often considered. Before radiocarbon dating, it was easy to think of the New World as recently populated from Asia, perhaps 3,500 years ago, and as a result, prehistoric indigenous cultures were viewed as structurally static, maintaining their behavioral patterns unchanged over the brief time they had been in existence.

The advent of radiocarbon dating changed all that. Short chronology thinking was out, replaced by a much longer chronology. Also abandoned was the notion that migration played an important role in shaping the North American archaeological record. Instead, archaeologists adopted, even became obsessed with, a key concept borrowed from the science of ecology: adaptation. By adaptation, ecologists (and archaeologists) mean the tendency of a species or a culture to modify its behavior to establish a good fit with its environment, and it was this concept that came to dominate archaeological thinking to the near exclusion of migration. The reaction was extreme. Archaeologists were given an explicit list of criteria that must be complied with to propose a prehistoric migration.[24] In effect, this discouraged any proffering of migration hypotheses until the 1990s.[25]

As is so often the case in science, the merits of adaptationist thinking seemed obvious to archaeologists once they had been suggested. Just as a species changes to become more suited to its environment, so too does a culture. However, while biological adaptation proceeds slowly by genetic change, cultural adaptation can be achieved rapidly through behavioral change under intellectual, not genetic, control. Cultures change their minds, not their genes. This rapid adaptability, anthropologists now agree, is what has made us the dominant species on earth.

Moreover, most human communities have local ancestry, so it is not surprising that interpretations of the archaeological record focused on how they were shaped through adaptation to changes in their environments. The search was on for local ancestry, and what had been seen as distinct, stable cultures were now plugged into hypothesized long-standing archaeological "traditions." For the Red Paint People, the first potential tradition was called the Laurentian Archaic, defined by Ritchie in the 1940s as a group of related early cultures centered on the St. Lawrence River beginning around 6,000 years ago. The second contender is variously referred to, but we shall call it the Coastal Archaic. It refers to a sequence

**FIGURE 3.** Archaic projectile points from various Maine sites, arranged chronologically, dating from around 8,500 to 3,500 years old.

of cultures, or waves of immigrants, that entered the Northeast from the mid-Atlantic region beginning around 8,500 years ago.

Many artifact types have been used to distinguish Archaic groups, the most popular being projectile point styles (figure 3), the Laurentian styles having mostly side-notched bases and the Coastal Archaic being mostly stemmed (figure 4). Other suggested criteria to distinguish the two have been more problematic. The Laurentian, for example, was said to possess tools and weapons ground from slate and heavy woodworking tools such as adzes and gouges, while the Coastal Archaic was not, but this distinction has not stood the test of time. In the 1970s, many archaeologists favored the Laurentian tradition ancestry model because of its ground slate technology. But I had worked with Ritchie in upstate New York, the heart of Laurentian territory. I knew what the Laurentian looked like and that there is very little evidence of it on the Maine coast. Working with Ritchie on Martha's Vineyard had also introduced me to the Coastal Archaic culture called the Small Stemmed Point tradition for its characteristic tiny stemmed projectile points often made of white quartz.[26] Once we encountered these at the Turner Farm site underlying the Moorehead phase midden, it became clear that this was a much more suitable ancestor than the Laurentian.

Let's now turn to regional continuity. This issue is relevant in our efforts

FIGURE 4. (*top*) side-notched Otter Creek points of the Laurentian tradition. Longest specimen is 4 inches (10 cm) long. (*bottom*) points of the Small Stemmed point tradition. Small triangular points are occasionally found with stemmed points in Maine. Longest specimen is 1.5 inches (3.75 cm) long.

to understand the Moorehead phase, because in 1967, evidence for a culture with strong resemblances to the Moorehead phase was discovered by Memorial University archaeologist James Tuck at Port au Choix, on Newfoundland's Northern Peninsula.[27] Some traces of this culture had been found previously, but the discovery of the huge cemetery at Port au Choix with grave goods closely resembling some from the Red Paint cemeteries convinced Tuck that he was dealing with essentially the same culture, which he included in what he called the Maritime Archaic tradition.[28]

In terms of impact, the timing of Tuck's assertions about a Maritime Archaic tradition model couldn't have been better. It was a beautiful theory with great appeal to a reviving discipline that was trying to make sense of the fragments left by earlier researchers. In a single stroke, it tied all the most interesting archaeological material in the Northeast into a neatly wrapped package. The Maritime Archaic model quickly became an orthodoxy that no counterarguments would dislodge for the next quarter century. To its detractors, mostly arguing from south of the Gulf of St. Lawrence, it was problematic because it ignored new information that was coming to light there. Tuck can hardly be blamed for this oversight, as little of that information had yet been published. Also fueling debate was Tuck's assertion that the Port au Choix cemetery was related to several older and contemporaneous sites along the Quebec-Labrador coast west and north of Port au Choix.[29] This implied that the Moorehead phase was but a recent extension of an ancient northern maritime cultural tradition. Those of us working in Maine and New Brunswick, on the other hand, increasingly believed that the ancestors of the Moorehead phase were clearly local. If Tuck's view was correct, we were dealing with a single culture with northern origins that covered a vast territory, albeit with some large spatial gaps. If we were correct, there were at least two locally derived highly maritime cultures, one in Maine and one in Newfoundland-Labrador, which, admittedly, had exhibited many close parallels.

Debates about which tradition a culture belongs to or which contemporaneous cultures are related to which have died down in recent years, the competing parties retiring to their corners of the ring, quiescent but, I suspect, unchanged in their views. Perhaps they share my sentiment that, when it comes to explaining the Red Paint People, these debates are irrelevant. They did have ancestors and they did have neighbors, but these facts will tell us nothing important about them. Instead, the Moorehead phase represents a remarkable cultural development, sui generis. These debates were conducted inside the box of conventional, late twentieth-century archaeological theories and have explained nothing. Archaeology must now figure out how to think outside that box. It is important to note that adaptationalist explanations have been falling short in ecology, too. Later in the book, we will see that just as twentieth-century archaeology found theoretical inspiration in adaptationalist ecology, so twenty-first-century archaeology can find similar inspiration in a postadaptationalist ecology known as niche construction theory.

## THE SHIFTING BASELINE PHENOMENON

Ecology is also shifting its perspectives on what problems were important and what scales of analysis were appropriate to solve them. These shifts have exposed to me some major errors in the ways I interpreted the faunal remains from the Turner Farm site. During the mid-twentieth century, marine ecologists not unreasonably became concerned about the recent impacts of pollution on marine ecosystems. Their focus was usually on changes in recent decades, and they tended to assume that their systems were at their "natural" levels of productivity until the onset of the impacts they were studying. In the late twentieth century, however, fisheries biologist Daniel Pauly of the University of British Columbia criticized this kind of short chronology thinking, claiming that these natural baselines were actually shifting baselines that had been unconsciously reset from generation to generation, as children lost sight of the system's richness in their parents' time.[30] The result of this collective amnesia, according to Pauly, is their inability to perceive the rate and extent of systemic decline over time. As a result, successive generations of fishers target successively smaller species as the larger ones become depleted in a process he and his colleagues called "fishing down marine food webs." Pauly characterized fisheries science as lacking "formal approaches for dealing with early accounts of 'large catches' of presently extirpated resources, which are viewed as anecdotes."[31]

Once I became aware of the shifting baseline phenomenon, I suddenly realized that in a way I had been taken in by it as well. Although I understood the size and abundance of the marine species I encountered at the Turner Farm site, my view of biological productivity in Penobscot Bay was based on observations made in the 1970s. I now suspect that the abundance of marine life in Penobscot Bay 4,000 years ago was probably an order of magnitude richer than it was in 1970, not to mention what it is today. This kind of research continues to resound among students of marine ecosystems everywhere, including the Gulf of Maine, and we shall return to it at the close of the book.

# 2

# THE WORLD 4,000 YEARS AGO

BEFORE CONTINUING OUR story, we should frame it in time and space. In my view, the Moorehead phase is a singular cultural event especially because no one would have expected it to emerge where and when it did. It had a clear ancestry and abutted other cultures to its west and south, but these facts explain very little about it. To understand how isolated from other dynamic cultures it was, we should take a quick look around the world of 4,000 years ago. We will then look at how the environment of the Red Paint People was changing during their times.

## THE OLD WORLD AND THE NEW

Between 110,000 and 12,000 years ago, the world was locked in an ice age known as the Wisconsin Glacial Period. Great sheets of ice covered most of Canada, New England, the upper Midwest, and parts of Idaho, Montana, and Washington as well as much of Northeast Asia and Europe. This was the last ice age of the Pleistocene epoch, which had seen the spread of modern *Homo sapiens* from Africa to Europe and Asia. As the ice sheets melted, an essentially modern climate emerged. This initiated the Holocene epoch, which continues to the present, and it is the period during which humans continued their expansion into Northeast Asia and from there into the New World, quickly populating both North and South America.

The ice sheets had a profound chilling impact on climate in the Northern Hemisphere, but as they melted, the weather both warmed and became locally variable. Most of the large mammals that had existed in the Americas and Eurasia during the Pleistocene era went extinct, either because they could not withstand the onset of modern climate or because humans hunted them to extinction. The combination of climate change and Pleistocene extinctions caused the widespread patterns of ice-age hunting to splinter into more varied lifestyles adapted to the kinds of localized ecological zones we recognize today.

## THE PACE OF HISTORY

The varied communities that emerged at the end of the Pleistocene started out small because hunter-gatherers rarely find enough food concentrated in one locality to allow for large ones. Small groups of hunter-gatherers like these probably lacked leaders. Instead, like more recent hunter-gatherers, they probably acknowledged and tended to follow the advice of a headman who possessed some useful quality—perhaps he was a good game finder or a good settler of disputes—but to whom allegiance was a personal choice. There was also likely to be a shaman, a person who could communicate with the spiritual world. Sometimes the headman was the shaman. But the main point is that leadership was attained through individual merit and was generally not passed on to offspring.

Soon, however, some of these small groups—bands, as anthropologists call them—began to grow. Anthropologists still debate the reasons for this growth, but an important one was probably an increase in female fertility caused by a decline in long-range, energy-consuming seasonal migrations. And with this growth came economic changes, especially agriculture, and, in the Old World, animal herding.

A basic fact of the Holocene world is that the pace of human history ran faster in the Old World, particularly in Eurasia, than in the New. Why this was so has bothered anthropologists for a long time. In the nineteenth century, racist arguments carried the day, and "primitive cultures" were thought to be the result of racial differences. In the early twentieth century, crude understandings of climate became popular among the so-called geographic determinists: vigorous populations developed in the cool climates on Europe and North America, whereas lethargic ones developed in the tropics.[1] More recently, Jared Diamond has argued that geography certainly does matter, but not in the way the determinists thought. In his book, *Guns, Germs, and Steel*, Diamond tackles the question using the principles of biogeography, the study of the distribution of plants and animals over the surface of the earth. He claims that the book was inspired by a question a native New Guinean friend named Yali once asked him. Yali's question was "Why is it that you white people developed so much cargo [technology and material wealth] and brought it to New Guinea, but we black people had little cargo of our own?"[2] To answer it, Diamond drew on the work of biologists like Robert MacArthur and E. O. Wilson who, beginning in the 1950s, demonstrated the close relationship between biological diversity and such factors as land area and rates at which species can extend their ranges over it. According to Diamond, the reasons for differences in the pace of New and Old World history lie not in different capacities of Old and New World peoples but in accidents of geography.

The key factors for Diamond are plant and animal domestication. Agriculture and animal herding were engines for technological change because they allowed increasingly large populations to live in stable settlements, which in turn led to political systems controlled by chiefs and eventually kings. Because they developed early in the Old World, history began to accelerate there before it did in the New World. The New World surely did develop agriculture, but only more recently and in more limited areas.

Let's examine the most important factors in Diamond's analysis: land area and climate. The number of species a landmass will sustain is limited by its size, and this relationship is not linear; larger landmasses have many more species than small ones. Climate is important too, and when it comes to domestication, one climate type is critical. It is called Mediterranean climate, and it is both highly seasonal and annually unpredictable. Let's examine how these factors affect plants and animals. First, let's look at wild grasses of the kind that produced domesticated cereal grains. These grains are especially important because they now provide half the calories consumed by all of humanity. The best candidates for domestication were those with large seeds. Of the world's 56 largest seeded grasses, 33 occur in the Eurasia, including North Africa, while only 11 are found in various parts of the New World. But that's only part of the story, for 32 of the 33 Eurasian species originated from wild grasses found in what ecologists call the Fertile Crescent, the world's largest region of Mediterranean climate, which extends from the western Mediterranean Sea to the Persian Gulf.[3] If we next look at large terrestrial mammals, we see a similar difference. Of the fourteen important large domestic mammals, only the common wild ancestor of the llama and alpaca occurred in the New World. Most of the rest originated in or near the Fertile Crescent, some elsewhere in Eurasia.

Related to the abundance of domesticated species is the ease of domestication. Because Eurasia had many more species suitable for domestication, they also had more that needed little genetic change to become domestic. Wheat, the first domestic grain in Eurasia, for example, originated 10,000 years ago in that part of the Fertile Crescent that now lies in eastern Turkey. As you can see in figure 5, the wild ancestor closely resembles the variety of domestic wheat called emmer, the most important difference being that the rachis, the brittle spike on which the kernels grow, has become flexible so that the grain does not fall to the ground and self-sew but stays with the

**FIGURE 5.** Wild versus domestic (emmer) wheat. (*Courtesy of Wolfgang Schuchert, Max Planck Institute for Plant Breeding Research.*)

stalk until the grain is threshed. Compare this close resemblance to the crowning achievement of New World agriculture, corn (*Zea mays*). Corn is now the world's most productive grain, but it had to make a long genetic journey to get there. The process began in southern Mexico 1,000 years later than wheat. The wild ancestor, a grass called teosinte, hardly resembles domestic corn, and the transition to the large ears familiar to us took millennia (figure 6).

**FIGURE 6.** Teosinte and maize. (*Courtesy of Dr. Peggy G. Lemaux, University of California, Berkeley.*)

In North America, a few varieties of seed-bearing plants were domesticated in the Southeast 4,000 years ago. These include squash (*Curcubita pepo*), sumpweed (*Iva annua*), sunflower (*Helianthus annuus*), and goosefoot (*Chenopodium berlandieri*), while three others—erect knotweed (*Polygonum erectum*), little barley (*Hordeum pusillum*), and maygrass (*Phalaris caroliniana*)—were partially domesticated. These developments, however, had little or no impact in the Gulf of Maine region. Even in the Southeast, the impact must be assessed against the fact that these plants went out of use soon after corn spread north from Mexico.

Differences in animal domestication are even more striking. In Eurasia, goats, sheep, pigs, and cattle were under domestication more than 10,000 years ago. Camels, donkeys, horses, chickens, ducks, and geese began the process 5,000 or more years ago. Only two animal species had been domesticated in the New World 4,000 years ago, both in the Andes of South America, the humble guinea pig (7,000 years ago) and llamas (5,500 years ago).[4] Only two more would be domesticated in later years, the alpaca in the Andes (3,500 years ago) and the turkey on Mexico's Yucatan Peninsula around the time of Christ and again, twice, in North America a few centuries later.[5] In sum, 4,000 years ago, Eurasia was a largely domesticated continent, while the Americas were still essentially wild.

Another important factor that influenced the pace of history is the impact of latitude. Longitude by itself has little impact on climate, which means that climatic zones in Eurasia where prehistoric agriculture and herding can be practiced extend from east to west for up to 6,000 miles (roughly the Strait of Gibraltar to Seoul, Korea) compared to agricultural North America's 1,000 miles (roughly from Washington, D.C., to Tulsa, Oklahoma). This meant that any domestic Eurasian species might spread within its zone without further modification. Thus, around 4,000 years ago, wheat was being eaten as far from its place of origin as northern China.

Unlike longitude, latitude has a strong effect on climate because it determines the amount of sunlight that falls on the earth's surface—more at the equator, less at the poles. New World domesticates, hemmed in by latitude, tended to spread slowly, if at all. Because it eventually became so productive, corn did spread southward rather quickly through the tropics to the Andes and was beginning to fuel urban settlement there 4,000 years ago.[6] Its spread northward, however, was greatly slowed by the need to adapt genetically to colder climates and shorter growing seasons. These changes took a long time, and corn agriculture had only recently spread into Maine when Europeans arrived. Finally, the impacts of longitude and latitude are enhanced by mountain ranges. In Eurasia, these run east to west, bordering climatic zones, not crossing or obstructing them. The opposite is true in the Americas, where mountain ranges run north to south, forming barriers to the spread of domesticates.

Let's now look at how differences in domestication impacted human societies in Eurasia and the New World. As early Holocene population growth put pressure on food resources, the human response in both the Old and New Worlds was similar, as local groups found plants and animals suitable for domestication. The process of domestication results in a new species that is hugely more abundant than its wild ancestor but that is unable to reproduce and survive without human intervention, and this interdependence has a further stabilizing effect on local communities. Unlike hunter-gatherers who met greater food needs by increasing their ranges, these agriculturalists and pastoralists had to settle down to increase their food supply, a process anthropologists call sedentism.

Anthropologists traditionally thought that prehistoric hunter-gatherers could not be sedentary because they needed to move their homes throughout the year to take advantage of seasonally abundant resources in different places. More recently, however, we have realized that some hunter-gatherers do settle down into year-round villages, particularly those living near the sea. This might be called opportunistic sedentism, allowed by an abundance of resources found in close proximity and therefore accessible year-round from a single village. Agricultural sedentism, however, is more obligatory because the farmer is tethered to his fields and a herder to his pastures. The process of agricultural sedentism was well along 11,000 years ago in Southwest Asia and soon began to spread, reaching Central Asia, North Africa, and Scandinavia by 6,000 years ago.[7] In Mexico and the Andes, agriculturally based sedentism was just beginning 4,000 years ago, or even a bit later.[8]

Sedentism almost universally leads to the making of pottery, though we've recently learned that pottery making began as early as 15,000 years ago in China, long before agriculture.[9] It became much more widespread in Eurasia after around 9,000 years ago.[10] The first New World pottery appeared in the Amazon Basin only around 7,500 years ago. A separate invention occurred in the Southeastern United States around 4,000 years ago, but did not spread into the Northeast until around 2,800 years ago.[11] In this very basic technology, Eurasia was once again way ahead of the New World.

The population growth caused by sedentism and agriculture led to towns and eventually to urban settlements. This happened more than 7,500 years ago in western Asia, leading to the invention of writing around the same time. Harnessing the power of domestic draft animals encouraged the development of strong materials such as metals. Four thousand years ago, the smelting and casting of bronze had been going on for 2,000 years in both Eastern Europe and western Asia, though the smelting of iron still lay 1,000 years in the future.

The great civilizations of the Old World had already emerged 4,000 years ago. The Old Kingdon of Egypt had just passed, both the Great Pyramid and the Great Sphinx of Giza were already more than 500 years old, and Minoan Crete was developing rapidly. In the Andes and Mesoamerica, the first urban settlements were still quite young.[12] Writing would not develop among the urban Maya for another two millennia. It remains unclear whether an equivalent to writing ever appeared in the Andes, although the smelting of metals developed there about the same time as Mayan writing. Neither urban settlements, nor writing, nor metallurgy ever emerged in prehistoric North America. In sum, the faster pace of history in Eurasia meant that settled, even urban life had begun there by the time the Red Paint People appeared on the scene and was only flickering to life in the New World thousands of miles from the Gulf of Maine, where it could have had no impact on them.

## THE GULF OF MAINE 4,000 YEARS AGO

The Red Paint People were quintessentially a culture of the Gulf of Maine, and so it is critical that we examine the properties of this semi-detached lobe of the northwest Atlantic 4,000 years ago. Historically, it was one of the world's most productive marine ecosystems. Its coastline extends in an arc from Cape Cod in Massachusetts to Cape Sable in Nova Scotia (figure 7). Its seaward limit is defined by Georges and Browns banks. The modern

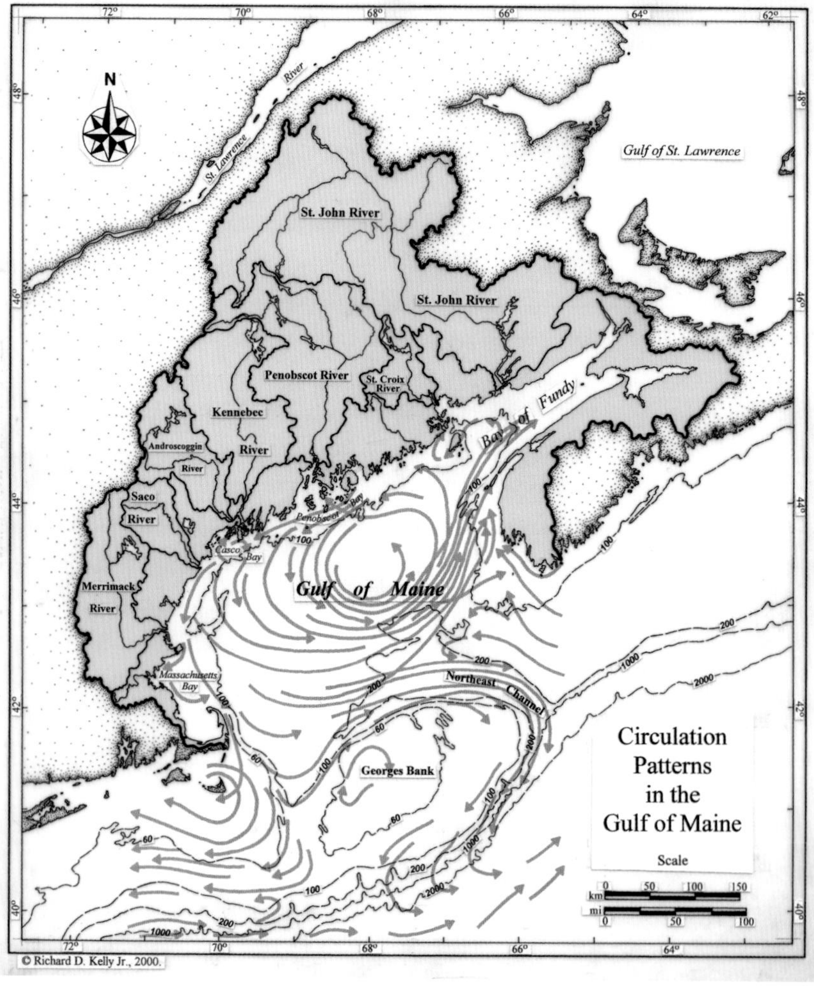


**FIGURE 7.** The Gulf of Maine region showing warm season water circulation patterns.

Gulf of Maine emerged around 13,000 years ago, at the end of the Pleistocene era, as a semi-enclosed sea that increased in depth by hundreds of meters as the world's oceans filled with water formerly frozen as glacial ice. By around 11,500 B.P. (before present [1950], or 9550 B.C.), relative sea levels along the coast of the gulf stood up to 250 feet (75 m) higher than at present (figure 8).[13] Note that we are talking about "relative" sea level. In fact, geologists remain quite unsure how much of this "rise" was due to actual worldwide sea-level rise and how much of it was due to depression of the land surface by the weight of glacial ice, which had reached thicknesses exceeding two miles.

Evidence for this relative high stand includes the skeletal remains of Arctic mammals such as whales, bearded seals, walruses, and mollusks that have been found on what is now dry land far from the modern seacoast. These fossils indicate that the early Gulf of Maine was a cold sea with shellfish species no longer found there but now abundant in northern Newfoundland and Labrador. It would also have been a forbidding

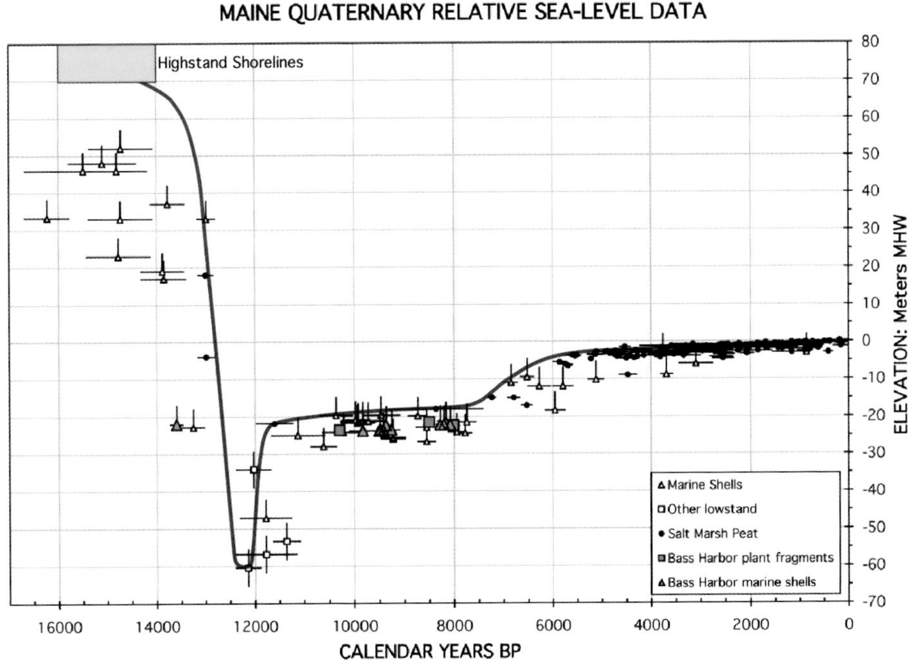


**FIGURE 8.** Maine quaternary relative sea-level data at Bass Harbor. (*Courtesy of Joseph T. Kelly, University of Maine School of Marine Sciences.*)

sea to any humans who wandered its shores, although current evidence suggests that their arrival postdates this high stand by at least a millennium. Then, around 11,000 years ago, as the earth's crust rebounded from the weight of glacial ice, sea levels fell rapidly as much as 200 feet (60 m) lower than at present (figure 8).[14] The rate at which sea levels dropped was so fast it may have been recognized during an individual's life span, and it is probable that there were some humans in the region by then. Since that time, sea levels have risen at varying rates up to the present.

The Gulf of Maine is connected to the northwest Atlantic Ocean by the Northeast Channel, which passes between Georges and Brown banks (figure 9). Eleven thousand years ago, it was quite isolated from the northwest Atlantic Ocean. As a result, oceanic tides had little effect on it, and marine life probably did not thrive under these conditions. By 9,500 years ago, however, as relative sea level rose to within 65 feet (20 m) of its pres-

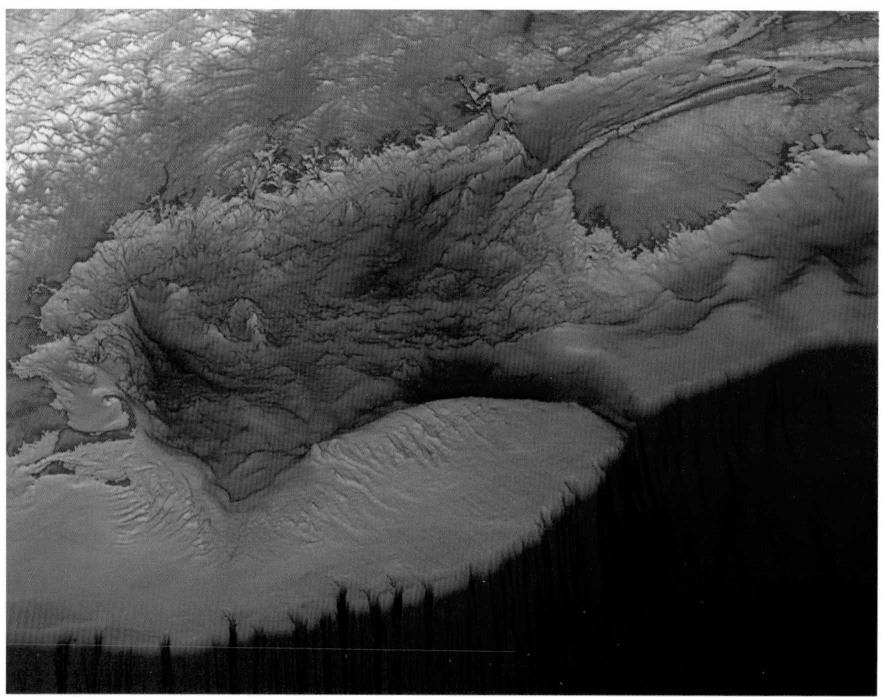

**FIGURE 9.** Digital bathymetry of the Gulf of Maine. (*USGS Open-file Report 98-801.*)

ent position, Atlantic tides increasingly ebbed and flowed in the gulf. Sea-level rise then slowed until 7,000 years ago, then accelerated again, reaching to within 16 feet (5 m) of modern levels by 5,000 years ago. At this time, the shape of the gulf actually amplified the tidal range of the adjacent Atlantic, creating some of the highest tides on earth. Sea-level rise slowed again thereafter, reaching nearly modern levels by 2,000 years ago. This sea-level rise, of course, has driven the coastal erosion, which has taken a heavy toll on the Gulf of Maine's archaeological resources.

FIGURE 10. Photo of two huge cod caught in the early twentieth century on the Labrador coast. They are in the size range represented by the cod bones from the Turner Farm site. (*Courtesy of the Provincial Archives of Newfoundland and Labrador.*)

The shape of the ocean bottom in the Gulf of Maine is such that the movement of water into and out of it, as well as within it, was highly sensitive to sea level, and it is these patterns of movement that are critical to the gulf's biological productivity. What is most relevant to our story is the fact that by around 5,000 years ago, something approaching the modern patterns of water circulation had been established in the Gulf of Maine. Tidal amplitude had risen to the point where deep, cold, nutrient-rich water originating in the Arctic flowed southward along the southeastern coast of Nova Scotia and was drawn into the gulf. High tidal amplitudes then mixed this nutrient-rich water upward to shallow depths, called the photic zone, where sunlight penetrating the water allows photosynthesis to occur. This photosynthesis allows phytoplankton to reproduce in huge numbers, called plankton blooms. Phytoplankton in turn feed zooplankton, tiny animals (small protozoans and large metazoans) that, in turn, support a food chain of larger and larger animals that prey on each other. Four thousand years ago the productivity of cod in the Gulf of Maine may have reached its peak.

Nutrient-rich food chains such as that found in the Gulf of Maine tend to produce large top predator species, which attract human predation. In the Gulf of Maine, those top predators were cod (*Gadus morhua*; figure 10) and swordfish (*Xiphias gladius*; figure 11). The story of swordfish in the gulf is more complex than that of cod. Surely they were abundant there 4,000 years ago but in a manner that requires detailed examination later on.

**FIGURE 11.** Profile of a swordfish showing its skeletal structure.

# 3

# Discovering the Turner Farm Site

As I undertook research on the Moorehead phase for my dissertation, the sad state of existing museum collections from those sites soon convinced me that after graduate school my first task must be to gather better ones. They would be essential to establishing a link between the mortuary ritual evident in the cemeteries and the lifestyle of the people buried in them. After completing my first draft in the winter of 1969, I set off for fieldwork in Maine.

A series of accidents took me to the island of North Haven, one of the Fox Islands in Penobscot Bay, and to a large shell midden now known as the Turner Farm site. I arrived there late in the summer, frustrated by my lack of success in identifying Moorehead phase sites elsewhere on the coast. I actually found North Haven by accident, a lucky one that shaped my field research for the next two decades. My first visit to that part of the Maine coast had been in 1957 on a family camping trip to Merchant's Island, near Deer Isle. I instantly felt at home there; I had always loved the outdoors, and this was my kind of outdoors. Everything about the place appealed to me; the salt air, the clear, cold water, the bold granite shorelines and delightful pocket beaches, the impenetrably dense spruce woods fill-ing in former pastures where thousands of merino sheep had once grazed, reduced to a few small herds by the time I first saw them. During subsequent visits to the neighboring island of Vinalhaven, I enjoyed hanging around the busy working waterfront and decided that I wanted a career that involved working on the water. When I decided to pursue archaeology, the decision to return to the Maine coast came easily, encouraged by the fact that the area had been the focus of some of North America's earliest archaeological research.

My goal for the summer was to examine and photograph all available artifact collections between Deer Isle and Mount Desert Island. Things had been going well. My modus operandi was to visit local post offices where the postmaster could be counted on to know who in the area liked to collect Indian artifacts. Following these leads, I'd met several collectors, some who had built their collections by digging in archaeological sites, a popular form of informal vandalism then endemic to the area, and others who had simply walked the local beaches, picking up artifacts washed out of the sites by winter storms. Some had organized their collections on backing and framed them; some kept them in boxes, drawers, and even old socks. I wasn't choosey and eagerly looked even at the ones obtained by trespass and vandalism. I figured that my looking couldn't unvandalize the site, and I needed all the data I could get.

These amateur collections were anything but systematic in a scientific sense. Scientific collections need not involve real excavations. Indeed, "surface collecting" is a standard archaeological practice. But scientific collection must follow rules designed to extract information from the process. For example, they must be from a defined research area, often from a category of site, such as shell middens. And the materials gathered must be clearly cataloged and kept identifiable as to place of origin. The amateur collectors I met in 1969 often followed none of these rules, making my task of extracting information from their collections a challenging one. Yet, they often developed a strong emotional attachment to their collections, and many were eager to cooperate with me. Beginning with a casual conversation to size each other up, there usually followed a long discussion during which the collectors showed me their favored pieces, revealing their perceived significance. I soon realized that I was subconsciously doing some fact checking on the reliability of my local informants. Sometimes their treasures were not artifacts at all, just oddly shaped stones. The stories they told sometimes conflicted with other information evident in the collection, things said to have been found together that should not have been, or attractive specimens like arrow and spear tips made of lovely colorful rocks that were obviously not from the local area but "salted" into the collection to spice it up. Sometimes a "find" might turn out actually to be a gift from a friend, or an heirloom passed down without the facts surrounding its discovery. On one occasion, I noticed inked-on numbers on some pieces and realized that these artifacts had been bought or stolen from another, better-organized collection.

Despite having to navigate these social difficulties, I'd gained much useful and, I thought, reliable information on which sites held the greatest potential for future excavation. The next phase was photography. I wanted the quality inherent in a large-format camera and so borrowed the anthropology department's Graflex Speed Graphic 4x5 camera, which I loaded with a newfangled Polaroid product—positive-negative film that produced both a print and a negative in one shot. These I backed up with color shots taken with a 35 mm SLR. The resulting prints were pasted into three-ring binders, the negatives slipped into glassine sleeves and the 35 mm slides into plastic mounts. The whole system worked well. I still refer to these images on a regular basis because many of the collections recorded in them are long gone—sold, lost, or scattered among relatives when their owners died. Gone too are many the archaeological sites from which they came, lost to vandalism. This loss is particularly poignant to the east of Penobscot Bay, where the long-established hobby of trespassing on private property to dig for "relics" in local "shell heaps" remains popular.

## A Happy Mistake: Finding the Turner Farm Site

Useful though this collection prospecting was, something was missing. The quarry that eluded me was archaeological evidence dating back beyond 3,000 years to the time of the Red Paint People. Old museum collections from this stretch of the coast contained a few artifacts from this early period, but each time I tried to follow up on the sites where they had been found, I failed to find enough promising evidence to warrant an excavation. What I needed was intact, undisturbed, early shell middens. I wasn't finding them, and realized by late July that I needed to look elsewhere. As the end of the field season approached, I thought I might as well try Vinalhaven, the largest of the Fox Islands in Penobscot Bay. I still had acquaintances there I hoped might put me up and connect me with local collectors. Then I missed the day's last ferry.

Plan B was to take the last ferry to nearby North Haven and cross over the narrow Fox Islands Thorofare to Vinalhaven on a smaller ferry that had run between them when I'd first visited the islands a decade before. The waterfront was quiet when I landed on North Haven, but I spotted eighteen-year-old Eric Hopkins standing on Hopkins Wharf and asked him, "Where is the ferry?" "My father stopped running that years ago," he replied. Stranded for the night, I explained to him why I'd come to North Haven. I told him I could make the best of my mistake if I could find a place to stay, a boat to look for archaeological sites with, and an artifact collection to photograph. He brightened as I went on and told me not to worry; I'd actually come to the right place. He then called out to a man about my age crossing the street nearby. He was David Cooper, and he offered me a room in his home, one wing of which he'd just opened as an inn. That took care of lodging. Hopkins next offered to rent me a beat-up Boston Whaler that had gone adrift and washed up on his beach a few days before, to which he'd attached an outboard motor. Finally, he pointed up the hill to a large summer cottage, telling me that it's owner, George Burr, and his boatman, Oscar Waterman, spent their summers combing the shores of the local islands collecting artifacts that had been washed out of shell middens onto the beach.

It turned out that Cooper was also an artifact collector, and when he learned why I'd come to North Haven, he enthusiastically offered to take me on a tour of the sites. The next morning, he took me on a boat trip around the island, showing me the Turner Farm site and nearly every other shell midden I would work on over the next two decades of research there. The site preservation on North Haven was extraordinary, with very little evidence of the kind of vandalism I'd so often encountered farther to the east. The next day, I took the rented Boston Whaler and returned to the Turner Farm site, looking carefully at its depth and structure, which were revealed by recent storm erosion, and satisfying myself that it looked old, undisturbed, and ripe for excavation.

The seaward edges of shell middens are subject to periodic episodes of erosion as storm-driven waves tear into them, washing away the edges and leaving an erosional scarp as vertical and clean as the wall of an archaeologist's excavation. When I first saw it, the Turner Farm site had recently suffered a bout of erosion, and I could see that the midden looked promising: deep and well stratified. Over time, these erosional scarps slump and become stabilized by vegetation until the next severe storm takes its toll. We saw this whole cycle during our time at the Turner Farm site. The bank became increasingly stabilized between 1969 and the summer of 1975. Then the ferocious Groundhog Day Gale of February 1976 tore into the midden, washing away up to five feet of the site's seaward edge. Over time, a great many shell middens must have been completely eroded in this manner, which leaves us uncertain how dense prehistoric populations along the Gulf of Maine coast were.

Cooper showed me his small artifact collection, mostly picked up on beaches, but he agreed with Hopkins that I really needed to look at the Burr-Waterman collection, and he called to arrange my visit. The collection was housed in handmade glass-topped cases, so very different from the old socks and shoe boxes that held the collections I'd been photographing earlier that summer. It was a wonder to behold. Unlike any other collectors I had met, Burr and Waterman understood the importance of systematic collecting. Each artifact in their collection had an identifying code, which could be matched to a master list of sites all over Penobscot Bay. Access to this collection saved me at least a full season of fieldwork and thousands of research dollars, and it was there that I found exactly what I'd been looking for, early artifacts from a handful of sites, most of them from the Turner Farm site. And, better yet, my tour of the island with David made it clear that local landowners had not allowed much digging into the shell middens on their properties.

From my first encounter with the Red Paint People in the basement of the Peabody Museum, I sensed that this material was highly unusual and very different from other cultures of the prehistoric Northeast. Even so, it also seemed to me quite at home there, not an alien intrusion from some other region. Intrusions of foreign peoples into the Northeast did occur repeatedly in the past, but this didn't seem like one to me. Rather, as I continued to work on it, I came to see it as a refinement, a distillation, and an intensification of an earlier widespread culture I had worked on with Ritchie. We called it the Small Stemmed Point tradition. Its artifact styles included several with clear local pedigrees, but added to these was a large group of unique elements that set it distinctly apart. Some of its most common artifacts, such as stone spear tips and fishing weights called plummets, were plain, utilitarian, and clearly derived from local prototypes. Others were basically utilitarian in design but raised to a much higher aesthetic or symbolic level by superb craftsmanship or engraved decoration. Still others seemed purely symbolic. Most fascinating of all, though, were those from far-off places. Nothing like these exotic pieces were known elsewhere in the Northeast. I knew those source areas needed to be pinned down as precisely as possible, another item in the long-range research project I was formulating.

In the meantime, I had to find new early sites, and it was that pursuit that took me to North Haven, that most fortunate mistake of my career. I've often wondered how differently things would have turned out had I not missed the ferry to Vinalhaven. It has a much larger land mass than North Haven, so I expected that it would have more sites, but I soon realized that land mass has little to do with site location, which is determined by a fairly strict set of criteria: right on the shore, on fairly level sandy to gravely soil (never clay), facing south to east, near a freshwater source, and behind a gravel beach, probably to facilitate the storage and launching of canoes. It turns out such locations are scarce on Vinalhaven, which has bold, rocky, south-facing shores that get viciously raked by storms. Suitable beaches are scarce for the same reason. As a high granitic island, freshwater sources are also in short supply. If early sites ever existed there, they were eroded away long ago, which is possible as Vinalhaven is exposed to the open sea around much of its shoreline and so is vulnerable to storm damage. North Haven, on the other hand, has a long southeast-facing shoreline on the Fox Island Thorofare, well protected from storms and lined with many beaches. North Haven's terrain is also less elevated, is covered with a thicker mantle of soil, and has numerous fresh water sources.

I returned to North Haven in July 1971, encouraged by the fact that, with a crew of twelve college students, I had the manpower to accomplish something useful. I had obtained permission to excavate some promising middens on North Haven, but not the Turner Farm site. Unfortunately, these sites had produced few of the early artifact styles I was looking for, but my research interests were ultimately broader than the Red Paint issue, and they were a useful place to start.

When I visited the Turner Farm site by boat in 1969, I saw that it lay on an abandoned farm owned by the Turner family. David Cooper told me that the Turners tended to be reclusive and that getting permission to work there was a doubtful proposition. I decided not to pursue permission by letter, as I had for other North Haven sites, because I wanted local coaching before initiating the process—a wise move as it turned out. I soon learned that, in addition to their reclusive habits, members of the Turner family had had earlier run-ins with archaeologists. In 1904, a party including Oric Bates, later a professional archaeologist but then an undergraduate at Harvard, were refused permission to excavate there but later returned surreptitiously only to be chased off by "the head of the Turner family being a lonely savage who . . . favored me with both barrels of his shotgun."[1] Islanders told me that ownership had recently passed to William Rice of Massachusetts and to his cousin, an island woman named Dorothy Ames, but they doubted this would make my task any easier.

As the summer progressed, curiosity about our work at other sites increased, and islanders began to visit our excavations, often and repeatedly, asking so many questions that we eventually had to assign a crewmember to act as docent. One day, a tall fellow stepped from the crowd and started probing me with questions. I eventually admitted to him that my heart was set on excavation at the Turner Farm, but that things didn't look too promising. He then told me he was Bill Rice, and that he'd have a word with co-owner Dorothy Ames about my interests. A few days later, Rice arranged my first meeting with Dorothy. The meeting was difficult at first because Dorothy was deaf, having lost her hearing to scarlet fever as a child. But once I learned to understand her, I sensed her deep pride in the lovely Turner Farm property and her willingness to let us work there. On the second of August, we were mapping the Turner Farm site and opening excavations there. That summer, we excavated a roughly one-hundred-foot-long test trench from which we expanded excavations during the next four seasons. Dorothy soon became a regular visitor to the site and a dear friend.

The fact that the Maine coast is slowly sinking relative to sea level is most obvious to archaeologists from the jagged erosional scarps, at the seaward edges of many sites. The erosional scarps at the Turner Farm site caused us to assume that it has been significantly reduced by erosion. But because the midden's surface sloped to the west, eventually to disappear into a salt marsh and gravel beach, we decided, in 1976 , to excavate these features to determine whether they had overrun and inundated the western portion of the site. We also dreamed of finding preserved wooden artifacts in ancient marsh peat, which is composed almost entirely of undecayed vegetable matter. By the end of summer, we'd confirmed that the midden had indeed been covered by beach deposits and salt marsh, but our trench into the marsh reached a depth of only six feet, not deep enough to encounter prehistoric peat.

We suspended operations at the site in 1976, turning our attention to other shell middens and other research issues around Penobscot Bay, but after a four-year hiatus we were asked to host a demonstration for a field trip of the American Quaternary Association, so we returned to the site to open an unexcavated area that promised—and delivered— important new Moorehead phase materials. That was our last excavation at the Turner Farm site, to which we'd devoted most of seven seasons of excavation.

Archaeological excavation strives for precise three-dimensional spatial control of where all recovered objects are found. For most sites, where the excavation is into soil, this process is relatively simple. A grid is staked out on the surface of the site, oriented to compass bearings. Excavation units within the grid are then opened. Artifacts and other items of interest are mapped with respect to the grid, so that their relative positions can be reconstructed during analysis. Depth is also important, and in stratified sites, both absolute depth and stratum location are carefully recorded. These procedures were developed by Putnam in the 1880s and have become standard throughout North America since then. During his Martha's Vineyard work, William Ritchie added some important refinements, including leaving unexcavated walls, called balks, between these units to preserve the midden's stratigraphy so that it could be recorded by photography and drawing, a practice I carried on at the Turner Farm site.

Troweling through a Maine shell midden is hard work and requires constant attention because, unlike shell-free sites where excavators can rely on screens to separate wanted materials from the unwanted soil matrix, shell middens can't be effectively screened because the largest and most ubiquitous objects recovered are the shells themselves. Archaeologists put up with these difficulties because of the significant payoffs mentioned earlier—the preservation of bone and the buildup of observable strata. But these advantages, too, have their drawbacks. Without screening, the collection of bone fragments is incredibly time consuming, and once an excavation unit is completed, recording its stratigraphy requires the combined efforts of a small committee. Added to this was the unfortunate fact that on a calm summer day, the site was one of the hottest spots on the Maine coast, protected as it was from breezes from every direction. Generally speaking, however, the crew shrugged off these difficulties because what we were finding was so extraordinary.

The Turner Farm shell midden is the best preserved and probably the oldest on the Gulf of Maine coast. It contains the remains of many episodes of occupation dating from before 5,000 years ago to the late 1500s, when European explorers and traders first entered the area. Well-preserved middens are so rare and precious to archaeologists that we excavate downward through all strata with equal care despite our intense interest in the earliest ones. The areas we chose to open at the Turner Farm site, however, were governed by where we thought were our best chances of finding remains of the Moorehead phase village. Our approach was to open small five-by-five-foot sections under the control of one or two crew members who were responsible for recovering all artifacts, samples, and data from it (figure 12).[2] After the stratigraphy had been recorded, we excavated the balks, and it was from them that we took systematic samples of midden material from all strata for subsequent compositional analysis.

Having quickly found what we'd come for during our first season at the site in 1971, our elation continued in subsequent seasons as we gathered bone specimens indicating diet and artifact making in amounts the Red Paint cemeteries had never provided, as well as artifacts that closely tied this village to Red Paint cemeteries in the area. Surely this was a major village, likely occupied by the very people buried in some of those cem-

**FIGURE 12.** Turner Farm site under excavation in 1972.

eteries. In the end we opened excavations covering roughly 25 percent of the site's surface area. We hesitated to open more because, having gathered what we thought were sufficient data to understand what went on at the site during Moorehead phase times, we were anxious to conserve the rest of the midden for future research.

One of the most gratifying and valuable aspects of our work at the Turner Farm site was the strong support shown us by the North Haven community. Ellen Nichols, one of our loyal volunteers, opened her home to us, including the kitchen and dining room, to work on the messy processes of examining, washing, conserving, and cataloging artifacts. Other islanders wined and dined us and invited the crew on weekend boat excursions. Best of all, at season's end, local contractor Eliot Brown provided equipment to backfill our large, deep excavations. In return, we offered tours of the site, and Sunday afternoon show-and-tell sessions at the town library, where the community could ask us questions about what we were finding. The bonds between some archaeologists and islanders created during those years have lasted to this day. Archaeologists return regularly or periodically to the island or get in touch with North Haveners who are traveling near their homes. Best of all, these bonds are now fostering a new generation of collaborative research between archaeologists, natural scientists, and the North Haven community.

## What the Faunal Remains Revealed

Our fieldwork was exciting but also hectic, and we barely had time to appreciate what we were finding. That had to wait until our off-season months back at the lab, when we could closely examine our finds, show them to colleagues, and begin to piece together their stories. Analysis of the site involved two processes: spatial/stratigraphic analysis and faunal identification. All artifacts and faunal remains were sorted according to the stratum they came from, then mapped horizontally by stratum. For the Moorehead phase strata, this allowed us to define what seemed to be household compounds. These had hearths, artifacts, and bone refuse near the shore. Behind them were areas with few artifacts but with a lot of evidence of stone toolmaking. These "backyards" also had several small pits, and some animal bone that looked gnawed, which suggested that dogs had been kept there.[3] With the faunal remains sorted stratigraphically, we identified as many as we could.

Most bones were fragmentary, the more fragile ones broken from the weight of the overlying midden and the larger mammal bones purposely broken to get at the marrow, one of the most nutritious and desirable parts of the animal. Identifying these broken bones by species was often not possible, so in the end we had large amounts of bones labeled "unidentified bird," "probably deer," and so on. The ones we could identify, however, yielded a vast amount of information, allowing us, for example, to compare changing hunting and fishing patterns over time. We also wanted to learn about the seasonal patterns of hunting and fishing. A characteristic of hunter-gatherers, especially those who live in regions with well-differentiated seasons, is that they consume seasonally abundant resources that vary over the year. In order to assess the seasonality of various Moorehead hunter-gathering activities, we paid attention to several indicators found in the bones. One is the mere presence or absence of a migratory species that was only seasonally available. The birds and some fish species are especially revealing in this respect. Other obvious indicators of seasonality include whether a deer antler was shed or removed while still attached to the skull and whether juveniles were present.

Useful as these standard indicators were for some types of animals, they couldn't be applied to other important species, such as female deer, clams, and cod. We therefore added to our analysis methods developed by wildlife biologists for examining annual patterns of growth in mollusk shells and animal skeletons (figure 13). These techniques work on the principle that many animals have parts that grow in regular annual increments over the course of their lives. Growth often stops for a brief period during the year, leaving a visible marker. Clams, for example, stop laying down new shell in the early spring when they spawn, while the bone tissue that attaches teeth to jaws in mammals, called cementum, often stops growing during breeding season. These growth arrests allow us to estimate the time of year when the animal died by measuring the amount of growth it added during its last year of life in comparison to previous years.

What we found out about seasonality surprised us. When we began work, we expected that, during all periods of its occupation, the Turner Farm site would turn out to be a temporary summer camp, but this turned out to be almost completely incorrect. Our conclusion from this research was that the site was apparently occupied during most of the year and that rather

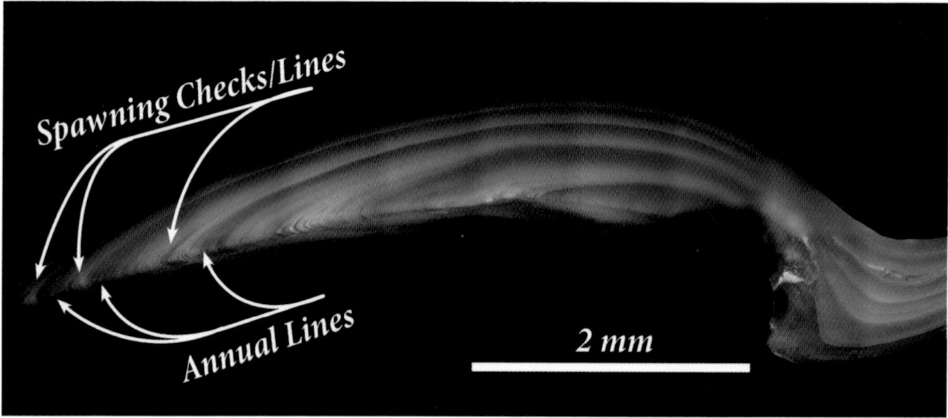


**FIGURE 13.** Cross-section of a clamshell umbo showing annual growth lines and spawning lines. (*Courtesy of Will Ambrose.*)

than having its highest population in the summer, this was actually the time when it may have been completely abandoned for brief periods (figure 14).

My 1995 monograph on the Turner Farm site barely touched on the important issue of biological productivity, which has since come to dominate my research interests. Essentially, I thought that the prehistoric Gulf of Maine looked pretty much like it did in the 1970s. This was before the recent overfishing in the last two decades of the twentieth century that brought fish stocks down to levels so low as to require federal intervention to save them. No one could have imagined this happening in 1970, but I should nevertheless have realized that there was something wrong with this "business as usual" idea even as I excavated the site. From the beginning, I'd been impressed by the sheer abundance of faunal remains we were recovering. I was pleased that so much bone would allow reliable reconstructions of prehistoric hunting and fishing, but as work progressed, I began to notice not so much the abundance of bone but their diversity and size.

Many of the species we encountered were not surprising. Deer bone, for example, was abundant, but island people still hunt deer. At first, I was surprised to find moose bone because today it is a rare event to see a moose on North Haven. However, I later read an early historic account of moose hunting on Mount Desert Island, suggesting that moose may have been present on the Fox Islands prehistorically.[4] There were bones from

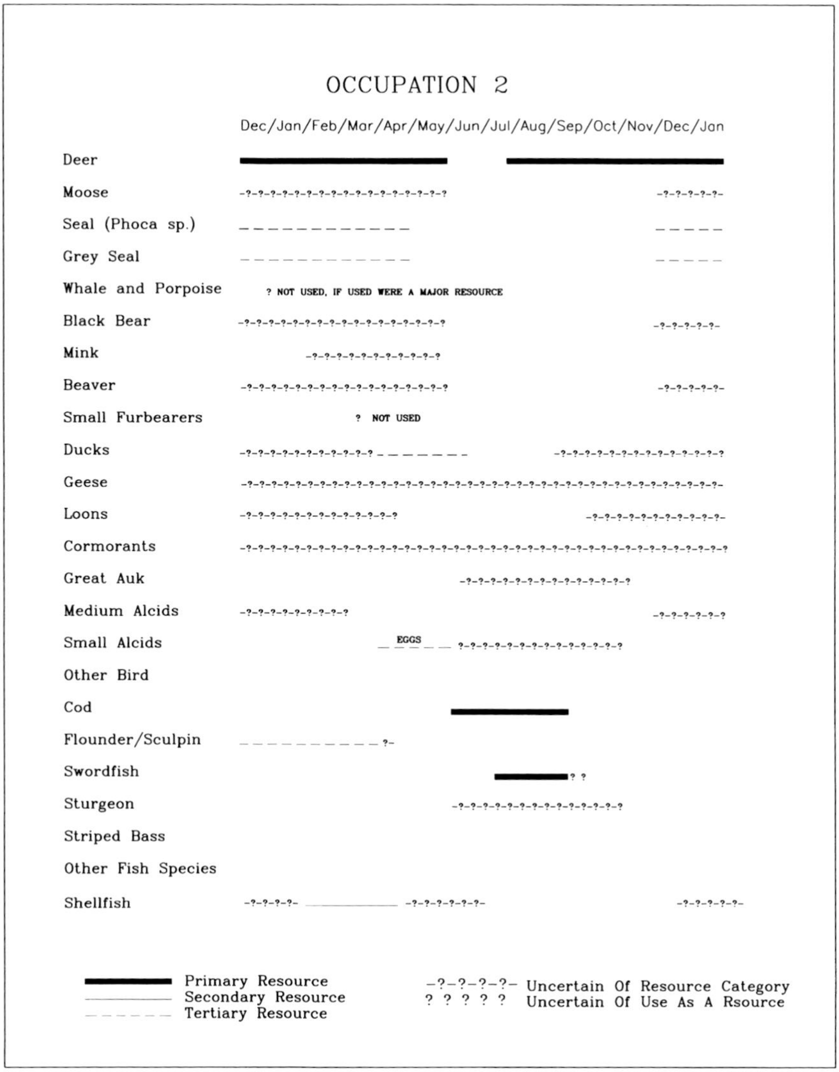

OCCUPATION 2

Dec/Jan/Feb/Mar/Apr/May/Jun/Jul/Aug/Sep/Oct/Nov/Dec/Jan

Deer
Moose
Seal (Phoca sp.)
Grey Seal
Whale and Porpoise — ? NOT USED, IF USED WERE A MAJOR RESOURCE
Black Bear
Mink
Beaver
Small Furbearers — ? NOT USED
Ducks
Geese
Loons
Cormorants
Great Auk
Medium Alcids
Small Alcids — EGGS
Other Bird
Cod
Flounder/Sculpin
Swordfish
Sturgeon
Striped Bass
Other Fish Species
Shellfish

Primary Resource
Secondary Resource
Tertiary Resource
-?-?-?-?- Uncertain Of Resource Category
? ? ? ? ? Uncertain Of Use As A Rsource

**FIGURE 14.** Seasonality of faunal remains, Occupation 2 at the Turner Farm site.

beaver (*Castor canadensis*) and bear (*Ursus americanus*), both of which are now absent from the Fox Islands but present on the nearby mainland, and it was not difficult to imagine hunting trips to the mainland to acquire any of these useful species. There were even bones of two species I could never observe firsthand: the great auk (*Plautus impennis*), a large, flightless, migratory penguinlike bird, and a large mink species known as the sea mink (*Neovison macrodon*), both of which were extinguished by overhunting during the nineteenth century.

The really interesting story, however, lay in the fish bone. The bones of cod were abundant, but we didn't immediately recognize them as cod because they were so large. As a teenager, I had caught what I considered to be good-sized, 30-inch cod off the Fox Islands, but many of these 4,000-year-old cod were simply huge, 5.5 to 6 feet (1.5 to 2 m) long and likely in the 100- to 130-pound range (220 to 285 kg).[5] Such giants were almost never taken in the Gulf of Maine in the late twentieth century, and today only small numbers of much smaller fish survive.

The vertebrae, fin rays, and swords (called rostra) of swordfish were also abundant. This was not a complete surprise because swordfish had been marginally noted in reports on two Moorehead phase shell middens excavated in the late 1930s and early 1940s, though neither report listed them among the food remains.[6] At the time I wondered about these omissions, but in hindsight, I now realize how focused these early workers were on sorting out issues of cultural identity. Moreover, they were working in an era when archaeologists did not yet understand the tremendous research potential of faunal remains.

Like the cod, many of these swordfish were really large. Judging by the widths of their rostra, some must have exceeded 10 feet (3 m) in length and likely approached the known maximum weight of 1,190 pounds (540 kg).[8] Actually, abundant swordfish remains of similar size had been recovered in at the Nevin site, but we didn't know that at the time because the excavators were of the opinion that the site was disturbed and perhaps not very old; they had published no report on the site, and the bones were not available for study.

As I began to publicize our discoveries at the Turner Farm site at conferences, fisheries biologists in some of those audiences expressed skepticism about our claims to have found abundant swordfish remains, suspecting that we had misidentified the remains of some other species of billfish such as marlin. Some asked for samples to examine and confirmed our identifications. Their confirmation dispelled any doubt in my mind about the importance of swordfish to people of the Moorehead phase. But even though I was surprised by the abundance of these large fish, as I looked out at fishing boats passing by the Turner Farm site, I still imagined that life beneath the waters of Penobscot Bay in the 1970s was not too different from what it had been 4,000 years earlier, a bit cooler perhaps, but populated with the same species in roughly that same abundance. My complacency regarding these large fish continued until soon after the Turner Farm monograph was published in 1995.

## Long Chronology and the Fishing Down of Marine Food Webs

Beginning in the 1990s, fisheries biologist Daniel Pauly of the University of British Columbia was the first to publicize the "shifting baseline" phenomenon, the unconscious process by which fishermen and marine ecologists lost track of a marine ecosystem's original productivity in the face of its actual decline. Pauly inspired a small group of marine ecologists to reassess what past oceans had been like. Placing their faith in historic documents, which were eschewed as unreliable by the majority of their profession, and in bone samples provided by archaeologists, they sought methods to construct reliable long chronologies for marine ecosystems. In the late 1990s, Oceanographer Jeremy Jackson of the Scripps Institution of Oceanography began to assemble a diverse research team, which included several of these innovators, to look at the deep history of marine ecosystems. This work took place at the National Center for Ecological Analysis and Synthesis (NCEAS) in Santa Barbara, California.

Jackson specializes in coral reef studies, and his original motivation was his personal experience of seeing Caribbean coral reef communities decline from the dazzling beauty of his youth to their sadly degraded condition today. This led him to suspect that the biological productivity of the world's oceans has been far more severely degraded by human overfishing for a far longer period of time than ecologists generally believed, and he hoped his team could help him prove it. I was invited to join Jackson's research team by Robert Steneck, a friend and former student of Jackson's, who now teaches at the University of Maine's Darling Marine Center in Walpole. My contribution was mainly to deal with issues of chronology and to provide faunal remains from Maine archaeological sites for comparison to modern samples.

As it turned out, data from the Turner Farm and other archaeological sites played a significant role in developing these long chronology paradigms of marine ecological history, and at the close of the book, I shall consider the future promise of this multidisciplinary approach for addressing pressing issues of marine ecosystem health.

The chronologies we reconstructed revealed that the species depletion and other systemic stresses now being documented for most of the world's marine ecosystems have deep historic roots, often extending back to early European colonial expansion or even beyond.[8] They revealed some startling facts. Columbus's ships, for example, plowed through so many now-endangered sea turtles that his crew feared they were running onto rocks. Jacques Cartier encountered so many now-vanished cod off Newfoundland that he said it slowed his ships. And who would believe that the now-depleted and polluted Chesapeake Bay once exported sturgeon caviar.

The NCEAS working group was a transforming experience for me. For one thing, I learned a tremendous amount about how marine ecosystems work and how so many of them have become depleted. This amounted to nothing less than a personal paradigm shift. I could never look at the Gulf of Maine in the same way again. Even more than the gulf's modern well-wishers, I truly began to understand what had been lost. Equally important to me was the recognition by the ecologists in the group that archaeological input could actually contribute to addressing a problem of global importance, in two ways. First, because ancient faunal remains are what scientists call voucher specimens because they bear accurate witness to the past state of ecosystems.[9] Their sizes, relative abundances, and chemical compositions provide a myriad of clues, which systematic biology and geochemistry are rapidly learning to decipher. Second, while the ecologists on our team struggled with time scales because the timing and rate of degradation was different for different ecosystems, my anthropological background quickly led me to realize that all these stories of decline had a common factor: major degradation began with the onset of European colonialism and proceeded stepwise as the colonizers began to sell first to regional, then national, and, finally, global markets. Long an avid consumer of the research output of marine ecology, I now felt that archaeology could also become a contributor.

The first report by our NCEAS group appeared in *Science* in 2001 and caused quite a stir. It laid out a strong case for drastic declines in four widespread kinds of ecosystems: estuaries, kelp forests, coral reefs, and open-ocean systems beginning with the arrival of European colonists and ending with the severe recent depletions caused by the global market for fish. Stated another way, the prehistoric oceans were vastly richer than anyone had thought. We regarded this as critically important because managers charged with restoring the productivity of these systems have been setting their restoration goals not to "natural baselines," as they thought, but to shifting ones that reflect depletions not detected earlier. Subsequent papers have explored some of these ecosystem depletions in closer detail, and I sense that our message has gotten out to the fisheries management community.[10]

It turns out that, even if we were correct in our assessment of the world's historic marine ecosystems, we probably made one incorrect assumption that has required subsequent correction. Because our NCEAS team focused on industrial fishing, we assumed that the subsistence fishing by indigenous populations occurred at a sustainable level and did not deplete local stocks. But Steneck pointed out something in our fish bone data that I hadn't noticed: the trophic levels of the major fish species found at the Turner Farm site had declined over time in a pattern that has the appearance of a system undergoing a prehistoric version of Pauly's fishing down a marine food web. During Moorehead phase times, the main fish species taken were very large swordfish and cod, keystone predators in the Gulf of Maine. During the next period of occupation, around 3,600 years ago, swordfish had completely disappeared and cod were also in decline, giving way to meso-predators like flounder, sculpin, and dogfish. This trend continued during successively later occupations of the site, the last of which dates to around the time of European arrival in the area. At this point, seal hunting underwent a sudden increase in popularity, perhaps because a resource-hungry local human population was forced to expand its resource base to include less-preferred marine mammals to supplement a depleted fishery. We had to face the possibility that even indigenous fishers might have impacted local fish abundance.

In a paper we published about this pattern, we admitted that we could not prove this was a case of prehistoric fishing down of a marine food web but argued that it had all the appearances of one. The inclusion of geochemist Beverly Johnson as an author reflects the growing importance of isotope geochemistry in tracking changes in prehistoric marine ecosystems, particularly the light stable isotopes of nitrogen and carbon and the trace element sulfur, which have the potential to track changes over time in the Penobscot Bay system extending back to the early Holocene, which is as far back as we can obtain bone samples.This research is ongoing and shows real promise. At the same time, marine ecologist Will Ambrose, also at Bates, is applying elemental and growth-pattern analysis to mollusk shells from the Turner Farm site and other Maine coastal sites to assess spatial and temporal changes in mollusk growth rates and oceanic temperature and salinity.

This kind of multidisciplinary research is exciting, and it may well help to explain the rise and fall of the Moorehead phase. Indeed, it has already demonstrated the capability of the system to support a fairly dense human population, which is probably a necessary condition for making something like the Moorehead phase economically possible. In the end, however, I suspect that marine productivity will not suffice to explain the Moorehead phase because its emergence is disproportionate in speed and magnitude to any changes in marine abundance we are likely to discover. We will return to this issue after establishing a temporal and spatial context for the Red Paint People.

# 4

# DISCOVERING THE MOOREHEAD PHASE

THE FIRST PRINTED reference to a Red Paint cemetery appears in Frederic Ward Putnam's preface to Willoughby's 1898 book on his excavations at Orland and Ellsworth, where he mentions that Hamlin had infirmed him about "an interesting Indian burial place" at Bucksport. This is no doubt a reference to Hamlin's presentation at the 1882 convention of the American Academy for the Advancement of Science. As mentioned above, the text of the paper is now lost, but according to Moorehead, Hamlin described many unusual tools found in red ocher.[1] He had apparently requested Willoughby's assistance in excavating the site in 1892.[2]

Given how spectacular Hamlin's and Willoughby's finds were, it seems odd that no evidence of this culture seems to have been recognized before then. This absence is underscored in a book titled *Primitive Industry*, published by Charles C. Abbott in 1881.[3] Abbott, a physician by training, was an admirer of Putnam and, like him, a long chronology man. Putnam had sponsored some of Abbott's excavations in the 1870s and communicated regularly with him thereafter. Both remained up-to-date on the latest archaeological finds throughout the East, and yet *Primitive Industry* includes no mention of bayonets, zoomorphic figurines, exotic projectile points, bone harpoons, or any of the other remarkable artifacts of the Moorehead phase. It does illustrate and describe the more mundane utilitarian artifact types now associated with it, but like the rest of the artifacts included in the book, these seem merely to be randomly collected objects whose significance neither Putnam nor Abbott understood. And how could Abbott have known what lay in the cloistered archaeological collection of the Ursulines at Three Rivers?

Willoughby's report on the Maine cemeteries, published by the Peabody Museum in volume 1 of its Archaeological Papers series, was a model of archaeological reporting. It was the first monograph to show in detail the spatial locations of each find, stratigraphic profiles of the pits, and illustrations of most artifacts. The cemeteries were soon introduced to a national audience in 1893 when Willoughby and Frederic Ward Putnam presented artifacts and models of Peabody Museum fieldwork in various parts of North America at the 1893 Columbia World's Exposition. These exhibits not only presented novel information about American prehistory but demonstrated methods of controlled excavation newly developed by Harvard archaeologists. Following Moorehead's excavations in the early twentieth century, the Red Paint sites came to be understood as cemeteries from which nearly all traces of bone had been dissolved by the region's generally acid soils. Besides the ubiquitous ocher, most graves in these cemeteries were furnished with several stone artifacts, most utilitarian but some that are highly unusual and beautifully crafted and some imported from faraway places. The special qualities of these cemeteries include their large size (seventy-two ocher-filled pits at the Emerson site in Orland) compared to other prehistoric cemeteries throughout the Northeast; their large numbers (fifty-four identified to date); the abundance of grave offerings found in them; and the technological quality, variety, and diverse geographic origins of their furnishings.[4]

## The Moorehead Phase

Only in the last two decades of the twentieth century did archaeologists develop a clear understanding of the origins of the Moorehead phase and its relationship to the Red Paint cemeteries. Granted that there are still a few thin spots in the archaeological record, we can trace the development of cultures of the Gulf of Maine coast from the entry of southern immigrants around 8500 B.P. to the end of the Moorehead phase more than four millennia later. At first, the immigrants seem to have maintained close ties with their ancestral homelands, and their artifact styles changed gradually in unison with those of the Southeast. After around 6,000 years ago, however, patterns more specific to the Northeast appeared. At the same time, there was sharp increase in site numbers, which probably represents a significant growth in population, though with the increase, these populations remained conservative, continuing the same pattern of generalized hunting, gathering, and fishing for millennia. Judging from archaeological evidence, their ceremonial lives were unremarkable. In only a very few places near the coasts of northern Massachusetts, New Hampshire, and Maine did they create small cemeteries of a few graves furnished with the kinds of goods found at their village sites—mainly spear points, adzes, gouges, and whetstones.[5]

Sometime shortly after 5,000 years ago, the pace of cultural change quickened, and more clearly defined, regionally specific groups began to appear, none more distinctly than in a small region along the Maine coast east of the Androscoggin River. There, people began to consciously differentiate themselves from even their near-neighbors to the south and west. They began as northern representatives of the Small Stemmed Point tradition, which is prominent in the archaeological record as far south as Long Island.[6] It's a ridiculous name, really, for the archaeological signature of any Stone Age culture amounts to far more than a projectile point style. But their projectile points, while fitting well into a long succession of evolving styles, suddenly became quite odd. They were tiny in comparison to earlier point styles, usually with stems that probably were set into sockets at the end of spear shafts. Points of this size are suitable for arrowheads, yet most archaeologists doubt that the bow and arrow had yet arrived in the region. Oddest of all, many were made of white quartz. Though among the hardest of minerals, quartz is very difficult to flake, and prehistoric people rarely used it. It's the distinctiveness of the projectile points that earned them their archaeological name.

Between 1972 and 1980, evidence from two sites shed new light on these strange small point makers. From the deepest parts of the Turner Farm site came hearth pits dated to around 5000 B.P. associated with cod, swordfish bone—hallmarks of the Moorehead phase—and small stemmed points. At about the same time from a partially submerged site in Seabrook

Marsh, on the New Hampshire coast, Brian Robinson discovered a group of five swordfish rostra along with cod bones and small stemmed projectile points. Human burials were also found at the site, one of which was radiocarbon-dated to 4780 B.P.[7] These two discoveries provide the earliest-known evidence of swordfish hunting in the context, not yet of the Moorehead phase, but in its ancestral Small Stemmed Point tradition. It is possible that both swordfish hunting and cod fishing may have greater antiquity in the region, but no earlier sites with bone preservation have been found, and possibly none survive.

These finds made it clear that within a few centuries of their emergence from a generalized Archaic background, Small Stemmed Point tradition people living in Maine began to exhibit an increasing distinctiveness not shared by their cousins to the south. They began to cluster near the coast and to hunt swordfish. They began to create cemeteries, some with well over a dozen graves amply furnished with finely made weapons and tools that differed from those of their ancestors. These cemeteries soon began to exhibit a complexity unparalleled in northeastern North America, with a few exceptions in Labrador and Newfoundland that we will discuss below. Their technology expanded to include a wide range of bone implements and stone artifacts sculpted into both functional and zoomorphic forms, some with very finely incised decorations, indicating an elaborate symbolic system. Soon thereafter they began to draw in symbolically laden artifacts from places as far as 1,000 miles away. The full range of distinguishing characteristics did not suddenly appear full blown, but it did develop quickly, reaching efflorescence after a few centuries. These innovators became the Red Paint People, now known to archaeologists as the Moorehead phase.

## How to Read a Cemetery

Archaeologists look at the world differently from other people. We find it hard merely to acknowledge the existence of a human artifact without wondering who made it, why, and how it got to where we encountered it. And so it is when, on occasion, I spend an afternoon strolling in a cemetery. Mount Auburn cemetery in Cambridge is my favorite. The first of America's garden cemeteries when it opened in 1831, it has since become the final resting place for over 93,000 well-to-do Bostonians. To most visitors, it presents a peaceful, parklike atmosphere. It is, in fact, an arboretum as well as a cemetery.

How different is Mount Auburn from the typical New England graveyard, with its uniform rows of headstones listing the bare facts of the deceased's life. When I walk there, my archaeologist's eye sees in the monuments and gravestones a flood of social information about prosperous Bostonians over nearly two centuries. The largest monuments announce social prominence. Many announce military service, even heroism. One says, "I died young but I was a favorite child."

Prehistoric cemeteries also have stories to tell, through using symbolic language that we don't fully understand. Let's begin with Mount Auburn cemetery, which started out as farmland and achieved its visual prominence through landscape design. Unlike the architects of Mount Auburn, hunter-gatherers never much bothered with shaping the landscape, preferring instead to place their ceremonial sites on naturally suitable, often elevated, landforms (figure 15). Most Red Paint cemeteries lie in prominent, though not dramatic, spots along the banks of small to large rivers, though some are on ponds, near the inlets and outlets of streams. Their orientations relative to water are more variable than village sites, which usually face south to east. A few have been found on the seacoast, and many more coastal cemeteries have probably been lost to erosion. The surprising number located along interior waterways, however, must indicate that even though the Moorehead phase was strongly marine oriented, some aspect of the interior landscape was symbolically important to these people. In this regard, it is worth noting that interior cemetery locations are generally not near significant interior village sites and instead are often near falls and rapids, good places to net and spear fish. That these were recognized as important places is supported by the presence at several cemeteries of other graves, both earlier and later than those of the Red Paint People. In a region with extensive heavy clay soils, the cemeteries are confined to soils ranging from fine sand to coarse gravel. Perhaps this choice of soils was simply for the convenience of grave digging, though a few cemeteries are on very coarse, boulder-strewn terrain, suggesting that clay soils were actively avoided, possibly for symbolic reasons.

Perhaps the most striking thing about the Red Paint cemeteries is the discreteness of their geographic distribution, which is even more circumscribed than that of their habitation sites. Indeed, when archaeological

**FIGURE 15.** The upper Ormsby site, which includes a Red Paint cemetery, is situated on a high terrace overlooking the Androscoggin River in Brunswick. This is probably the most prominent landform with a Moorehead phase cemetery.

research in the Northeast revived in the 1970s, many expected new discoveries in adjacent areas, particularly in the relatively unexplored Maritime Provinces. Four decades later, however, their limits remain as understood in 1970, clearly clustered between the lower reaches of the Kennebec and St. John rivers. Only the recent discovery of two small cemeteries on the previously unexplored lower Androscoggin River has expanded this range slightly westward.

The grave count at Red Paint cemeteries is highly variable; one site in Union apparently had only a single grave, while Moorehead claimed up to two hundred at the Haskell site in Blue Hill. A fairly typical one is Soper's Knoll on Lake Alamoosook in Orland (figure 16). The graves are generally well clustered, covering an area of 100 to 200 square meters, but generally they do not overlap, suggesting some form of surface marker. They apparently range in depth from 10 centimeters to 2 meters. Overall, there is no perceptible pattern to the arrangement of the graves or of their contents at most cemeteries. Moorehead claimed to have found a large communal

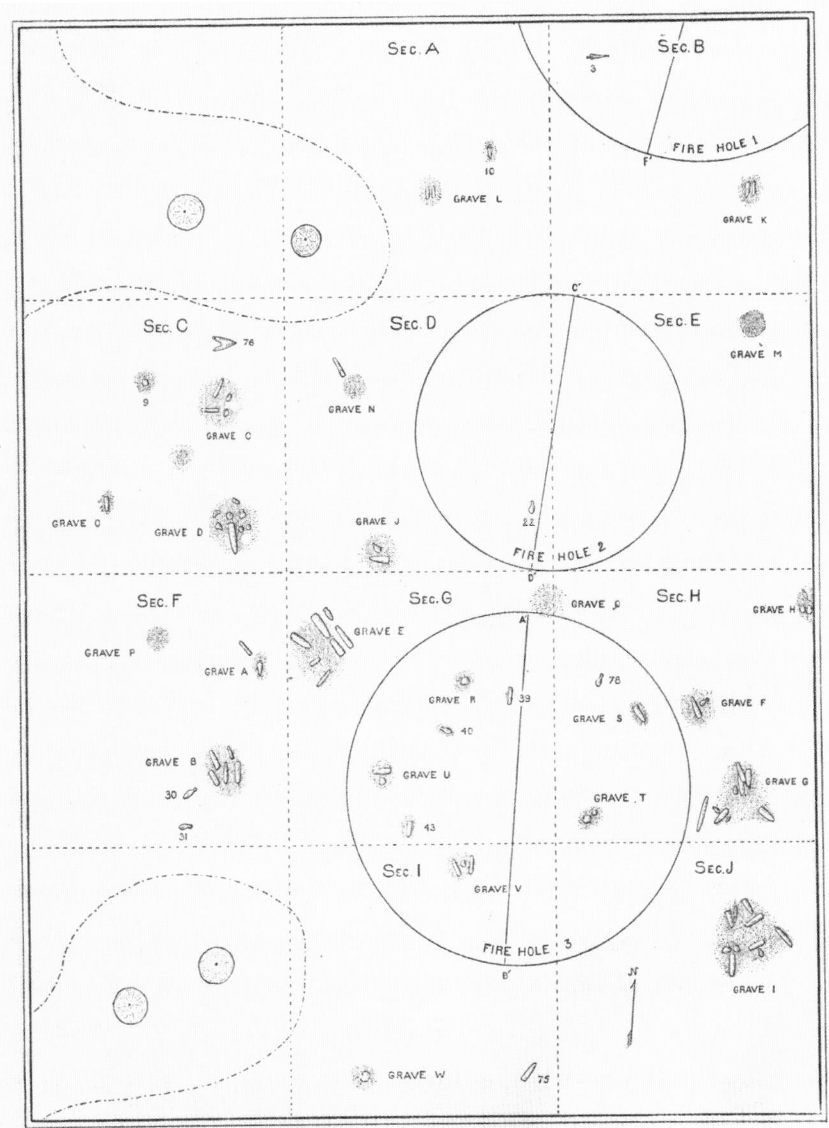


**FIGURE 16.** Plan view of Willoughby's excavation at Soper's Knoll.

ocher-lined pit containing multiple burials at the Hathaway cemetery in Passadumkeag, but his published diagram is less than convincing.[8]

The number of grave furnishings ranges from none to over twenty. Ocher content varies in amount and brilliance (figure 17). Regarding the placement of human remains, only traces of decayed bone were present

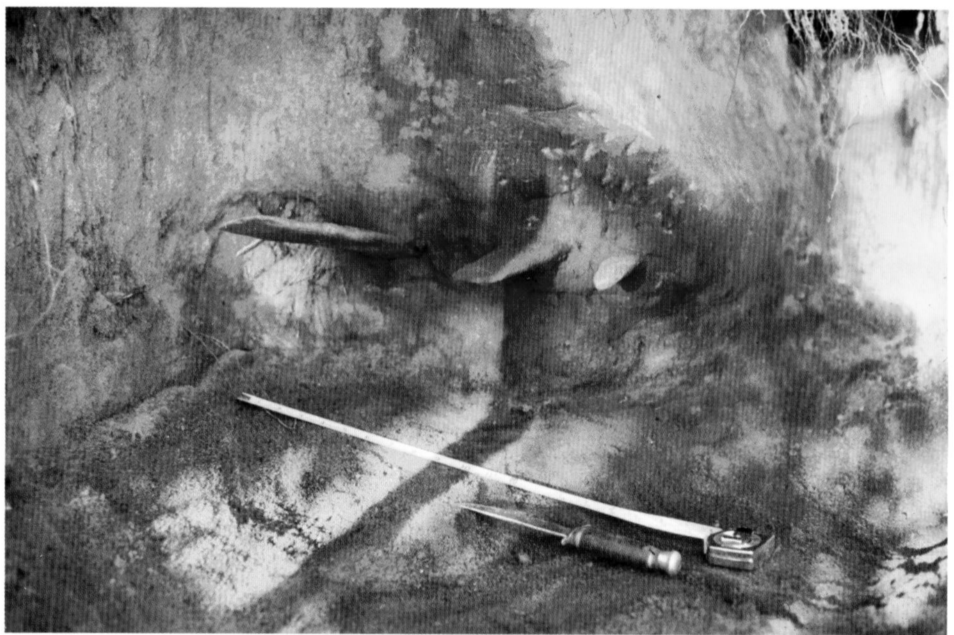

FIGURE 17. Red ocher in an eroding grave at Atkins Bay.

at most cemeteries, except in cases where later burials occurred there as well. The only cemetery with real bone preservation is the Nevin site, in Blue Hill, where the graves were dug into, and later covered by, shell midden deposits, which provided excellent bone preservation. Some Nevin graves held single adult skeletons in the fetal or flexed position, while others contained multiple disarticulated clusters of bones, called bundle burials, of individuals ranging from adult to infant (figure 18). These seem to have been individuals who died during the winter, when burial was not possible, or perhaps individuals who died far from home with only their bones retained for later burial next to their relatives.

What social messages might we take from all this cemetery variability? I am inclined to view the cemeteries as those of kin groups and their variability as reflecting the differential success of these groups in maintaining their corporate identity. The cemetery locations suggest family ties to favorite places in the landscape, perhaps because they were important for subsistence. The cemeteries may even have marked ownership of these places by a group in the face of competition from neighboring kin groups. Because even successful hunter-gatherers usually have small group sizes

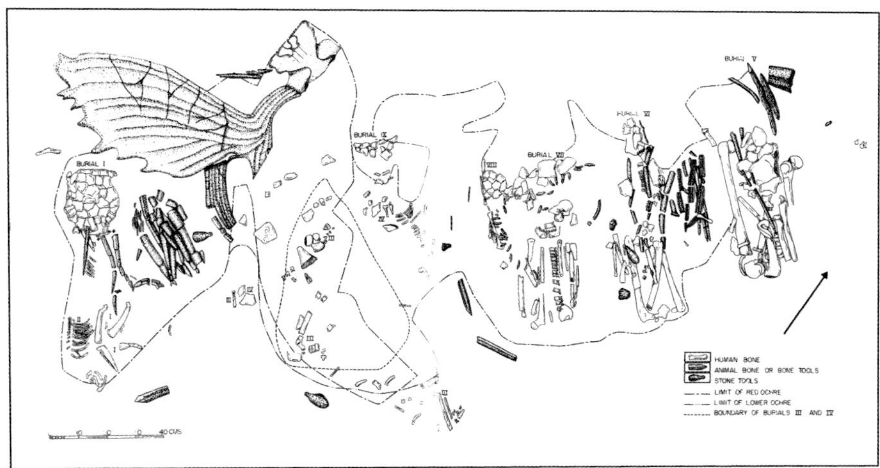


**FIGURE 18.** Byers's drawing of bundle burials at the Nevin cemetery.

and low overall populations compared to agriculturalists, the vicissitudes of their collective lives probably meant that these kin groups often did not maintain their territorial claims over long periods, and they abandoned their cemeteries when forced to move or to reorganize in the face of competition or other kinds of misfortune. Such a scenario is supported by the presence of multiple episodes of use at several cemeteries. In the case of the carefully excavated Cow Point cemetery in New Brunswick, for example, the later users were apparently unaware of where earlier graves were located and cut into some of them with new grave pits.

Turning to individual burials, if we were to excavate the graves at Mount Auburn cemetery we would likely encounter well but simply dressed corpses in caskets, and not much else. In keeping with its Judeo-Christian origins, social statements at Mount Auburn are placed mainly aboveground, not under it. In prehistoric cemeteries, however, social meaning more often lies in what is placed in the grave. Of course, there may have been surface monuments of wood or some other perishable material, but no clear indications of these have been found at the cemeteries. Two excavated by Willoughby at Ellsworth and Soper's Knoll in Orland had large shallow depressions at the surface, but their relationships to the burials, if any, are unclear.[10] Willoughby also claimed to have found evidence for extensive burning over and around the graves at Ellsworth and Orland, but the features he describes were more likely the results of natural podzol formation. In fact, the grave outlines at most cemeteries were difficult to determine and even the number of burials is somewhat uncertain.

Whatever might have been visible above the ground at a Red Paint cemetery, it is abundantly clear that what went into the ground had great significance. The deceased were laid to rest in the presence of those who mattered in their lives, and with their placement of grave furnishings, those people gave meaning to the funeral ceremony in each other's presence. Let's take a look at the Red Paint cemeteries from this perspective to see if we can read social history from them.

## THE MEANING OF OCHER

To begin with, the most obvious and ubiquitous element we must consider is red ocher, which was found in nearly all pit features at the cemeteries. Red ocher is a powdered form of the mineral hematite and is the pigment used in such traditional paints as "barn red" still seen on outbuildings throughout rural America. It remains in use as an artists' pigment today. Red ocher has been associated with human ritual behavior for a very long time. Even the Neanderthals of Europe ground red ocher for pigment.[11] Hematite ocher has been used in burial rituals by many prehistoric people around the world, and the practice may have been brought by the first humans to enter the New World, for Paleo-Indians used it in their burials.[12] Its use in the Northeast before and after the Moorehead phase was sporadic, however, and few, if any, prehistoric North Americans used it as lavishly as did the Red Paint People. It is now also clear that, ubiquitous as it is in their graves, red ocher was associated with their nonburial rituals as well.

What might ocher have meant to the Red Paint People is difficult to say. Blood symbolism is one likely ritual meaning. In fact, the term *hematite* is derived from the Greek word for blood, *haema*. Where the ocher came from is also uncertain. Its ubiquity in the cemeteries has led most, including me, to assume it had local origins. There are clear favorites as to where it may have originated. For example, large amounts of ocher or iron oxide exist at Katahdin Iron Works; so large, in fact, that it was smelted commercially in the nineteenth century.[13] But the iron oxide at Katahdin was mostly a yellowish iron sulfite called pyrrhotite, not red hematite.[14]

Moorehead thought that Katahdin was the source of the cemetery ocher, stating that

> near Katahdin Iron Works, up Pleasant river, a tributary of the Piscataquis, the source of the red paint was found. Mr. Walter B. Smith, formerly of the United States Geological Survey, who is familiar with the surface geology of the Penobscot valley, informed me that in his opinion there was no possible source in Maine for powdered hematite except at the Katahdin Iron Works. Mr. Smith accompanied the expedition and his opinion was verified. The outcrop consists of soft, powdered, brilliant carmine hematite, and extends along the side of a high ridge.[15]

Later, however, Moorehead presented a different account, claiming to have personally found both yellow and red ocher at Katahdin Iron Works.[16] He also states that local buildings had been painted with this red ocher. Moorehead again related information from Smith, but in this version of the story, the discovery had been made a century earlier by an unnamed French geologist who found there "soft powdered hematite of such fine character that it was used for paint without preparation." Since Moorehead felt compelled to mention it in this way, it probably is precisely what he personally did not find. Likewise, other well-known ocher localities, such as those near the Androscoggin River in Rumford, are not hematite.[17]

I am now not sure the ocher was locally produced. True hematite is widespread in Maine but mostly in trace amounts, which could not have produced the copious volumes of fine, powdered material found in the cemeteries. It could possibly have been produced by roasting pyrrhotite or bog iron, an impure form of iron that forms in bogs and swamps, but we have no evidence for this kind of processing in prehistoric north America. A more likely mode of production is that it was ground from specular hematite, a form that does not occur widely in Maine but is common in Quebec, Labrador, and Newfoundland. Hematite nodules are found along with powdered red ocher at Late Archaic cemeteries in Labrador and Newfoundland, and the fact that no nodules have been recovered from the Red Paint cemeteries suggests that it may have been imported in powdered form.[18] Moreover, many hearths excavated by William Fitzhugh on the Labrador coast have ocher-stained fill, suggesting that these may be production sites. If so, ocher joins the growing list of imports from the north found in the cemeteries. All these imports would have been expensive to transport in terms of human effort and given the amounts of ocher used during the Moorehead phase, more expense was incurred in its importation than was the case of the other exotics.

If the ocher is the single universal inclusion in Red Paint graves, the artifacts they contain are highly variable, clearly not conforming to any simple formula of appropriate grave furnishings. Let's now turn to them to see what they tell us about the people they accompanied.

# 5

# Gleaning Information from the Artifacts

WHAT HAS MADE the Moorehead phase so difficult to understand for over a century is the desultory way in which it has been explored. According to Moorehead's calculations, as of 1916, of the eighteen known cemeteries, Willoughby had excavated three and Moorehead, nine.[1] Nine or ten others had been excavated by various "citizens of Maine," and one of Willoughby's and six of Moorehead's had been considerably damaged by untrained collectors, including total destruction in three cases. Worse, the collections resulting made by both professionals and amateurs were often widely scattered and rarely ended up in situations where their value was institutionally recognized. Moorehead, for example, passed parts of his collections on to several small museums and historical societies with a checkered history of collections care. I have even purchased at a garage sale a Penobscot Indian basket full of plummets with Moorehead's catalog numbers on them, and the seller thought I wanted the basket, not the plummets! Amateur collections are notoriously unstable and often handed out piecemeal to relatives when the owner passed on. One collection from an important early Red Paint cemetery was offered to a Boy Scout troop. Fortunately, an anthropologist overheard the conversation and managed to get the collection redirected to the University of Maine's archaeology lab.

I was exceptionally fortunate that the Peabody Museum of the late 1960s and early 1970s still had artifact storage cabinets interspersed with offices and classrooms throughout the building, open to any interested student. Dubious as this arrangement was from a collections security perspective, it provided me an unparalleled opportunity to examine all of Willoughby's cemetery collections, as well as other relevant finds donated to the Peabody over many decades. I was also able to examine Moorehead's collections at the R. S. Peabody Foundation in Andover along with some of what curators Douglas Byers and Frederic Johnson had recovered from the Nevin site. Slowly, during many a lunch hour, I poured over them trying to commit each artifact to memory. From this process came what archaeologists call a typology, a set of definitions or visual impressions that allow archaeologists to mentally push collections of artifacts into piles of those that look alike. Here's a brief typology for the Moorehead phase. The numbers of artifacts given are based on Robinson's dissertation; they do not reflect additional examples recovered subsequently.

## Bannerstones

Some artifact styles are highly formalized and beautifully made, suggesting that they are not merely utilitarian, but were also symbolically charged and probably intended for ceremonial purposes. The oldest, originating well before the Moorehead phase, is the bannerstone, a form widespread in eastern North America beginning at least 7500 years B.P.[2] Its actual function remains unclear, and the term *bannerstone* indicates a belief among some early archaeologists that these stones were mounted on staffs to serve as symbolic standards or banners. To most archaeologists, however, these artifacts imply the use of a weapon system known as the spear thrower, also known by its Mexican name *atlatl*. This inference is based on the discovery of what are clearly spear throwers with attached stone weights found in very dry cave sites of the American Southwest, where organic materials are well preserved. A spear thrower is basically a hand-held shaft that serves as an extension of the hunter's forearm. A hook at its end fits into the socketed end of a fletched spear or dart, which resembles a large arrow.

The stone weight is thought by some to increase the force with which the dart could be propelled. Atlatl darts were often armed with a stone-tipped foreshaft, which could rapidly be replaced for another shot.

Modern experimenters have demonstrated that the atlatl is a highly effective weapon system. It likely came to the New World with the first human immigrants, to be replaced by the bow and arrow in eastern North America only around 2000 B.P., continuing in use among native Mexicans until the Spanish conquest.[3] The earliest bannerstone forms have a crescentic shape and a tabular cross section notched on both sides at the midpoint to facilitate lashing to the atlatl shaft. Most later styles, however, have a thickened central mass with a carefully drilled perforation ranging from one-quarter to one-half inch (.6 to 1.2 cm) in diameter to accommodate the atlatl shaft. The five examples attributable to the early Moorehead phase include both a winged form and a less-common, late, spheriodal form (figure 19).[4] Most spheroidal bannerstones have a facet or groove on one side, apparently to allow the dart shaft to be held parallel to the spear thrower shaft.

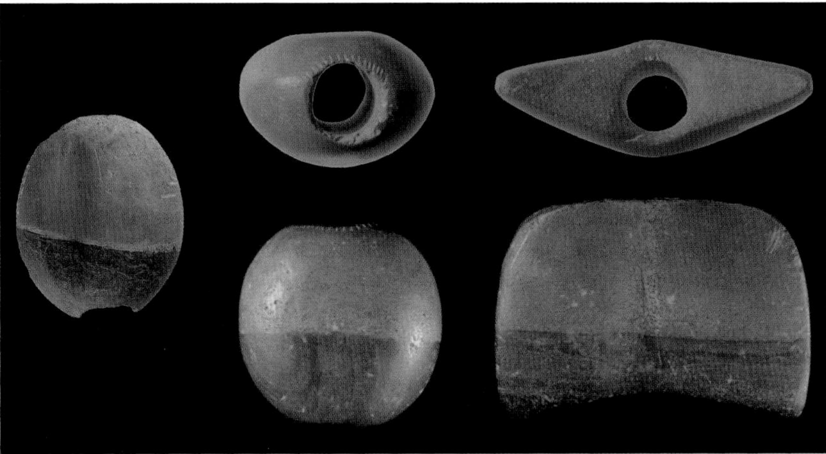

**FIGURE 19.** Early Moorehead phase atlatl weights. Left: weight from the Davis-Tobie site in Alna, 2 inches (5cm) in diameter. Right: weights from the early Godfrey Red Paint cemetery in Old Town. (*Courtesy of Brian Robinson.*)

The presence of at least three bannerstones in early Red Paint cemeteries is perhaps our most concrete clue that the Moorehead phase descended from preceding cultures in the region, particularly the Small Stemmed Point tradition mentioned above. This link is made even stronger by the fact that all Maine bannerstone found in sites of these two groups are made of an unusual bicolored gray and green slate or siltstone of unknown origin.[5]

## ADZES, GOUGES, AND WHETSTONES

Adzes were widespread among Stone Age people living in wooded environments, but gouges are rare, being found only in small numbers across northeastern North America and a few places in northern Europe. In eastern North America, adzes and gouges have a long history, extending back over 7,500 years. They are icons of Archaic cultures throughout the Northeast, but are most abundant by far along the midcoastal region of Maine. Moreover, those found elsewhere tend to be generalized in form, lacking the special features, graceful shapes, and fine finishes that typify most of the roughly four hundred specimens recovered from Red Paint cemeteries. Many are among the world's most aesthetically appealing prehistoric stone artifacts. The extraordinary abundance of gouges and adzes as well (roughly five hundred) suggest that they were extremely important. The frequent cooccurrence of adzes and gouges suggests that they were used together in wood-shaping tasks, likely including dugout canoe construction—the gouges for hollowing out the inside and the adzes for shaping the outside. Their size ranges suggest different scales of utility. One can imagine

**FIGURE 20.** Gouge hafted to a wooden handle.

the larger ones were used to shape a dugout canoe while the smaller ones were used to carve decorations on it.

While they vary in form, most gouges and adzes were probably hafted in a manner similar to that shown in figure 20. Today there are many hobbyists who have experimented with replicas of these tools, making handles from a tree branch with a piece of the trunk attached at the distal end as a platform to which the stone tool was lashed. An interesting feature of gouges and adzes is that, no matter how graceful their overall form, most have battered butt ends. This battering suggests that while they most likely were swung, they were also driven with a mallet.

**FIGURE 21.** Susquehanna tradition–style grooved axe hafted to a wooden handle.

Gouges, in particular, but adzes as well, are northern tool forms, quite different from the woodworking technology of the Southeast, where the grooved stone ax dominates (figure 21). Fine examples of stone axes do occur in the Northeast as far as the south shore of the St. Lawrence River, some of the finest from Maine sites, but they are present only during periods both predating and postdating the Moorehead phase, when strong intrusions of cultural influence and even populations from the Southeast are obvious in the archaeological record.[6]

Most gouges and adzes were formed by pecking, a process whereby a hard hammerstone was repeatedly tapped against the artifact surface so that each blow shatters a small amount of stone, leaving a characteristic pitted surface on both the artifact and the pecking stone. The technique itself was common among Archaic hunter-gatherers of the Northeast, and the hammerstones used to execute it are usually expedient tools of amorphous form, with most wear being evident on the more protruding parts of the surface. Those used by the Red Paint People are most often of a hard rhyolite, also commonly used for flaked stone tools.[7] What is remarkable about them is that many were so extensively used that, more than any I have seen in North America, they became almost perfectly spheroidal

**FIGURE 22.** Pecking stones from Moorehead phase midden deposits at the Turner Farm site. Diameter of specimen at top right is 2 inches (5 cm).

(figure 22). As mentioned above, once the gouge or adze was formed, it was sharpened with a whetstone.

There is a small subset of adzes and gouges that appear to be imports from the far north. The clearest example is the gouge of a lovely blue-green slate shown in figure 23 from the Emerson cemetery in Orland. I first saw this artifact in 1969, illustrated in an early paper by Douglas Byers on northeastern prehistory.[8] Later that year I actually held it at the R. S. Peabody Foundation. To any who appreciate beautifully executed stonework, it was captivating, wonderful to hold, smooth, almost polished, nearly flawless, and, I now realize, probably the best example of its type known to us. Byers called it "the acme of perfection in polished tools."[9] In those early years, both Byers and I assumed that it was a local product, and I expected to encounter others in the many Red Paint cemetery collections I had yet to research. But I never saw anything like it again in a Maine collection, although I have since identified a few other fine gouges that are likely imports from the far north. Someone else shared my fondness for this object; the person who, in the 1980s, stole it along with several of the R. S. Peabody Foundation's treasures during a time when its parent institution, Phillips Academy at Andover, had let its guard down. Most of

**FIGURE 23.** (*right*) Slate gouge from the Emerson cemetery. It is a combination gouge/adze (no scale available). (*Courtesy of the R. S. Peabody Museum.*) **FIGURE 24.** (*above*) Slate gouges from the Rattler's Bight cemetery in Labrador. Specimen on the left is 8 inches (20 cm) long. (*Courtesy of William Fitzhugh.*)

the stolen artifacts eventually were sold at auctions in the Midwest, later recognized as stolen, and returned to the R. S. Peabody. This one never reappeared.

It was more than twenty years later that I finally realized where this wonderful artifact had originated. I was at the Canadian Museum of Civilization in Hull, Quebec, examining collections that were then coming into the new institution from Atlantic Canada. Excavations along the Newfoundland and Labrador coasts had begun more than a decade earlier, but with a few notable exceptions, reports on these excavations had not been published, and the collections were temporarily housed in places not easily accessible to me. One such collection came from the Curtis site at Twillingate, Notre Dame Bay, Newfoundland, and it was in this collection that I saw several specimens that, had they not been broken and damaged, would have matched the R. S. Peabody specimen in raw material, form, and

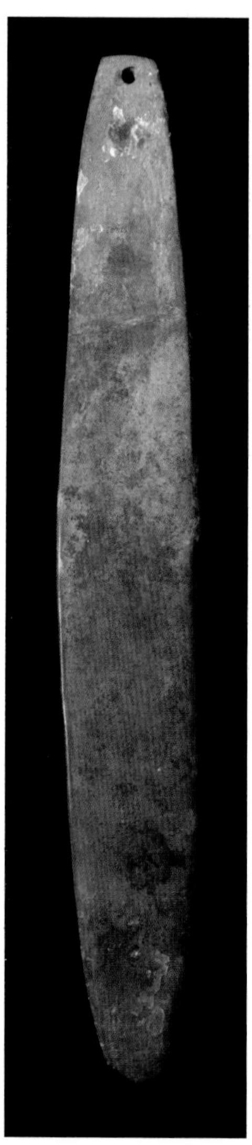

**FIGURE 25.** Early Moorehead phase whetstone from the Eddington Bend cemetery (length: 16 inches [40 cm]). These elongate oval whetstones are quite standardized in form.

quality. Similar as the Emerson gouge is to those from Twillingate, the home of this form is more likely to be Labrador, where they are most common (figure 24). By this time, most of the profession knew that the Maine's Red Paint cemeteries reflected connections to the far north in some way, but it was exciting to find that such heavy, utilitarian tools had actually been transported nearly eight hundred miles from their source to Maine.

Whetstones, presumably used to sharpen gouges and adzes, are common in the cemetery collections, numbering 228. The most distinctive style is a highly standardized elongate tabular form with a perforated end, probably for suspension by a thong (figure 25). It is the earliest whetstone style, being found at a single site of the antecedent Small Stemmed Point tradition and at only a small number of Moorehead phase sites. The whetstones of later times are generally less regular in shape.

Did the heavy woodworking tools placed in graves hold more than utilitarian value, or were they merely items the deceased would need in the afterlife? Many clearly resemble those found at village sites, and it is not surprising that some are in unused condition because grave furnishings often were made specifically for funerary purposes. Still, the overall size and quality of those placed in graves sometimes suggests extra care in their making. I know of no adzes or gouges from village sites, for example, that have carefully shaped longitudinal facets, such as those shown in figure 26. And clearly, the imports from the north have never been found outside the cemeteries, so they must have been accorded special symbolic importance.

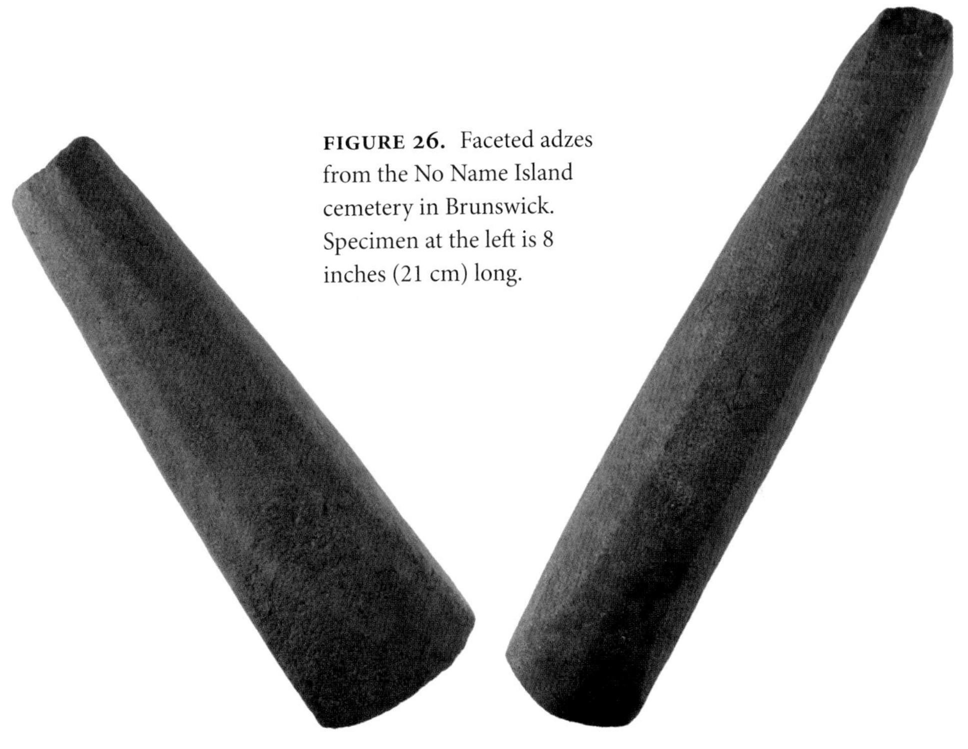

**FIGURE 26.** Faceted adzes from the No Name Island cemetery in Brunswick. Specimen at the left is 8 inches (21 cm) long.

## PLUMMETS, FIGURINES, AND WEATHERED PEBBLES

Also very common in the cemetery collections, and in village sites as well, are teardrop-shaped stone weights known as plummets. Robinson analyzed 234. Like gouges and adzes, they are shaped by pecking, with a ground groove at the top forming a knob. Rare specimens have a perforated top for line suspension. Plummets were especially numerous at the Turner Farm site, and using that sample, we were able to define two weight classes: the smaller weighing between 420 and 20 grams and the larger weighing between 1,260 and 610 grams.[10] The larger plummets (figure 27, bottom) most likely served as cod fishing sinkers. The function of the smaller ones is less clear (figure 27, top). Many seem too light to have been useful as line weights at all, and as a class, they intergrade with more carefully crafted zoomorphic and abstract sculpted forms found mostly in Red Paint cemeteries (figure 28). Like gouges, plummets are rare throughout the prehistoric

**FIGURE 27.** Small and large plummets from the Turner Farm site. Specimen at bottom left is 6 inches (15 cm) long.

**FIGURE 28.** Small plummets and figural forms. Elongate specimen at right is 6 inches (15 cm) long.

world, fairly common in northeastern North America, and very abundant in Maine's midcoast area. In northeastern North America they appear sometime before 7500 B.P., but become far more numerous during the Moorehead phase, after which they completely disappear from the record.

Among the more fascinating Moorehead phase artifacts are a handful of small zoomorphic figurines of stone, including small plummets (figure 29). Most depict aquatic creatures, including the porpoise, seal, and cormorant, but terrestrial animals are also represented. As all date

**FIGURE 29.** Zoomorphic figurines from various Red Paint sites. Bird's head is 1.4 inches (3.6 cm) tall.

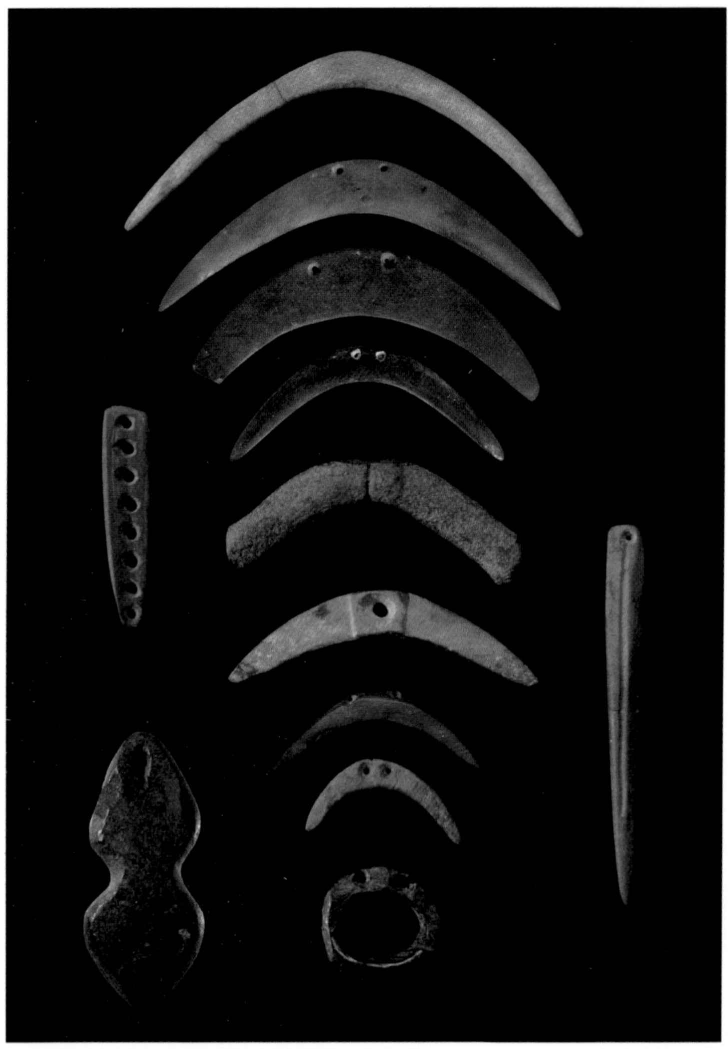

**FIGURE 30.** Ground stone pendants from various Red Paint cemeteries. Crescent at the top is 4.7 inches (12 cm) wide.

to around 4000 B.P., they are among the oldest such figurines in North America. On the same diminutive scale are a handful of graceful crescentic and other pendant forms ground from slate (figure 30).

Water-rolled pebbles, most of which are oddly shaped, or quartz-banded (figure 31), are common in some cemeteries. Though naturally formed, it is clear that they were purposefully included as grave offerings, perhaps as talismans.

**FIGURE 31.** Water-rolled pebbles from the No Name Island and Ormsby cemeteries. Quartz-veined specimen has a maximum diameter of 3 inches (7.6 cm).

## Ground Slate Bayonets

Of all the fascinating and dramatic artifacts from the Red Paint cemeteries, however, the most compelling are the 157 long, delicate "bayonets." Long lance tips or knives of ground metamorphic stone are common at early interior sites in Maine, less so near the coast, perhaps because coastal erosion has destroyed most older sites there. The ages of these ground stone lance tips is often unclear, but at a deep, stratified site in central Maine, they may date back eight millennia, over three millennia before the rise of the Red Paint People.[11] These early lance tips from village sites are variable in shape, length, and raw material, but on the whole, they look like functional artifacts. While some examples from the cemeteries resemble these early, generalized forms, most are quite different. They are almost universally made of slate and ground—some almost polished—to precisely defined forms. Their purpose remains open to question. They would have been deadly if thrust into the vital organs of an animal, but many are very fragile and would have been very prone to breakage.

A striking characteristic of the bayonets is that so many are clearly divisible into four standardized styles. The most dramatic and perhaps the earliest is the long, narrow hexagonal form, which reaches a maximum length of over 15 inches (38 cm); figures 32 and 33). They somewhat resemble specimens made from swordfish rostrum found in Moorehead phase village sites which may be their functional prototypes (figure 34). Some narrow hexagonal bayonets bear extraordinary engraved geometric decoration, such as the spectacular examples from the Cow Point cemetery in New Brunswick (figure 35). Most narrow hexagonal bayonets are made of dark gray slate, similar to that found in the vicinity of the commercially quarried deposits in Monson, Maine, though a few are made of a red slatelike stone of unknown origin. Unlike

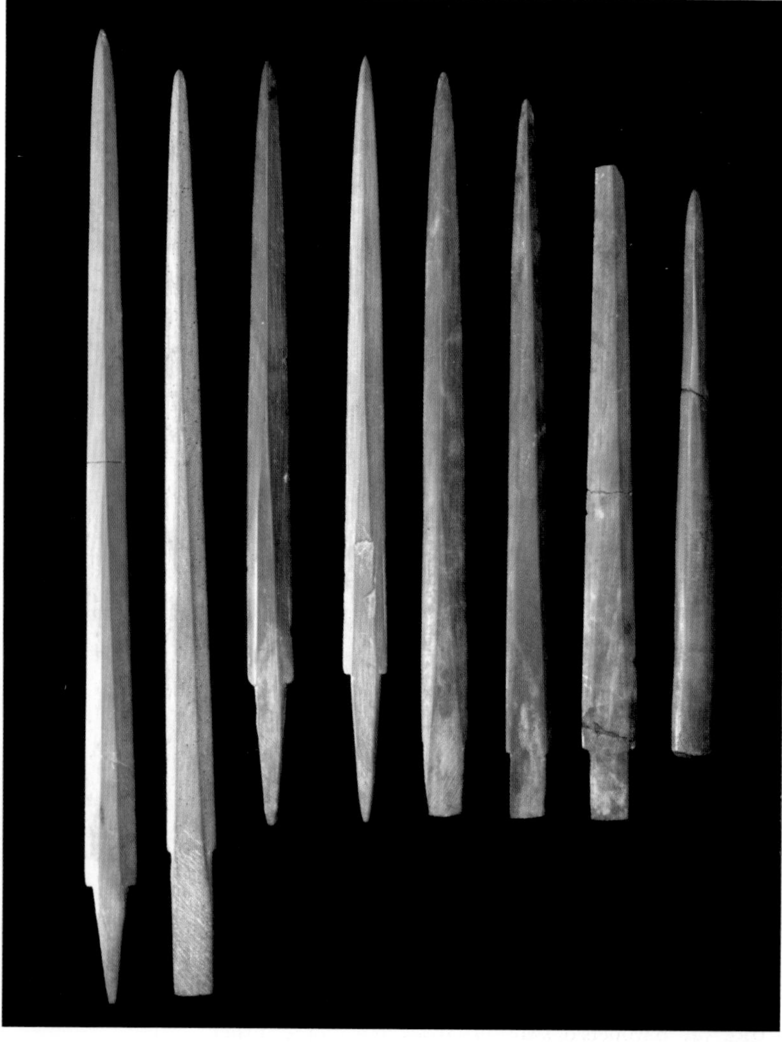

**FIGURE 32.** Narrow hexagonal bayonets from the Lancaster cemetery in Winslow. Specimen at left is 16 inches (41 cm) long, the longest yet found.

the other forms, very few narrow hexagonal bayonets occur outside the range of the Moorehead phase. Aside from four found around Sebago Lake, there is only a single specimen from the Ursuline collection at Three Rivers, Quebec, and few small fragments from between Massachusetts and Newfoundland. Their beautifully precise faceted surfaces and precise overall workmanship are hard to appreciate until held in the hand. Two narrow hexagonal specimens were impressive enough that they were included in the exhibit "Indian Art of the United States" at the Museum of Modern Art in 1941.[12]

Another bayonet form is called broad pie-wedge because of its broad trianguloid, pie-shaped cross section, with a well-defined

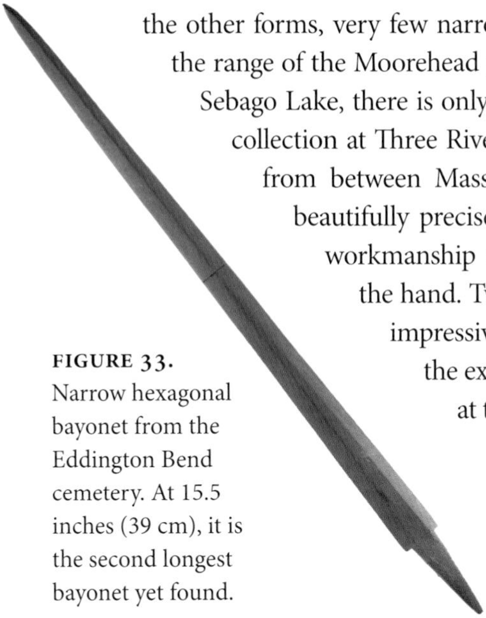

**FIGURE 33.** Narrow hexagonal bayonet from the Eddington Bend cemetery. At 15.5 inches (39 cm), it is the second longest bayonet yet found.

**FIGURE 34.** Bayonets of swordfish rostrum from the Turner Farm site, North Haven Island. Length of the second specimen from the left is 6.7 inches (17 cm). Specimen second from the left is 7 inches (18 cm) long.

**FIGURE 35.** Details of incised decoration on bayonets from the Cow Point site, Grand Lake, New Brunswick. (*Courtesy of the Canadian Museum of Civilization.*)

medial ridge on one side only, the other being gently convex.[13] The ridged side often has a ground facet at the base, probably to aid in fitting it to a handle or shaft (figure 36). Specimens that best exhibit these characteristics are often made of visually striking banded slate. Wide pie-wedge bayonets were found in only three Red Paint cemeteries at the Grand Lake Stream, Nevin, and Cow Point sites. Those from Grand Lake Stream (figure 36, second and third from left) are of black slate and only weakly express the characteristics of the type, suggesting that they may be local imitations. Although rare in the Red Paint cemeteries, this is the most widely distributed style outside the Moorehead phase range, occurring as far west as southern Ontario and as far to the northeast as the Port au Choix cemetery in northern Newfoundland (figure 37). The available sample suggests that the wide pie-wedge form originated south of the St. Lawrence and Great Lakes and west of New England. The origin of the banded slate used to make many of them is unknown, but the immediate source is likely the upper Midwest, where cobbles of banded slate occur in glacially deposited gravels. The ultimate source probably lies farther north on the Canadian shield. In the Midwest, it was highly favored as well for other special artifacts, such as atlatl weights.[14]

The smallest of the ground slate point styles reach only around four inches (10 cm) in length and have sharply barbed shoulders. While most have been found in cemetery contexts, these are fairly common in habitation sites as well (figure 38). All known specimens are apparently made of the same gray slate as the narrow hexagonal bayonets, and their range is similarly tightly constrained by the range of Moorehead phase sites. Unfortunately, it is not possible to determine their age relative to other bayonet forms.

The fourth and least numerous style has a wide blade and a hexagonal

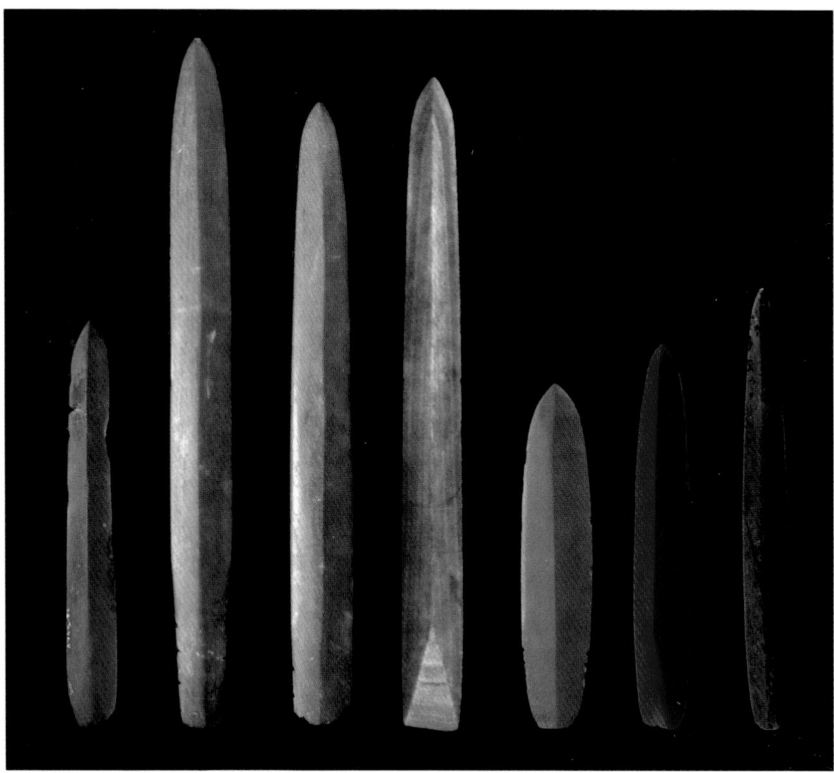

**FIGURE 36.** Wide pie-wedge bayonets from several cemeteries. The first on the left is from Nevin. (*Courtesy of the R. S. Peabody Museum.*) The next two are from Grand Lake Stream. The two following are from Cow point. (*Courtesy of the Canadian Museum of Civilization.*) The last two are from Port au Choix. (*Courtesy of The Rooms.*) Longest specimen is 9 inches (23 cm) long.

cross section with very sharp edges and usually eared stems (figure 39). Nearly all have a snubbed tip. Their association with Red Paint cemeteries is tenuous in that only two have been found associated with typical Moorehead phase artifacts, but the available evidence suggests that they were contemporaneous. The two specimens on the left in figure 39 came from an isolated ocher-stained pit in Warren that was likely an late Moorehead phase grave. Like the wide pie-wedge form, these are made of lovely banded slate not found in Maine. The third specimen in figure 39 was found in a red ocher patch at the nonmortuary Davis-Tobie site on the Sheepscot River in Alna and appears to be a local copy made of schist. Like the wide pie-wedge style, the broad hexagonal style also seems to have

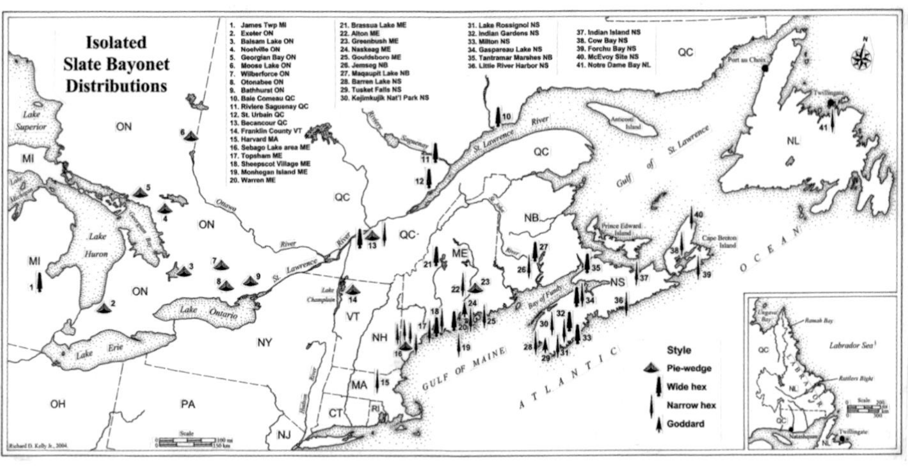


**FIGURE 37.** Isolated bayonet finds.

been developed to the west and been incorporated into the Moorehead phase through importation and local copying.

While there is evidence that the three longer bayonet styles are not precisely contemporaneous, the remarkable set in the Ursuline collection at Three Rivers suggests they must be nearly so. In sum, the available data suggest that bayonets were created during the life span of the Red Paint People, but not necessarily by them. Narrow hexagonal and small barbed forms seem to be completely indigenous, whereas wide pie-wedge and wide hexagonal forms seem to have outside origins and were imported and locally copied. The available data raise more questions than they can answer, but what we know suggests that bayonets were meant to encode some very specific information about their makers or owners, such as status or kin group, and that the social forces that produced them extended in some diffuse way over a large region of the Northeast.

Though unusual, the bayonets are not unique. Somewhat similar ground stone forms are found in a few places around the Northern Hemisphere, including the coasts of Newfoundland and Labrador, the North Pacific coast of North America from Washington to Alaska, Scandinavia, Lake Baikal in Russia, and on the Korean peninsula.[15] In Newfoundland and Labrador, cemeteries of comparable age with many red ocher graves have produced numerous bayonet-like forms, including some identical to those found in the Red Paint cemeteries. We will look further into these north–south similarities below.

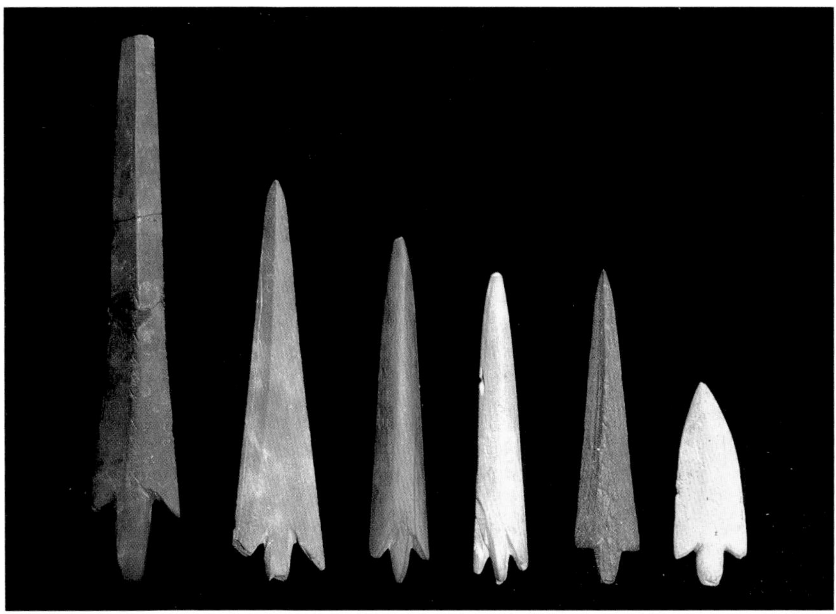

**FIGURE 38.** Small barbed slate points from various Maine sites. Specimen at left is 5 inches (13 cm) long.

Somewhat similar specimens occur along the Norwegian coast, generally as isolated finds in village sites (figure 40). They are usually less well made and more variable in form and size than bayonets, and also are thought to be substitutes for flaked stone projectile points. Finally, from South Korea come beautifully made ground slate lance tips that are comparable to bayonets in workmanship though different in style, thought to be modeled on cast bronze lance tips from farther down the Pacific coast (figure 41).

The bayonets also resemble the long slate whaling lances of the Alutiiq peoples of Kodiak Island in Alaska (figure 39), which were rubbed with vegetable poison (aconite from monkshood) and actually intended to break off inside a wounded whale, paralyzing and thus drowning it.[16] A similar use of bayonets can't be ruled out, but we have no evidence of whale hunting during the Moorehead phase, and their size seems unnecessarily long for smaller marine mammals. Moreover, unlike Alutiiq whaling lances, they are rarely found outside cemetery contexts, suggesting that they were more important symbolically than as functional weapons.

To some, the rarity of this technology and the fact that it is found only in the high latitudes of the Northern Hemisphere and often in

coastal localities meant one of two things. Either it must have a single point of origin, perhaps somewhere in the Old World, and spread from group to group via cultural diffusion, or it must be a manifestation of a suspected ancient and widespread circum-boreal culture.[17] As better data became available, however, it became clear that such artifacts from different regions did not have either the similar ages or the kinds of continuous distributions that one would expect if they had spread by diffusion. In comparison to the ceremonial nature of Moorehead phase slate work, most of these look-alikes are later and have a markedly utilitarian appearance. None surpass the bayonets in their number, length, and overall quality of execution.

**FIGURE 39.** (*top*) Two wide hexagonal bayonets of banded green slate from the Bickmore site, Warren, and a local copy made of schist from the Davis Tobie site, Alna. Specimen at right is 10 inches (25 cm) long. **FIGURE 40.** (*middle*) Bayonet-like lance points from the northern coast of Norway. Length is approximately 7 inches (18 cm). **FIGURE 41.** (*bottom*) Ground slate points from the Korean Plain Pottery culture dating after 3000 B.P. Central specimen is 4.7 inches (12 cm) long. (*Courtesy of the Lithic Castin Lab.*)

**FIGURE 42.** Alutiiq whaling lance tips, Kodiak Island, Alaska. Longest specimen is 8 inches (21 cm) long. (*Courtesy of the Alutiik Museum.*)

## PROJECTILE POINTS

The next most common forms are flaked stone projectile points that likely functioned as spear tips and knives (figure 42). Of the 154 Robinson dealt with, nearly all have a contracting stem at their base, suggesting that they were set into socketed handles and shafts. Most are sharp and effective looking, but are generally thick and crudely made, without the attention to design and finishing so apparent in other artifacts of the period. Local rhyolite is the most common raw material.

Other projectile points, however, are quite different. They are broader, thinner, and more carefully made of visually appealing, high-quality stones from remote sources. All are from Red Paint cemeteries. They fall into two distinct categories. The first includes eighteen specimens imported from over two hundred miles to the west in the Lake Champlain basin (figure 43). Their form is alien to Maine. Most archaeologists would call them large Normanskill points, a type defined in eastern New York by Ritchie, though in the Maine context I refer to them as Bradley points after a cemetery in Bradley where they were relatively common.[18] They are made of chert or quartzite,

**FIGURE 43.** (*top*) Moorehead phase projectile points. Specimen at left is 8 inches (19 cm) long. **FIGURE 44.** (*bottom*) Projectile points of quartzite (top) and chert (bottom) from Lake Champlain. Specimen at top left is 6 inches (15 cm) long.

closely resembling varieties found in the Lake Champlain area. The other includes twenty specimens that originated at a far more distant source, a single outcrop atop a mountain 1,000 miles to the north at Ramah Bay on the north Labrador coast (figures 43 and 44).[19] The term that is emerging for these beautiful projectile points is Rattler's Bight, a 4,000-year-old cemetery site on the southern Labrador coast where they were particularly abundant (figures 45 and 46).

Projectile points originating from far off places turn up occasionally throughout prehistoric North America but usually as unique finds in ordinary contexts. These cases are different in that specific cultural sources repeatedly supplied finished artifacts for importation and inclusion in the cemeteries. There is no "trail" of finds in intermediate areas. This is, perhaps, not too surprising for the Normanskill points because of the thinly inhabited, mountainous region that separates the Champlain Lowland from the Maine coast, but the distribution of Rattler's Bight points is remarkable.

The only comparable pattern of prehistoric long-distance lithic procurement in North America occurred some 2,000 years later, when the mound-building Hopewell culture obtained obsidian from western Wyoming and eastern Idaho sources some 1,400 miles to the west, which

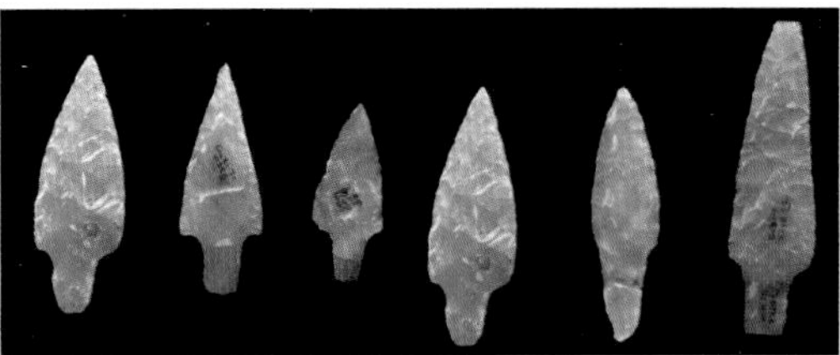

**FIGURE 45.** (*left*) Ramah chert projectile points from Red Paint cemeteries. Specimen at bottom left is 5 inches (13 cm) long.
**FIGURE 46.** (*above*) Ramah chert projectile points from the 4,000-year-old Rattler's Bight cemetery on the south Labrador Coast. Specimen at left is 2.75 in (7 cm) long.

they flaked into ceremonial knives. We can't be sure of the route by which the Rattler's Bight points traveled to Maine. The shortest would be down the Labrador coast, across the Strait of Belle Isle to Newfoundland, down the west coast of Newfoundland, and then across the Gulf of St. Lawrence to the isthmus that separates Nova Scotia from New Brunswick and into the Gulf of Maine, but this is not the likely route because only two Rattler's Bight points have ever been found on the island of Newfoundland. There is, however, a very thin scatter of Rattler's Bight points along the Lower North Shore of the Gulf of St. Lawrence, extending as far west as Natashquan, Quebec.[20] If this was the jumping-off point for crossing the Gulf of St. Lawrence, the trip would be about as long as that traveled by the obsidian found in the Hopewell burial mounds.

## Mica and Fire-making Kits

Large fragments of muscovite mica, called books, were found at three cemeteries, though they may have occurred at others and not been recognized as grave inclusions (figure 47). None have been reported from village sites. They do not appear to have been shaped in any way. Two sites where mica

**FIGURE 47.** Large book of mica (muscovite) from the No Name Island cemetery in Brunswick. Maximum dimension is 3 inches (8 cm).

was present are the westernmost of the cemeteries, and they lie near pegmatite formations that could easily produce these books of mica.

One artifact, class so far found almost exclusively in the cemeteries, is more difficult to identify because all examples show signs of advanced decay (figure 48). It is comprised of 127 lumps of amorphous, yellowish, concreted material that archaeologists recognize as the remains of fire-making kits. They functioned much like the flint and steel of later times. The kits were originally composed of two small rocks, one of rhyolite, for striking, and the other bearing crystals of iron pyrite, particles of which ignited when struck by the rhyolite. Once buried, the chemically unstable pyrite decayed, producing corrosion products (mostly the mineral limonite) that cemented surrounding material together into a yellowish mass and, in the process, often incidentally mineralized fragments of organic substances such as textiles or birch bark, at least some of which were parts of containers that held the fire-making kit.[21] The identity of these kits was first confirmed by Willoughby, who found a well-preserved fire kit at a Bucksport cemetery which still possessed uncorroded pyrite crystals.[22]

In the prehistoric world, pyrite fire kits are unusual. Far more common are techniques that rely on heat generated by the friction of wood on wood (including various forms of the fire drill). In the New World, starting a fire by striking rock on rock (mainly using pyrite) is best known among northern peoples such as the Eskimo/Inuit, Athabaskans, and northern Algonquians. Aside from a single earlier Maine example, no known pyrite fire kit predates or postdates the Moorehead phase, the next later instances anywhere in North America being around 1,000 years later.[23]

Like red ocher, the source of the pyrites used in these fire-making kits is unknown. In Maine, pyrites are uncommon and generally smaller than

**FIGURE 48.** Decayed iron pyrite fire kits from various Red Paint cemeteries. Maximum diameter of specimen at lower left is 3 inches (8 cm).

those used in Red Paint fire kits. Moreover, according to senior Maine geologist Woodrow Thompson:

> It's hard to imagine how the Indians would have found fresh pyrites of any great size in the Northeast, unless they mined them from solid rock. Pyrites in surface outcrops, or weathered rocks, will quickly rust and be replaced by brown limonite.[24]

Similar fire kits have been found in cemeteries of about the same age in Newfoundland and Labrador, and it is possible that those from the Maine cemeteries originated in that northern region.

## Significance of the Grave Goods

When considering what symbolic value the grave furnishings may have possessed, we must consider Ramah chert points, mica, and perhaps pyrites together, for all have visual qualities that were valued for ceremonial use by several prehistoric and historic prestate cultures around the world. Such materials were commonly associated with shamans, who have the ability to "see within, through, and beyond" the spirit world.[25] These materials mimic those abilities and so are frequently adopted by shamans for ritual use. In addition, we should consider together all exotic materials from the cemeteries, including the projectile points, the polished northern woodworking tools, and the exotic bayonets of banded slate. These, too, are likely to indicate shamanistic practice. Shamans commonly undertake transformative journeys over long distances, beyond the lands of known peoples. These journeys are seen as approaching the sacred or supernatural, and the materials shamans bring back from a journey are evidence of the journey's transformational nature.[26] The presence of these materials exclusively in the cemeteries seems a fairly strong argument for the burials of shamans in them.

There may be one additional indication of shamanism from the contents of the Nevin graves. One Nevin burial was furnished with multiple beaks of the pileated woodpecker (*Dryocopus pileatus*).[27] Several facts about this species suggest that this may have been a shaman's burial.[28] The flight of birds in general frequently symbolizes shamanistic trances, which are often likened to soul flight. Woodpeckers in particular have been held as sacred by many cultures around the world, and in North America, the large, swift-flying pileated woodpecker was esteemed by cultures ranging from the Cherokees of the Southwest to the prehistoric Mississippians of the Midwest, to the Pawnees of Nebraska and Kansas. Creek or Muskogee shamans used their beaks to "extract" foreign objects from the bodies of people who were ill. Other faunal remains possibly associated with shamanism are the shells of periwinkles (*Littorina obtusata*), probably sewn onto a garment as decorative trim in one burial at the Nevin cemetery,

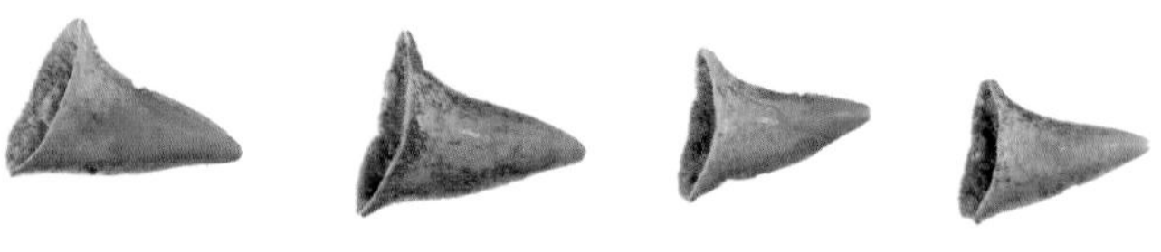

**FIGURE 49.** Shark teeth from a burial at the No Name Island cemetery in Brunswick. Average length is about .45 inch (1 cm).

and several teeth of the shortfin mako shark (Isurus oxyrinchus) from two graves at the No Name Island site (figure 49).

Shamanistic-like materials, however, are fairly rare in the cemeteries, so it is not likely that only shamans were buried there. What other significance might the grave goods have to the people who placed them in the graves? The standard response is that they were intended for use in the afterlife, and this may well be the case. But they probably meant much more than that.

A death is a significant event in all cultures. In large, complex societies, it impacts at least friends and kin, if not a broader range of people, and in small societies, it impacts the whole population, most of whom are kin. Mortuary rituals nearly always ensue, to satisfy the emotional loss of the bereaved and to attain closure on a lost life for all affected parties. Rules for mortuary ritual usually must satisfy some basic body disposal requirements, but beyond that, there is room for a vast array of symbolic behavior to emphasize whatever the affected group collectively thinks important.

According to Shryock and Smail grave goods "became containers for meanings that express social relations across both time and space. . . . In this context the grave goods likely represented not merely useful things but extensions of the deceased's body; a system for communicating information about status and prestige as well as identity and belonging."[29] They probably include what Shryock and Smail call "membership goods" which "unite, triggering emotions like affection, trust, and possibilities of marriage or cooperation" and "prestige goods," which "by contrast, pull apart and trigger emotions like envy, fear, and tension."[30] The adzes, gouges, plummets, fire kits, locally made spear tips, and water-rolled pebbles seem likely to have been membership goods, reflecting activities and beliefs that bound the community together. On the other hand, the exotic spear points, banded slate bayonets, and polished gouges from far-off places may have been, if not the property of shamans, prestige goods—"signals by virtue of the materials they are made of . . . the effort of collection added value." The acting out of the mortuary ritual likely symbolized the social contract of the whole community. Shryock and Smail call this "kinshipping."[31]

Archaeologists have often succeeded in sorting out people of different social categories according to their grave goods. At Port au Choix, Newfoundland, for example, women were buried with fishing gear while men were buried with hunting weapons. Lacking human skeletons as the Red Paint cemeteries do, the task becomes much more difficult, and no one has yet succeeded in doing this. However, we are not quite done learning from them and will later return to the question of who was buried there. For now, I hope readers will agree that we can accurately "read" a considerable amount of social information about the Red Paint People from their cemeteries. But the cemeteries tell us much less about their daily lifestyle. For that information we must turn to their bone technology and to the one remarkable cemetery where bone was well preserved.

## BONE TECHNOLOGY

With the notable exception of the Nevin site, the cemeteries lack not only human bone but all traces of bone technology. The Nevin cemetery provided many wonderfully preserved bone artifacts, and the fact that many more were found in the midden there indicates that these were not merely ceremonial objects but functional equipment in daily use. Additional specimens came from the Turner Farm midden, where undisturbed Moorehead phase midden deposits shed useful new light on how these bone objects were used.

The Nevin site was excavated by Douglas Byers and Frederic Johnson in 1936 and 1937, after road construction disturbed it. The presence of the overlying shell midden at the Nevin cemetery meant that skeletons and bone artifacts were well preserved, uniquely among all Red Paint cemeteries. The cemetery included twenty-five individuals in twelve graves.[32] Despite the amazing artifacts found there and in the midden, the site remained little known outside regional archaeological circles because, as I was later told by William Ritchie, Byers and Johnson were unsure of their grasp of the site's stratigraphy and therefore of the age of the burials and because of the unprecedented artifacts they found in them, thought they might be quite recent. In any case, they never prepared a report on their work there, and even when I visited the R. S. Peabody in 1969, doing research for my dissertation, Byers revealed only a small portion of the collection to me.

Most of the stone objects from the Nevin site are unremarkable and typical of the Moorehead phase, but the bone artifacts are startling in their beauty and diversity. Some were simple utilitarian forms, such as harpoon heads, awls, and beaver incisor woodworking tools. Others, however, were unlike anything previously recovered from a Maine shell midden. Most impressive are thirty-five long, double-bladed artifacts made from moose leg (metacarpal) bone. Their sharp edges and wear marks along their basal portions suggest that they were knives or daggers with handles of wrapped cordage or hide thongs, though they may have been lashed to longer shafts for use as thrusting spears (figure 50). Very similar specimens were later recovered from Moorehead phase strata at the Turner Farm site. Like some narrow hexagonal slate bayonets, many daggers from the Nevin and Turner Farm sites bear very precisely incised decoration.[33] Elaborate though this decoration is, however, the daggers were likely serviceable tools or weapons because many show signs of heavy wear and breakage. Several other daggerlike forms made from different moose and deer bones also came from the Nevin and Turner Farm sites, as did a variety of other long, well-executed pointed bone objects. Broken and badly worn examples of all indicate that they, too, were utilitarian objects.[34]

Another interesting form was rodlike with forked or socketed ends found at both the Nevin and Turner Farm sites, as well as at a few other Moorehead phase middens (figure 51). Their lengths ranged from less than ten to over twenty centimeters. All are made

**FIGURE 50.** Bone daggers from the Nevin site. Specimen at left is 28 cm long.

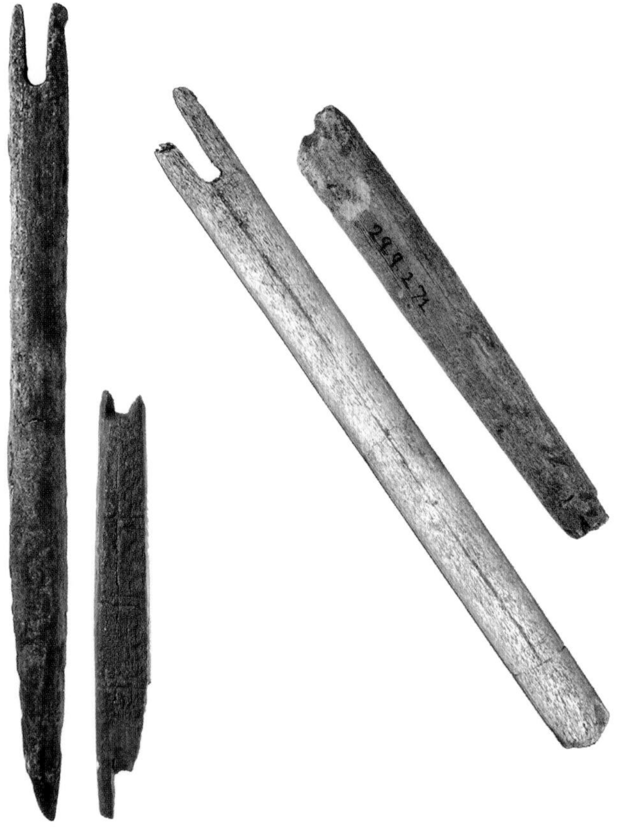

**FIGURE 51.** Swordfish rostrum foreshafts from the Turner Farm and Nevin sites. Specimen at left is 9 inches (22 cm) long. (*Nevin foreshafts courtesy of the R. S. Peabody Museum.*)

of swordfish rostrum and probably were foreshafts mounted at the ends of wooden harpoon shafts and armed with bone harpoon tips. This identification is based on very similar foreshafts of bone known from several more recent northern hunting cultures. Probably these harpoons were used mainly for swordfish hunting.

Several small-eyed bone needles were found in the Nevin burials (figure 52). Again, a very similar needle from the Turner Farm site suggests that they were in general use during the Moorehead phase. No similar artifacts are known from any other prehistoric Maine culture. They suggest either the sewing of tailored leather garments or the sewn application of decoration to draped garments such as robes.

**FIGURE 52.** Bone needles from the Nevin site. Specimen on the lower left is 1.4 inches (3.6 cm) long. (*Courtesy of the R. S. Peabody Museum.*)

Another utilitarian form found in great abundance at both the Nevin and Turner Farm sites is the modified beaver incisor. Natural incisors were distally ground, apparently to form cutting edges for woodworking (figure 53).

The bone tools from the Nevin and Turner Farm sites bespeak a technology that is considerably more diverse than any earlier or later one in the region. It accords well with Peter Rowley-Conwy's characterization of complex hunter-gatherer technologies generally, "overdesigned, well constructed and sturdy, and the tools are composed of numerous redundant parts which can function as a backup so that the system keeps running even if some of the parts wear out or break."[35]

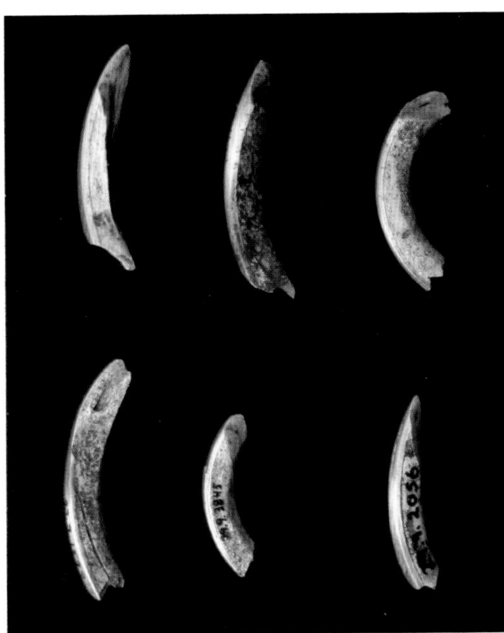

**FIGURE 53.** Beaver incisor knives from the Turner Farm site. Longest specimen is 1.6 inches (4 cm) long.

# 6

# Parsing the Moorehead Phase

THE APPARENT SUCCESS of Moorehead phase technology in sustaining a vibrant culture can be seen in the sheer abundance of artifacts we now have available for study. In 1922, Moorehead—who had himself overseen the excavation of 440 graves at twelve sites—estimated that a total of 1,440 graves containing more than 5,500 artifacts had already been excavated, all in a limited area between the Kennebec and Frenchman's Bay.[1] Since that time, the number of excavated cemeteries has nearly doubled, and excavations at Moorehead phase shell middens have added many thousands more artifacts.

As my familiarity with this large sample increased, I began to perceive patterns of association between artifacts and to understand that, while the contents of the cemeteries and the individual graves could not be crisply divided into different classes, neither were they simply random selections from the Red Paint artifact repertoire. Moorehead himself sensed this but never was able to pursue it very far. For my dissertation, I attempted to subject the fairly complete sample I had examined to seriation analysis, a simple technique for comparing the occurrence of all artifact types to all other types on a grave-by-grave basis. What I found was surprising; some artifacts were found in a great many grave lots, together with nearly every artifact style in the sample, but many were not. Some styles were often found together, while others never were. One such pairing was between the long, smooth perforated whetstones and a particular style of gouge made of lovely green metamorphosed volcanic rock, which we now know comes from the local Ellsworth Formation (figure 54, left). Another was between Ramah chert points and slate bayonets. But neither chert points nor bayonets were ever found with perforated whetstones or green gouges. These patterns of association, however, did not have a detectable spatial dimension. Rather, they were evident at many sites throughout the culture's entire range, suggesting a sequence of unknown duration over which Red Paint mortuary behavior had changed systematically.

I made considerably more progress than had Moorehead in defining these patterns, but with a new field research program to build, my progress on unraveling the Red Paint puzzle stopped in 1971, leaving many details unresolved. Matters improved in the 1990s, however, when Brian Robinson tackled the problem again as a dissertation project at Brown University in the 1990s. Robinson was able to add several "lost" and previously unknown collections to the corpus. Whereas I had managed to demonstrate some kind of change over time, Robinson was able to define three fairly coherent subperiods, dating from around 5000 to 3700 B.P. Through careful observation, Robinson defined subtle style changes that I had not noticed, which enabled him to place the sites more precisely in relative chronological order. As a result, we now have a much more detailed understanding of the Moorehead phase as a discrete, coherent, cultural phenomenon that evolved in place for over roughly five hundred years.

Robinson's subdivisions are based on stone artifacts from the cemeteries, but his subdivisions apply equally as well to habitation sites. The majority of artifacts in Robinson's sample are simple but well-crafted woodworking tools: concave-bitted gouges and straight-bitted adzes. Identical forms have also been found at habitation sites, indicating that these were functional tools. Most gouges conform to three basic styles.[2] The earliest style is made from metamorphic rock with a concavity that slopes evenly from the ventral surface to the bit. The most abundant and generally later gouge form is made from igneous rocks and has a scoop-

**FIGURE 54.** Gouges of the Moorehead phase, left to right: early, middle, late. Specimen at the left is 6 in (15 cm) long.

shaped concavity. Finally, the latest style, also made from igneous rock, has only a slight ventral concavity (figure 54). While Robinson's chronological interpretation of gouge style changes fits the data fairly well, one site suggests something else was at work. At the Cow Point cemetery in New Brunswick, which is generally considered the youngest of all the cemeteries, the early metamorphic style suddenly returns.[3] Whether this was a conscious readoption of an obsolete style or whether it reflects some other social dimension remains to be determined. Adzes are made of a similar suite of rocks but are more variable in form . Robinson's analysis did not include the polished slate forms likely imported from Labrador or Newfoundland, which have a dorsal ridge and a gracefully scoop-shaped concavity that is quite different from the locally made form (figures 23 and 24).

Artifact forms that appear during only part of the sequence are bannerstones, which are early, and bayonets and exotic projectile points, which appear in the middle. What these changes signify is unclear. One can imagine changes in shamanistic practice accounting for the presence or absence of exotic artifacts, but changes in the style of utilitarian objects like gouges seem less likely to be explained in this way.

## Village Life of the Red Paint People

As we noted earlier, the roughly 1,500 graves excavated by the mid-twentieth century had not been very informative about the lives of people buried in them. The wide variety of gouges and adzes point to the importance of large- and small-scale woodworking, while both the plummets and marine animal effigies suggested an interest in marine species, but few such artifacts had yet turned up in shell middens or other village sites in the region.

As significant interest in the Red Paint problem revived in the 1970s, numerous field projects supported by Maine-based institutions, including the Maine State Museum, used modern techniques to locate early coastal sites and to reanalyze older cemetery collections. The total number of coastal Moorehead phase sites then stood at only around ten, the Turner Farm site being the most recent addition to this list. This low number presumably reflects the complete destruction of many more by coastal erosion, an inference that is supported by the presence of a few isolated Moorehead phase artifacts at the bases of many later middens, presumably all that is left of more substantial deposits.

My initial assessment of the Turner Farm site was that it was likely to be the largest and least disturbed of the surviving Moorehead phase middens. The goal of my excavations there, then, must obviously be to clarify many issues raised but left unresolved by earlier fieldwork, such as the age of the Moorehead phase, its relationship to the Red Paint cemeteries, the day-to-day lives of its people, and how that lifestyle compared to that of the site's earlier and later occupants. For now, let us focus on the latter two questions.

The Moorehead phase midden deposits at the Turner Farm site date between 4300 and 4000 B.P. They overlie traces of an earlier occupation left by inhabitants belonging to an earlier culture known as the Small Stemmed Point tradition that date to around 5000 B.P. These traces are likely all that remains of more extensive midden deposits, which have now been eroded by a rising sea level and resulting bank-face erosion (figure 55). Even earlier occupations, extending back as far as around 7000 B.P., are suggested by a few artifacts found in subsoil beneath the midden and on the beach in front of it.[4] The Moorehead phase midden deposits are overlaid by deposits that resulted from several later occupations.[5]

The sequence of deposits at the Turner Farm site is generally similar

**FIGURE 55.** Shell midden erosion at the Turner Farm site after the Groundhog Day Gale in 1976.

from bottom to top. Strata composed of mollusk shells, most of it softshell clam (*Mya arenaria*), constitute most of the midden. These are often interbedded with shell-free strata made up of beach gravel, humus, and hearth rock fragments. All of these strata contain artifacts typical of the cultures that deposited them, as well as larger features, such as hearths and beach-gravel house floors (figures 56 and 57).

At first glance, one could take the abundance of shell in the midden as an indication that clams were the predominant food source, but there are three reasons why this is unlikely. First, the protein their flesh would provide is not the priority in hunter-gatherer diets that is often assumed; the critical need often turns out to be fat, and clam meat contains very little of it.[6] Second, clams would have been brought whole to the site to be processed, and their shells discarded there in direct proportion to the number processed. Nonmolluscan remains, however, are probably significantly underrepresented in shell middens. Many mammal bones, in particular, were likely left where the animal was butchered; used to make tools; eaten by scavengers, especially dogs; or broken up and boiled to extract marrow fat. Finally, the presence of bone fishhooks at the site suggests that, as in

FIGURE 56. Stratified shell midden deposits at the Turner Farm site.

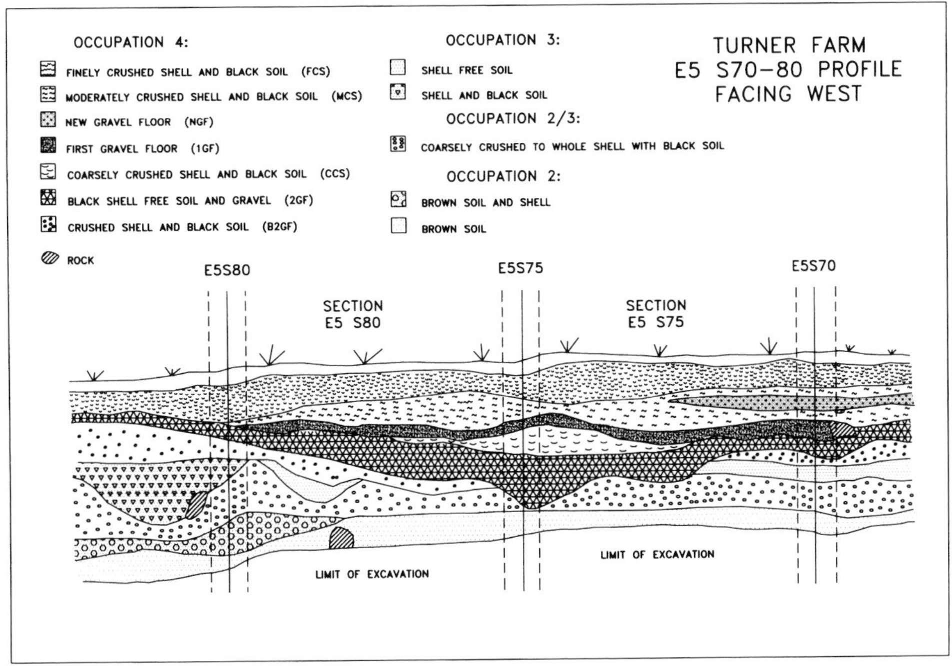


FIGURE 57. Stratigraphic section of the Turner Farm shell midden.

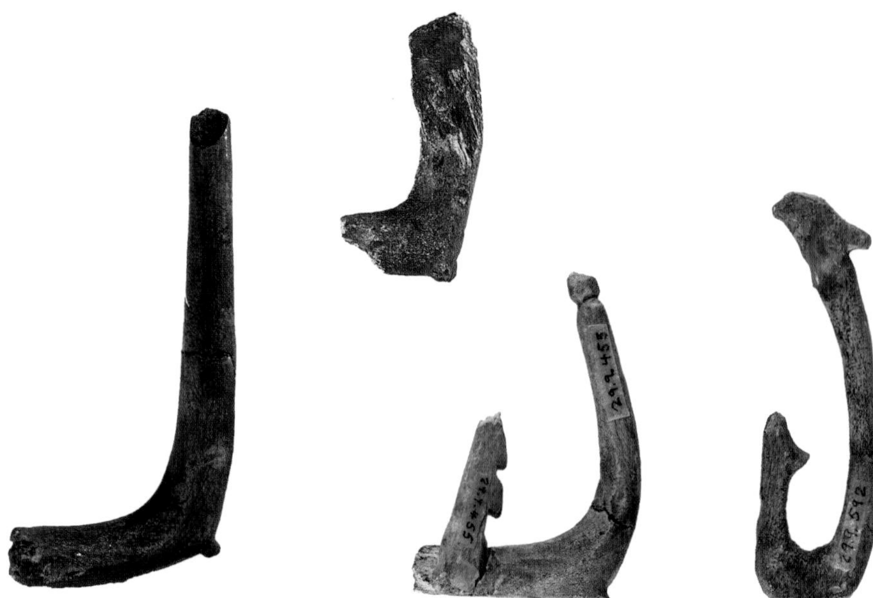

**FIGURE 58.** Bone fishhooks from the Nevin and Turner Farm sites. The complete one on the right is just over 2 inches (5 cm) tall. (*Hook fragment at the left courtesy of the R. S. Peabody Museum.*)

the historic hand-lining cod fishery, a significant proportion of clams were used as fish bait (figure 58).

This is not to say, however, that mollusks were insignificant in the diet. Archaeologists have analyzed the annual growth layers of mollusk shells and can determine the season of death by comparing the amount of the last annual layer to form relative to fully formed layers of previous years. Such analysis indicates that mollusks were seasonally important, being gathered mainly in the late winter and early spring, as was the case among the region's Indians when the first Europeans arrived.[7] At that time of year, when fish had not yet returned close to shore and deep snows made larger species hard to hunt, mollusks may have been a critical food resource.

The abundant bone refuse found in the midden was in excellent condition but often broken. Small, fragile bones suffered more breakage than larger ones, but even these were often complete enough for identification. While it is likely that the proportions of bones from different species does not directly reflect the ratios in which they were hunted, bone refuse remains a wonderfully rich source of information on daily subsistence activities.

A major difficulty in interpreting archaeological faunal remains is determining the relative importance of the species represented in it.[8] We observed that the most abundant bones from all strata of the midden were those of large mammals, mainly white-tailed deer (*Audocoileus virginianus*) and moose (*Alces alces*). Seasonality indicators *from all strata* point to nearly year-round deer hunting, while moose were hunted mainly between December and May.

We reasoned that, among all the abundant species represented in the midden, deer were the most likely to have been about equally important during all periods when the site was occupied, whereas cultural preferences might have led some species to be more heavily pursued or perhaps ignored during different periods of occupation. We also felt more confident that we could better identify the number of individuals represented by the deer bones than for most other species. For example, except for ribs, most deer bones are shaped differently from each other, whereas most bones from a fish look alike. Thus, we were much less likely to mistake two deer bones from the same animal than we were two fish bones. We therefore used deer abundance as a standard against which all other species were compared.[9]

We learned about two things through these comparisons. The first was which species were important to each group of occupants. The second was how patterns of animal exploitation changed over time. For example, we learned that during Moorehead phase times, the mollusk harvest included the quahog (*Mercenaria mercenaria*), which was completely absent during later times. It turns out that this change may reflect decreasing water temperature in the Gulf of Maine after around 3,800 years ago. We learned that large cod and swordfish were easily as important as large mammals like deer and moose to the site's Moorehead phase occupants, but also that fish were about equally important to all later occupants as well; the difference over time being in the decreasing average size of the fish, mainly as flounder and sculpin replaced first swordfish and then cod over time. Atlantic sturgeon (*Acipenser sturio*) was an exception to this pattern in that this large species became more abundant over time.

Beaver was well represented in the midden, increasing slightly in relative abundance over time, but how it was used is not clear. Beaver can provide significant amounts of meat and fat, but its fur was preferred for clothing by Indians of the Gulf of Maine coast when Europeans first met them, and beaver incisors were resharpened for use as carving tools during the Moorehead phase and again much later in the sequence. Given the near absence of beaver habitat on the Fox Islands, the latter two uses may have been more important.

The bones of small fur-bearers were present throughout the stratigraphic sequence, but only those of mink were abundant. Mink have little food value, but their fur is beautiful and still popular today for garments. Prehistorically, the Gulf of Maine region supported two varieties of mink, the common mink (*Mustela vison* or *Neovison vison*) and the now-extinct sea mink (*Neovison macrodon*). Debate continues about whether the two were really different species, but the most recent literature suggests that they were.[10] The Red Paint People hunted or trapped many mink, nearly all sea mink, which they must have used to make clothing. Mink teeth were also sometimes perforated and used for ornaments, either sewn onto garments or strung on necklaces.

Moorehead phase dogs deserve special comment. Dogs came with humans to the New World, and most prehistoric North Americans kept

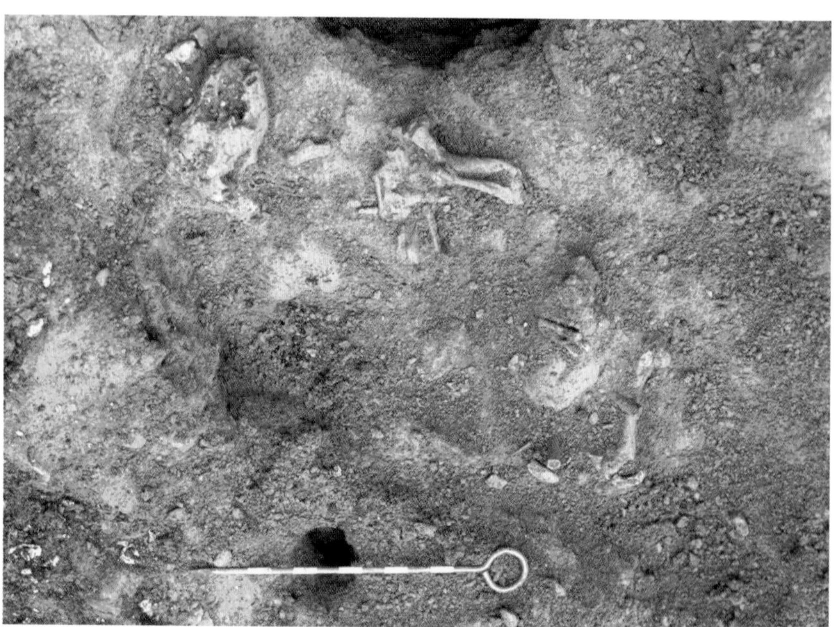

**FIGURE 59.** Red ocher dog burial in Occupation 2 midden deposits at the Turner Farm site.

FIGURE 60. Artifact cache found near a dog burial from Occupation 2 midden deposits at the Turner Farm site.

dogs, though they used them in a great variety of ways, as hunting companions, symbolic sacrificial victims, and emergency food sources, among others. Most dog bones encountered archaeologically in the Turner Farm and other Maine middens are scattered among other refuse, but the six dog burials at the Turner Farm site include two furnished with red ocher and one of which was apparently buried next to a ritualistic cache of artifacts (figures 59 and 60). These finding suggest that during the Moorehead phase, dogs were highly regarded by their owners.

Nearly all seal bones found in the midden came from the harbor seal (*Phoca vitulina*) or the larger gray seal (*Halichoerus gyrpus*). Formerly under heavy hunting pressure, both species are increasing in the Gulf of Maine today, though harbor seals are far more abundant. It seems likely, then, that they would have been comparably abundant throughout the Turner Farm sequence, and because they could easily have been clubbed during the seasons when they haul out to bear young and to molt, they would have been taken in large numbers. In fact, this was the case for the site's later occupants, but not during Moorehead phase times. Two different explanations may play a role. First, the few seal bones we did recover appear to have been chewed by dogs, suggesting that, during Moorehead phase times, seal meat served more to nourish dogs than humans.[11] This is in accord with general food preferences among hunter-gatherers, who prefer terrestrial mammals for food when they can get them. Second, faunal remains from later occupations reflect an intensification in the pursuit of species that were less important during the Moorehead phase, probably because of a growing regional population. Seals seem to be one of the lower-preference resources added to the human diet as a result of this pressure. Steneck, however, thinks we should not assume that seals were abundant during Moorehead phase times because, as fish eaters who must occasionally cease their food quest to come to the surface to breathe, they would probably have been at a comparative disadvantage relative to the abundant large cod we found.[12]

By and large, faunal exploitation patterns at the site remained fairly stable through time. They make ecological sense in that all occupants procured food and other animal resources from the species most suitable and abundant in the area, and it happened that they were mainly able to do this without shifting their residence throughout the year. Most changes over time, such as the increase in seal hunting, can be seen as reactions to slowly increasing regional populations. There are, however, two striking exceptions to this stability in faunal exploitation. The first is the disappearance of swordfish bone after Moorehead phase times. No younger swordfish remains were found at the site or at any other coastal site in the Gulf of Maine. The hunting of swordfish ceased with the Moorehead phase, never to be resumed by any later people. The second is the sharp decline in overall cod size and abundance after the Moorehead phase, a decline that continued through time until the site was abandoned. Both have implications for our understanding of the Red Paint People, which we will consider below.

## LIFESTYLE OF THE RED PAINT PEOPLE

From its beginnings, American anthropologists recognized that "that study of the handicrafts of primitive people affords the only key to prehistoric art."[13] This sort of comparison is known as ethnographic analogy, and it remains a basic element of the archaeologist's tool kit. Today, ethnographic analogy is applied to much more than art, extending even to whole cultural styles. One style widely recognized as very ancient and widely distributed around the inhabited world until recent times likely fits the Red Paint case, that of the hunter-gatherer.[14] The term became current while I was in graduate school, just after Richard B. Lee and Irvin Devore had organized the "Man the Hunter" conference in 1966, mainly to present the results of the Kalahari Research Project. The conference was soon followed by a book of the same title.[15]

That project and book powerfully challenged prevalent ideas that the lives of those who lived without the benefit of domestic crops or animals were, in the famous words of philosopher Thomas Hobbs, "solitary, poor, nasty, brutish and short." Instead, anthropology learned through the Kalahari project that the Khoisan-speaking inhabitants of South Africa lived generally peaceful lives of abundance. The importance of this discovery was neatly summed up in anthropologist Marshall Sahlins chapter, titled "The Original Affluent Society," which gave my generation permission to consider hunter-gatherers as worthy of scholarly attention. Hunter-gatherer studies burgeoned and have remained vibrant, in part because most anthropologists understand that this ancestral lifestyle of all of humanity is what shaped us as human beings.

Although hunter-gatherers may generally lead affluent lives, the seasonal and spatially dispersed resource base that they depend on nevertheless forces them to remain mobile. The Khoisan, for example, traditionally led highly mobile lives. I expected that the residents of the Turner Farm site, like the Khoisan, would turn out to be both affluent and seasonally mobile, including summer residence at this coastal site. What our studies of seasonality instead showed us was that they apparently remained at the site throughout the year.

This is not to say that such communities are entirely stable throughout the year. At the Turner Farm site, for example, the site's population dropped, perhaps nearly to zero, during the spring, when spawning runs of salmon must have attracted at least the more able-bodied to take a an up-river spring fishing trip, much as modern Maine fishermen have traditionally done.[16]

## Fishing and Sea Hunting

It turns out that around the world, hunter-gatherers of recent times who depended on aquatic resources, particularly in northern latitudes where such resources tend to be abundant, have relatively high population densities, as well as permanent or semipermanent villages. They also tend to have well-defined territories compared to their terrestrial neighbors.[17] With this in mind, let's examine whether and how the Red Paint People's economic activities affected their population, settlement patterns, and territoriality.

All the groups who had ever occupied the Turner Farm site had relied extensively on large terrestrial game, so I thought it unlikely that clues to the uniqueness of Moorehead phase lifestyle lay in that activity. A more fruitful approach, I thought, would be to think about their maritime exploits, including their cod fishing and swordfish hunting, which we knew were different from the site's later occupants.

The near-shore waters of the Gulf of Maine, like many shallow, rocky, cool temperate environments around the world, are dominated by a kelp forest ecosystem. It has historically been extraordinarily productive, but it is relatively species depauperate, with only one or a few species occupying each trophic level.[18] Thus, cod, the main keystone predator in the system, were historically so abundant that they provided nearly the entire economic underpinning for the region's traditional coastal culture. Moreover, the hook-and-line technology, which the commercial fishery was originally based on, survived until the mid-twentieth century. The large bone fishhooks we found in the Moorehead phase strata at the Turner Farm site suggest that hand-lining was probably as productive prehistorically as it was historically. The abundant swordfish bone, however, presented a more difficult problem. Swordfish will bite a baited hook, but we found no hook that looked like a match for a swordfish. At first I thought that they might have been harvested from carcasses that washed ashore, as do the carcasses of dead marine mammals today. For example, we had found fragments of large whalebone at the site, which we presumed came from beached carcasses, and I thought perhaps swordfish got there in the same way. However, swordfish are oceanic, rarely coming near shore, so it is unlikely that any would wash ashore when dead as do marine mammals like seals and porpoises.[19] That had to mean that swordfish hunting must have played an important role in the Moorehead phase. That conclusion

**FIGURE 61.** A warm core ring approaching Georges Bank.

raised two questions: How did the Red Paint People encounter swordfish, and how did they manage to catch them?

Today, swordfish live in tropical, temperate, and sometimes cooler waters around the world.[20] They are diurnal visual predators that feed on demersal fish and cephlapods (mainly squid), although they occasionally prey on other organisms, including seabirds. In the Atlantic Ocean, they are strongly associated with the Gulf Stream, but during the warm months they follow warm gyres, called core rings, that detach from the Gulf Stream and drift toward the much more productive waters off Georges Bank, where upwelling, nutrient-rich, Arctic-originating waters support large plankton blooms and, in turn, populations of their prey species, including fish and squid (figures 61 and 62).[21]

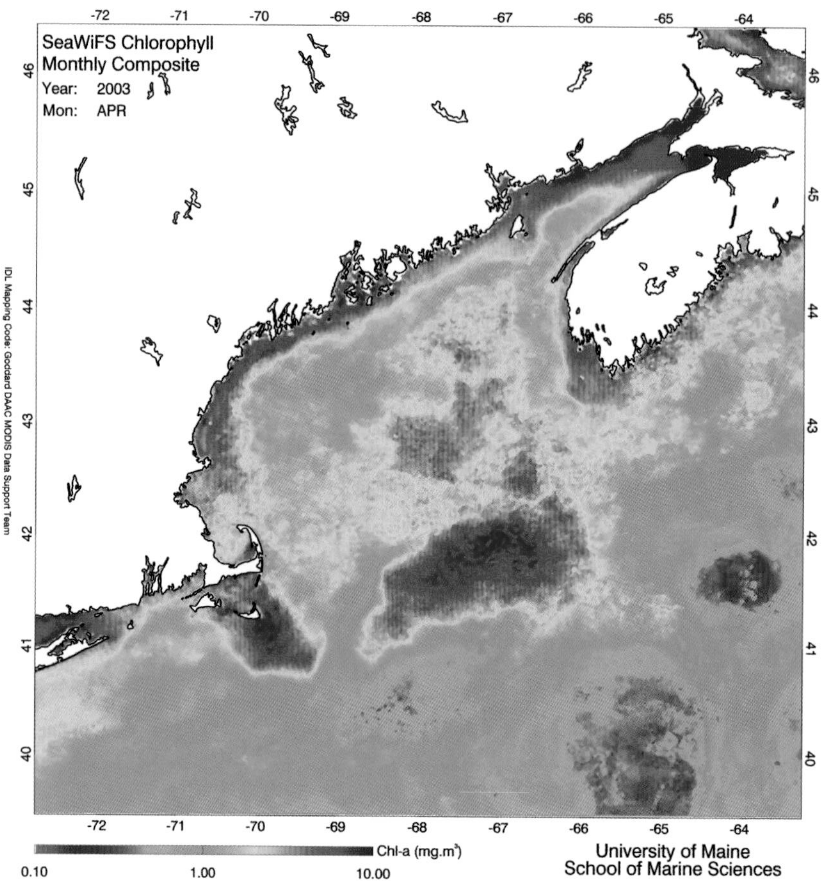


**FIGURE 62.** Plankton bloom in the Gulf of Maine. (*Courtesy of Andrew Thomas, University of Maine School of Marine Sciences.*)

It is highly unlikely that Moorehead phase swordfish hunters paddled over two hundred miles over the open ocean from the Maine coast out to Georges Bank where the fishery now takes place. So how, then, could they encounter their prey? The answer may lie in a puzzling change in swordfish behavior noted during the late nineteenth century as commercial sword fishing was becoming popular. Until 1884, the best fishing was in a one-hundred-mile stretch of water roughly twenty-five miles offshore and northeast of Jeffrey's Ledge. The fishery to the south of that was much less productive. In that year, for example, 1,062,500 pounds of swordfish were landed at Portland, Maine but only 350,000 pounds were landed at the much larger port of Boston. After 1884, however, swordfish disappeared from these inshore waters, forcing the fishery out to Georges Bank, where it persists today.[22] This shift may have been caused by fishing pressure because swordfish seem averse to feeding close to one another.[23] Before large-scale fishing began, this aversion would likely have forced some fish farther inshore than their optimal feeding area on the eastern slope of Georges Bank. If similar conditions prevailed prehistorically, swordfish may have been within easy reach of their Moorehead phase hunters. Moreover, as they apparently resorted to island fishing stations such as the Stanley site on Monhegan and the Candage site on southern Vinalhaven which are discussed below, this would have put then within fifteen miles of the productive zone. Fishing trips would have been even more feasible if they were undertaken by groups of boats that could provide aid to any that were in trouble, as was the practice among the swordfish-hunting Ainu of Japan.[24]

But even if this scenario is correct, the effort and logistical complexity of conducting such a fishery would still be significant. A surprising alternative solution has recently been suggested by geochemist Beverly Johnson, who compared carbon and nitrogen isotopes from archaeological Moorehead phase swordfish bone with bones from freshly caught swordfish from Georges Bank, and found them to be very different. The explanation for this difference is not yet clear, but they are consistent with the former living in a coastal, kelp-dominated system, while those from Georges Bank reflect life in an oceanic, planktonic system. If further research bears this dichotomy out, the likely inference would be that the Red Paint People hunted a separate, now-extinct population of swordfish that lived close to the Gulf of Maine coastline not just seasonally but throughout much of the year. Such an inference may seem unlikely, but in fact it appears that swordfish in the Gulf of Mexico may be semipermanent residents there, and two other populations (or subspecies) in the Mediterranean and in the Atlantic south of the equator are similarly isolated.[25]

Whatever the explanation, the archaeological data from all Moorehead phase sites with bone preservation are clear: the Red Paint People did, in fact, encounter large numbers of large swordfish. The size of the rostra we found at the Turner Farm site suggests that many were very large, perhaps nearly 1,000 pounds, the upper end of the swordfish body size range. This is actually to be expected because female swordfish, which dominate the North Atlantic stock in summer, are larger that males.[26] But how did the hunters capture them?

Today, most swordfish are taken by hook on trawl lines, but as mentioned above, the bone hooks we found at the Turner Farm site seem better suited to cod than to the powerful swordfish. Greeks of the Bronze Age attempted to wound the fish with lances, then to tie a line to it and tow it to shore, while the Romans used purse seines.[27] It is doubtful that the Red Paint People would have employed either of these techniques, however, as the size of their canoes was likely insufficient. Nineteenth-century swordfish hunters took swordfish with harpoons thrown from sloops or small schooners. The technique is still practiced from motorized vessels today. Archaeological evidence of harpoons and foreshafts suggest that the Moorehead phase swordfish hunters used a similar technology (figures 63, 64, and 65).

Swordfish are easily frightened when approached by a boat. In modern harpoon fishery, the harpooner's station is in a pulpit at the end of a plank that projects from the bow. In the warm waters of the Mediterranean and along the California coast, this plank must be nearly as long

**FIGURE 63.** Hunting swordfish from a fishing schooner off the Atlantic coast, early twentieth century.

as the fishing vessel itself to place the harpooner far enough ahead of the vessel to avoid startling the fish. In the northwest Atlantic, however, swordfish pursue their prey in deep, cold waters where they are unable to maintain body warmth, unlike other large predatory species such as tunas and some sharks. This forces them to rise to the surface where they can warm. There they loll quietly, with their dorsal and caudal (tail) fins exposed, a behavior called finning.[28] They are lethargic in this state and oblivious to their surroundings, making them easy to harpoon.[29] As similar water conditions likely prevailed prehistorically, approaching and harpooning the fish may not have been difficult.

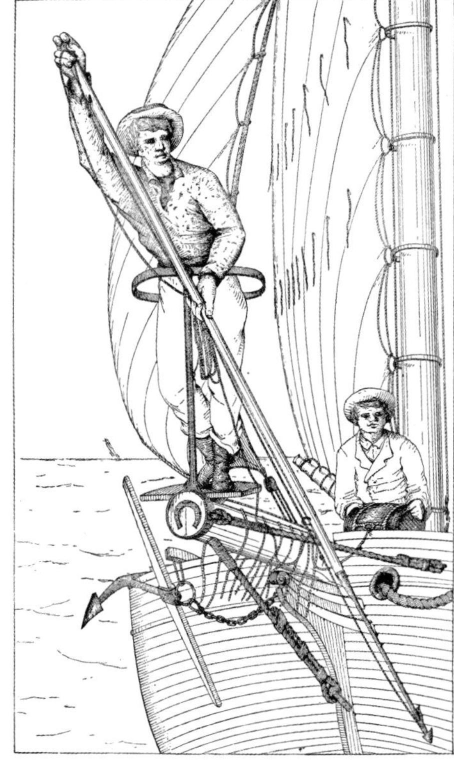

**FIGURE 64.** Harpooner from Goode 1883.

The successful harpooner then faces the possibility that the wounded fish will attack his boat with great force, possibly driving its sword through even a thick hull. Bigelow and Schroeder state that:

> full grown swordfish are so active, so powerful, and so well armed that they have few enemies . . . fish that have been harpooned often turn on their pursuers, and it is a common event for one to pierce the thin bottom of a dory. We have, indeed, known several fishermen of our acquaintance to be wounded in the leg in this way, but always after the fish had been struck with the harpoon. Under these circumstances swordfish have been known to drive their swords right through the planking of a fishing vessel.[30]

In the late nineteenth century, the British naturalist Sir Richard Owen testified that a swordfish "strikes with the accumulated force of fifteen double-handled hammers. Its velocity is equal to that of a swivel shot, and is as

**FIGURE 65.** Franklyn D'Entremont preparing to harpoon a swordfish. At less than 500 pounds (227 kg), it is much smaller than the average swordfish represented in the faunal remains from the Turner Farm site. (*Courtesy of Franklyn D'Entremont.*)

dangerous in its effects as a heavy artillery projectile."[31] The question that thus arises is how a prehistoric Stone Age population could have landed swordfish, particularly the large individuals evident in archaeological bone samples from Moorehead Phase sites.

They probably employed two risk-reducing strategies. The first was the design of their boats. Good boats are critical to maritime hunters. As archaeologist Kenneth Ames put it, they are "numerous, ubiquitous, and central to life" because they greatly increased the amount of food that could be returned to home sites compared to foot transportation.[32] If, in addition, their boats were rugged enough to hunt swordfish from, then the potential payoff, both of calories and in bragging rights, may have been impressive. But what kinds of boats would these have been?

No Moorehead phase watercraft, indeed no direct indications of prehistoric watercraft at all, have been recovered in the region. I suspect that some may actually be found in the future, however, perhaps deep in the wet peat of the salt marsh that flanks the Turner Farm, which began to accumulate at least 4,300 years ago.[33] However, descriptions of the indigenous watercraft written by early explorers in the region mention two likely types, birch-bark canoes and log dugouts. It is unlikely that the third major New World boat type, the hide-covered kayak and the larger *umiak* of the far north, would have been made here because hide coverings would quickly have deteriorated in this region's temperate climate.

Historic sources mentioned birch-bark canoes in glowing terms, and many were brought back to Europe as souvenirs by early visitors. They are light but surprisingly strong and seaworthy. Penobscots, Passamaquoddies, and Micmacs formerly used them to hunt porpoises, an active marine mammal roughly the size of an adult swordfish. Despite these qualities, two factors suggest that they were not the kind of craft used by Moorehead phase hunters.

First, making a bark canoe necessitates shaping small wooden gunwhales, thwarts, and ribs and cutting and stitching birch bark. The tools needed to accomplish this include stone scrapers to use as microplanes for shaping the wood and numerous bone awls to pierce the birch bark in preparation for sewing with split conifer roots, which were widely used to sew together the bark canoe skin.[34] No such tools are found archaeologically until roughly 1,000 years after the Moorehead phase disappeared. Second, it is unlikely that a bark canoe could withstand an attack by such a formidable and well-armed adversary as a swordfish.

When Europeans began to write descriptions of the Maine coast in the early 1600s, bark canoes were the only watercraft mentioned east of the Kennebec River, but farther west another kind of boat was encountered—the dugout. Samuel de Champlain, who visited the region in 1607, encountered both bark canoes and dugouts along the western Maine coast.[35] Archaeological evidence that dugouts were constructed during the Moorehead phase includes the robust stone adzes and gouges found in so many Moorehead phase sites. These were clearly designed to shape solid wood—the adze for convex surfaces and the gouges for concave. While the Red Paint People were neither the first nor the last to make such woodworking implements, they must hold a world record for their sheer abundance, variety of sizes, and care taken in finishing them. Moreover, gouges virtually disappeared from the archaeological record at the end of the Moorehead phase around 3800 B.P., and adzes become far less abundant, just as stone scrapers and bone awls become more common.

What might these dugout canoes have looked like? They had to be large enough to go into open water to reach the swordfish. Most likely, they were made from large white pines (*Pinus strobus*) like those still to be found in Maine's forests, some of which are over four feet in diameter at the butt

**FIGURE 66.** Old-growth white pine, Gero Island, Moosehead Lake, Maine. *(Courtesy of the Maine Department of Conservation.)*

(figure 66). To judge from the abundance of very small, narrow-bitted gouges found along with larger ones in many Moorehead phase sites, such dugouts might have been elaborately decorated with engravings, perhaps in the manner of decorations found on Moorehead phase bone daggers and slate bayonets.

The second technology is the harpoon. Some elements of this weapon system survive archaeologically, but we must speculate about others. Harpoons are distinguished from spears by their detachable heads, which remain imbedded in the prey as the shaft is withdrawn or falls away. Referring to them as systems reflects their likely composition of many separate elements, including the harpoon tip, the shaft (probably composed of a wooden shaft with a foreshaft made of bone or swordfish rostrum), and a line that connected the harpoon head to either the harpooner or to a float. Given the strength of a large swordfish, once harpooned it could only have been directly retrieved with great difficulty, so it is likely that the line was attached to a float, leaving the harpooned fish tethered to tire or die from blood loss before being retrieved. Float technology was used to hunt whales by Northwest Coast Indians and Inuits (figure 67). A wooden keg served the same purpose for nineteenth-century swordfish hunters.[36]

**FIGURE 67.** Makah whaling canoes with sealskin floats, Neah Bay, Washington, 1900. (*Courtesy of the Museum of History and Industry.*)

The Red Paint People made two kinds of harpoon tips from deer and moose bone. The first is the barbed form, a style made by humans for the past 20,000 years or more and widespread throughout prehistoric eastern North America. Much more unusual is the toggling harpoon, which is designed to twist inside the harpooned animal. The toggling harpoon is a sophisticated weapon system that has great holding power. It is best known ethnographically among northern peoples, particularly the Inuit of Arctic Canada and Alaska, where they are used in hunting marine mammals. Somewhat surprisingly, then, is that the archaeological evidence suggests that they originated with prehistoric Indians of the northwest Atlantic.

There are two candidates for the earliest toggling harpoon. The first is from a small burial mound at L'Anse Amour on the south Labrador coast near the Quebec border. Radiocarbon-dated to around 7500 B.P., it is actually the oldest burial mound yet discovered in North America. It entombed a single adolescent individual accompanied by dozens of stone, bone, and antler artifacts.[37] One antler piece is interpreted by the excavators as a toggling harpoon head, but if so, it is an unusual one, lacking features typical of other known prehistoric Indian examples (figure 68). Its toggling spur juts prominently from the pointed tip portion in a way that would make

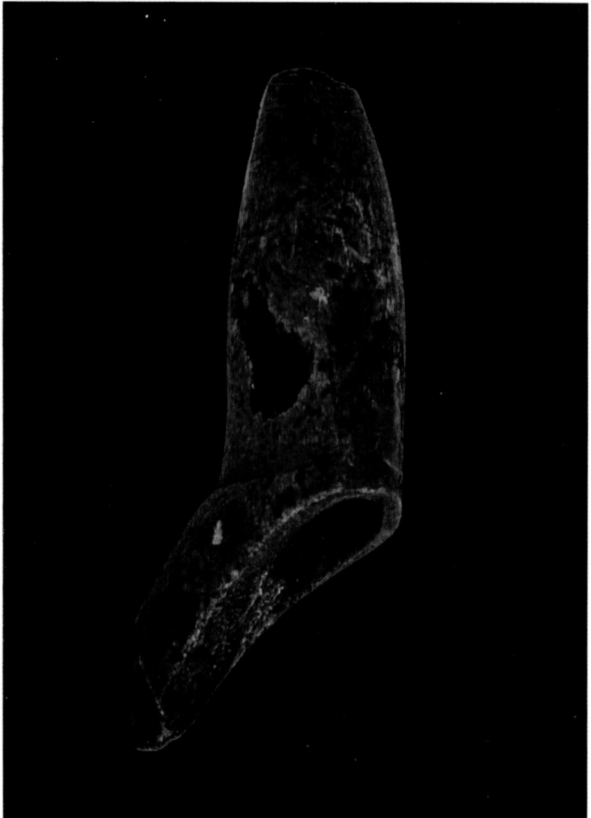

**FIGURE 68.** Object from a burial mound at L'Anse Amour, Labrador, claimed by its finders to be a toggling harpoon.

imbedding it fully beneath the skin of its prey more difficult than the more streamlined spurs of other known harpoon tips. It also lacks either the line hole seen in other examples or a lashing groove. The absence of a line hole cannot be explained by the lack of a drilling technology among its makers, for another tool found with the body has a very precisely drilled hole. Finally, it is the only known specimen with a completely enclosed socket. Such closed-socket harpoons are known among Paleo-Eskimo and later northern peoples, but all other prehistoric Indian examples are open-socketed. Still, it may represent an early pattern that later fell out of favor.

Other candidates that clearly are toggling harpoons include one from the Nevin site and one from the Turner Farm site (figure 69). Both predate 4000 B.P., making them earlier than Paleo-Eskimo toggling harpoons, and they are likely the lowest latitude examples. Possibly these harpoons were used as in the North, to hunt marine mammals such as whales, porpoises, and seals. Moorehead phase sites have produced few seal bones and no remains of porpoise or whales, though a single juvenile harbor porpoise (*Phocoena phocoena*) may have been included in a burial at the Nevin site.[38] What is abundant in these sites is swordfish bone, suggesting that the latter was likely the species targeted by harpoons, both barbed and toggling.

A final interesting observation remains to be made about Moorehead phase harpoons from the Nevin site, particularly the barbed specimens. It is their remarkable resemblance to those recovered at the slightly later Port au Choix cemetery in northern Newfoundland (figure 70). They are so similar, in fact, that it is hard to believe that they were independently developed. This is an instance of the mysterious close links between the Moorehead phase and Port au Choix site that we will discuss later.

The difficulties and dangers of swordfish hunting raise an interesting

**FIGURE 69:** (*left*) Port au Choix cemetery, 3.5 in (9 cm) long; (*center*) Turner Farm site; (*right*) Nevin cemetery. (*Left, courtesy of The Rooms. Right: courtesy of the R. S. Peabody Museum.*)

**FIGURE 70.** Barbed harpoons. Left: Turner Farm site; next three: Nevin cemetery; next two: Port au Choix cemetery. Longest specimen is 5.5 inches (14 cm) long. *(Nevin cemetery harpoons courtesy of the R. S. Peabody Museum. Port au Choix harpoons courtesy of The Rooms.)*

question. How many other prehistoric hunting and gathering peoples around the world engaged in this activity? The answer seems to be "not many," even where swordfish were abundant. Prehistoric sword fishing might be expected in any coastal region of the world where the upwelling of deep, nutrient-rich water raises plankton productivity that, in turn, supports large schools of fish and cephalopods. These conditions are found in many parts of the world, including the Florida Keys, the Mediterranean Sea, the coast of West Africa, and the coasts of Peru and Chile, but none of these has produced evidence of prehistoric swordfish hunting (figure 71).[39] High near-coastal marine productivity leads to swordfish abundance, but it is not a useful predictor of swordfish hunting.

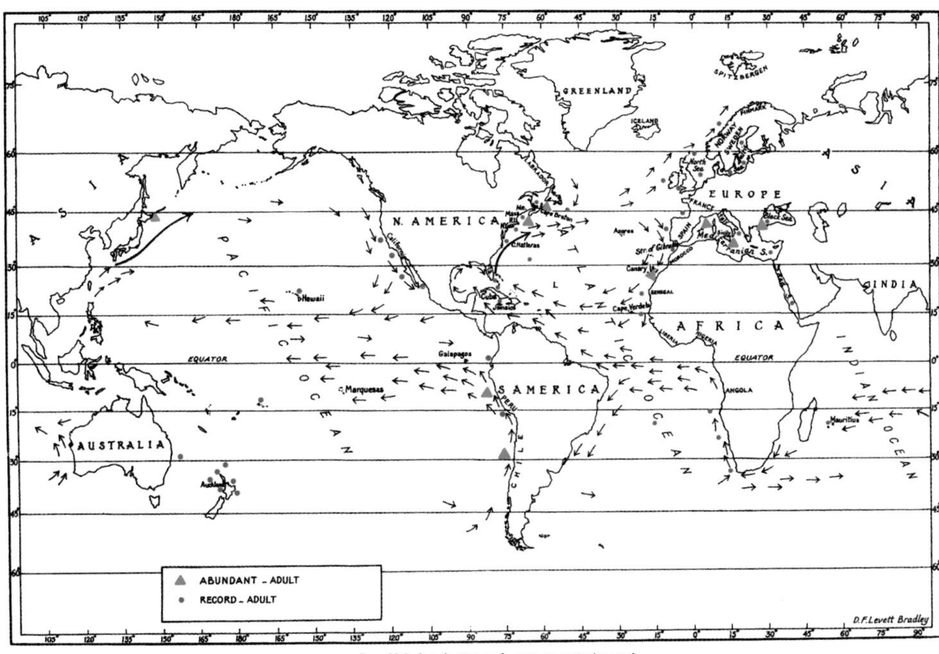


Swordfish distribution and ocean currents (arrows).

**FIGURE 71.** Worldwide distribution of swordfish (from Nichols and LaMonte 1937).

The earliest archaeological evidence for sword fishing comes from the early Bronze Age of the eastern Mediterranean, roughly 5,000 years ago, but these swordfish hunters had already been agriculturalists for millennia and, as the term implies, had mastered the use of metals.[40] Another contender for "earliest swordfish hunters" are the prehistoric Jomon people of Japan who passed the practice down to their historic descendants known as the Ainu. Recent research, however, indicates that Jomon swordfish hunting began only around 3500 B.P., a millennium later than in Maine.[41] Moreover, recent chemical analyses of coastal Jomon skeletons indicates that they didn't rely on marine protein to nearly the extent of those buried at the Nevin Red Paint cemetery in Blue Hill.[42]

Turning to North America, the group best known for swordfish hunting were the ancestors of the Chumash, who lived along the coast and islands of southern California. They hunted from *tomols*, boats unique in North America in that they were made of planks fastened by cordage and caulked with asphaltum and pine pitch. A recent survey of the archaeological data, however, reveals that Chumash sword fishing may not not predate the tomol, which appeared around A.D. 500, roughly 4,000 years after the practice began in the Gulf of Maine.[43] Thus it seems that the Red Paint People were among the earliest swordfish hunters in the world. Certainly, they were the earliest hunter-gatherers to do so.

A puzzling question about Moorehead phase swordfish hunting is why they apparently ignored other large species that could have been taken with the same harpoon technology. Other historically recorded swordfish hunters took multiple species, including tuna, sharks, and small cetaceans. In the Gulf of Maine, one might expect to see the remains, at least, of bluefin tuna (*Thunnus thynnus*), harbor porpoise, and even small whales such as the blackfish (*Globicephala melaena*), all of which have been taken in historic times by harpoon. Yet, these species are absent from the archaeological record, or nearly so.[44] It is likely that at least some sharks were taken. Their cartilaginous skeletons would not survive archaeologically, but shark teeth, including those of the white shark (*Carcharodon carcharias*) and shortfin mako (figure 49) have been found in Moorehead phase contexts, including burials. This nearly single-minded focus on the large, powerful swordfish suggests that it held some importance beyond its utilitarian desirability. We will turn to this question in the next chapter.

# 7

# Explaining the Moorehead Phase: Part 1

It is now clear that the Moorehead phase developed locally from the Small Stemmed Point tradition. Unlike its ancestor, however, the Moorehead phase occupied a very specific territory, so we must ask why this happened and why it remained focused there after it developed instead of spreading along the coast to the east and west. I suspect the answer lies in the geography and ecology of the Gulf of Maine.

## The Environment of the Red Paint People

To begin with, some of the largest plankton blooms today occur in this area, and that was probably the case prehistorically. They are based on deep, nutrient-rich water originating in the Arctic, some of which flows into the Gulf of Maine, where tidal mixing brings it to the surface. Still, the entire eastern Gulf of Maine has roughly comparable biological productivity, so this is probably not an adequate explanation. Added to this basic productivity are the many islands, some quite far out to sea, that cluster along this stretch of coastline. Though swordfish are now rarely seen in the Gulf of Maine, this was not the case when commercial sword fishing began in the late nineteenth century. As noted above, then the most productive hunting grounds lay within twenty-five miles of the coast.[1] If this was the case prehistorically, fishing stations on the outermost islands would have placed Moorehead phase hunters close to their prey. We know of two sites located on such islands that appear to be neither villages nor cemeteries, the Stanley and Candage sites.[2] Unlike the Turner Farm and Nevin sites, which are located well up estuaries in protected areas where swordfish were unlikely to be found, both the Stanley and Candage sites are in exposed settings that would have facilitated access to the hunting grounds. This combination of high productivity and easy access may thus have combined to create an ecological "sweet spot" that the Red Paint People found ideal compared to coastal areas to their east or west.

However, the culture's local origins in a sweet spot do not explain why its salient characteristics fall so far outside the expected range, not merely of its local ancestors but of many prehistoric hunter-gatherer cultures around the world. How did this happen? The first part of this explanation lies in its maritime adaptations. If we compare it to other maritime hunter-gatherers, we find some suggestive parallels. Candidates include the late prehistoric and early historic peoples of the Pacific Northwest, the Chumash of California, and the 8,000-year-old Mesolithic cultures of Scandinavia and of the Jomon of Japan.[3] All had roughly comparable, complex technologies as well as evidence for complex social structure and ritual behavior. In the case of the Pacific Northwest and the Chumash, these survived long enough to be historically recorded, so we know that these societies also had large stable populations and complex political structures. It is more difficult to determine in detail whether the prehistoric examples resembled them in these regards. According to Kenneth Ames, maritime hunter-gatherers become more complex than their more terrestrial cousins when their economies become focused on a limited range of high-yielding marine resources, acquired by developing relatively large-scale and complex technologies, including boats, which are linked to complex rituals and symbolic systems.[4]

But how does this happen? Ames and many others see this process as one of the intensification of preexisting patterns over time, and his arguments are appealing for these cases because the roots of complexity are apparent in the ancestry of these cultures. By intensification they mean that over time the culture learns the benefits of maritime—or some other kind of—adjustment to its environmental circumstances.

For the last several decades, archaeologists have viewed such processes as intensification through the lens of cultural ecology. The principles of ecology were developed by biologists to study the interactions of plant and animal communities, and we have seen how cultural ecology extends these principles to the study of human cultures. Cultures make environmentally driven adjustments and they do so much more rapidly than plants or animals because they do not depend on the slow genetic process of natural selection. In the larger picture of cultural evolution, this allows for incredibly quick responses to environmental challenges and opportunities.

Proper research into cultural ecology requires multidisciplinary teams of scientists that focus on how a prehistoric group used its technology, among other factors, to meet environmental challenges in order to survive. Thus, archaeologists try to explain changes in material culture as adaptations to changing environments. From the beginning of my fieldwork on North Haven, I have maintained close ties with several geologists, zoologists, and botanists interested in the terrestrial and marine ecosystems of the Gulf of Maine region. These contacts have been richly rewarding to me, and I think to my colleagues as well, and cultural ecology has been tremendously helpful in explaining the broad outlines of cultural change in prehistoric societies around the world. An example from eastern North America was the appearance of heavy woodworking tools 8,000 or more years ago as a cultural adaptation to the spread of forests. Another would be the development of toggling harpoons in the Northeast when people decided to hunt large marine animals.

There is no denying the crucial role the natural environment plays in shaping a culture, and successes of cultural ecology oblige us to review evidence about the environment in which the Red Paint People lived to see what influences it might have had on them. The first place archaeologists turn for environmental explanations is the climate. Climatic warming at the end of the Pleistocene, for example, caused Alaskan and Canadian glaciers to melt, which in turn allowed humans to enter the New World from Siberia around 11,300 B.P. A more recent example is the Medieval Warm Period, which lasted from around A.D. 950 to 1250. Its beginning coincides almost exactly with the Norse colonization of Greenland, which continued to grow throughout the Medieval Warm Period, reaching a peak of between 3,000 to 5,000 people before it started to decline around A.D. 1300, reaching total collapse early in the 1400s. But it turns out that climate isn't of much use in explaining the emergence of the Moorehead phase; it emerged during an era of warming in the Northern Hemisphere.[5] While I was initially attracted to the idea that this warming influenced the ancestors of the Moorehead phase, I soon realized that hemispheric warming couldn't explain events that occurred only in the Gulf of Maine unless we can demonstrate that it triggered local changes in resources important to humans there.

Evidence for ancient vegetation comes mainly from two sources, microscopic pollen and macroscopic fragments of plant materials called macrofossils. Pollen is usually collected from the bottom sediments of ponds and marshes. Grains of pollen carry the sperm cells of seed-producing plants, and the pollen of many species is designed to be carried by wind, which brings it into contact with the female organ of another plant. The vast majority miss the mark and fall as "pollen rain," some onto land but some onto the surface of ponds or marshes, where it sinks and is incorporated into the bottom sediments. Palynologists, those who study pollen, extract tubular cores of these sediments and take pollen samples every few centimeters from the bottom of the core upward. They then compare the frequencies of pollen species from sample to sample to reconstruct patterns of vegetational change over time. They also sometimes add an analysis of insect parts, which can provide additional, more specific information about local environmental conditions. Because pollen in a given pond has been blown there from a larger area, pollen analysis provides only a general picture of vegetation for that area.

Macrofossils tend to come from the immediate area where they were found. In ponds, and especially marshes, they tell us what plants grew in the immediate area but not whether they were important to humans. The most common macrofossil from shell middens is charcoal from campfires, and most other macrofossils from shell middens are also carbonized. These kinds of remains, however, were nearly absent in the Moorehead phase deposits at the Turner Farm site, which underscores the importance of marine resources during that period. One interesting fact did emerge from the identification of wood charcoal: on the Fox Islands, the forests of ancient times included a wide variety of hardwoods, quite unlike the spruce-dominated woods of today, which developed when spruce overtook extensive pasturelands as sheep raising declined in the late nineteenth century.

Pollen evidence is now quite abundant for North America,[6] and for the Maine coastal region, it supplements analyses of plant macrofossils from archaeological sites to confirm a general pattern of vegetational change since the end of the ice age. What it tells us about the era of the Moorehead phase is that forests were generally similar to those encountered by the first European colonists. The land was covered by a diverse forest dominated by broad-leafed (deciduous) trees and shrubs, which was probably modified by the human inhabitants, who set fires on a regular basis to keep underbrush down and to improve browse for deer. The forest was also similar to that of neighboring regions, with the relative proportion of broadleaf species increasing to the south, and with conifers increasing to the north.[7] One trend evident during the era of the Red Paint People is that the abundance of nut-producing trees was on the rise, which presumably meant more browse for mammals and more food for humans. Initially, I was among those who thought this trend might help to explain the Moorehead phase, but I now doubt that this is the case, for two reasons. First, like hemispheric warming, the rise in nut-bearing species was far more widespread than was the Moorehead phase, and second, the strong maritime focus of the Moorehead phase would likely have swamped any subtle increase in terrestrial resources.

Turning next to terrestrial animals, the evidence comes mainly from the Turner Farm site. The amount of bone we recovered there was staggering compared to what I had seen while excavating shell middens on Martha's Vineyard with William Ritchie in the 1960s. But there was also a huge volume of mollusk shell. This left me uncertain about the relative importance of large mammals, which took some effort to hunt, versus clams, which are easy to procure.

By the 1970s, ecologists had figured out that animals tend to acquire calories as efficiently as possible. In fact, during the 1960s a whole branch of ecology, ambitiously named optimal forging theory (OFT), has developed to study this phenomenon. OFT tries to predict, for example, which animals make sense as prey, assuming that over time, evolutionary pressures will drive the predator species toward obtaining the most food for the least effort. Because humans are predators, this efficiency model predicts that they will focus on the largest animals they can kill without undue effort or threat to themselves. Alternatively, they may focus on smaller organisms, such as schooling fish, which can be captured en masse.[8] But, in fact, efficiency alone rarely succeeds in predicting what animals actually eat.[9] Moreover, humans have needs that other animals don't. For example, they may need hides for clothing, lovely furs for ornamentation, sinew for sewing, and bone for toolmaking, so that calories alone do not completely shape hunting patterns.

For those who lived near the Gulf of Maine during the last several thousand years of prehistory, however, it seemed to me that this kind of simple efficiency argument came close to explaining how Moorehead phase hunters operated on land, focusing on large abundant herbivores, like deer and moose, that were easy to locate and kill and would deliver large amounts of meat, fat, hide, and other useful products. Their massive bodies mean that the bones in their legs would be strong and dense, useful for making artifacts, as are their antlers. Bear, too, were hunted for food and fur, but because they are omnivores, their populations would have been smaller. But if the Red Paint People used their terrestrial environment in a theoretically predictable pattern, so did the other groups who lived at the site, and there was nothing elsewhere in the regional archaeological record to suggest that any prehistoric group deviated from this pattern. What this tells us is that the cultural distinctiveness of the Moorehead phase probably does not arise from the Red Paint People's activities on land.

What about the sea? Might the Gulf of Maine have been significantly different during those times? Perhaps. If the area inhabited by the Red Paint People was indeed an ecological sweet spot, then one would expect to find such a cultural development there. But this correlation seems too pat, both geographically and temporally. Geographically speaking, why, for example, is there no evidence of the culture along the coast to the west, toward nearby Casco Bay, with its abundant islands? And temporally speaking, we see nothing in the oceanographic record to suggest a sharp upward swing in productivity as the Moorehead phase was emerging.

## A Robust Culture of Maritime Hunters

The fact that environmental factors seem too vaguely focused on its territory underscores how temporally and spatially discrete was the Moorehead phase. What might have caused this discreteness? There have been other reported cases of rapid cultural development leading to highly distinct cultures in the past. As early as the 1950s, archaeologists coined the term *X-factor* to explain the sudden emergence of the Mississippian tradition, which burgeoned throughout the American Midwest around A.D. 800. The X-factor was seen as "a kind of cultural and social gestalt wherein communities change through a process of new and varied experiences, at all social levels, emanating either internally or externally and synthesizing with conventional experiences and elements. The result is not a combination of the old and the new, but something entirely new."[10]

By its very name, however, the X-factor sounds alien, inscrutable, and imprecise in determining what was novel about the Mississippian tradition. Anthropologists have since developed more precise and user-friendly terms to explore such phenomena. Morton Fried, for example, used the term *pristine* for cultural situations where "development occurs exclusively on the basis of indigenous factors . . . [and] . . . there is no external model of more complex design to help shape the new society."[11] He contrasted pristine with secondary to cover cultures whose development was the result of outside influence. His specific concern was the development of civilizations, but the pristine-secondary dichotomy can be helpful here. For example, Tuck's view, I suspect, was that the Moorehead phase was not pristine because it was derived from his Maritime Archaic tradition.

More recently, anthropologists have adopted from ecology the term *robustness*. According to ecologist William C. Wimsatt, "things are robust if they are accessible (detectable, measurable, derivable, producible, or the like) in a variety of independent ways."[12] Robustness also implies the quality of resilience, that is, of maintaining characteristic patterns in the face of perturbations.[13] My main argument in this book is that the Moorehead phase possesses this quality to a greater extent than any other Archaic culture in northeastern North America. Let's examine some factors that might explain its exceptional qualities.

In my view, swordfish hunting must somehow be closely linked to Red Paint mortuary ceremonialism. Let's consider what that linkage might be.

Even if we assume that the bathymetry and oceanography of the Gulf of Maine "sweet spot" made swordfish hunting optimally possible, I don't think it ever made sense economically. The hunting efficiency concept was developed to explain animal behavior in terrestrial ecosystems, but some have extended it to the marine world. For marine hunter-gatherers, then, pursuit of large predatory fish, such as cod, seems predictable. Cod are abundant, large, and easy to catch and preserve. Swordfish, on the other hand, were far less abundant, less predictable to encounter, and difficult—even dangerous—to capture. We have seen that efficiency arguments alone often fail to predict what animals actually eat, and I think they are even trickier when applied to humans, who develop cultural preferences about which prey to pursue and which to avoid. Because we are such successful animals, we can get away with this discretionary attitude, and that, in turn, means that we can imbue our hunting and our diet with social significance beyond their economic utility. Carried to extremes, nonoptimal prey choices might destroy a culture, but within tolerable limits, they may actually benefit a culture in subtle, noneconomizing ways.

Today, swordfish are a highly sought-after food, but historically this was not always the case. It was not even offered for sale in American markets until the mid-nineteenth century, whereas cod and its relatives have been consumed by humans around the globe for more than 10,000 years. Swordfish are also large, powerful, and dangerous to hunt, and from an economic efficiency perspective, the energy expended in pursuing them, including maintaining the boat, the crew, and the weapons, as well as in the actual pursuit, would probably have been better spent pursuing more cod. That the Red Paint People nevertheless did so suggests that some economically irrational factor influenced them. This seems true even had swordfish been more abundant than we suspect. As mentioned above, if we look at nonindustrial swordfish-hunting patterns around the world, swordfish abundance in coastal waters is a very poor predictor of swordfish hunting. This incongruity accords well with ethnographic accounts telling us that, while most coastal cultures know about swordfish, incorporating them into their myths and folklore, only a few actually hunt them, mainly in the Pacific where navigational technology was unusually well developed.

To get some idea about why the Red Paint People hunted swordfish, let's look at ethnographic cases where hunter-gatherers sought other kinds of large, challenging prey. Smith and Bleige Bird, for example, compared several big-game hunting groups and concluded that, while big-game hunting may not make economic sense, it can be very useful to a society in sending unambiguous signals about who is a competent leader. They call this phenomenon costly signaling, and it seems to explain many cases better than economic efficiency.[14]

Speth has also examined cultures that hunt large, potentially dangerous terrestrial game. Focusing on food preferences, he notes that in nearly all cultures, meat is always preferred, and that providing it always confers prestige to the provider. Speth agrees with Smith and Bleige Bird that such preferences must trump considerations of efficiency because hunting absorbs a great deal of time and effort, can be deadly to the hunters, produces far more meat protein than the population can use, and is not the most efficient way to obtain fat, a more important dietary element than meat. Moreover, Speth argues that costly signaling is common among hunters and that, when it comes to big-game hunting, despite its riskiness, it delivers big payoffs, not in the domain of economics but rather "in the social, political, psychological, and/or reproductive domains."[15] He elaborates this point by quoting Bird and O'Connell:

> Hawkes and colleagues argue that big-game hunting is often a form of costly signaling, a means by which men establish and maintain social position relative to their peers and competitors, not just among the Hadza but among foragers in general. . . . To the degree the hunter is successful, two ends are achieved. First, because big-game hunting is a risky, skill-intensive undertaking, the good hunter marks himself as a powerful ally and dangerous adversary. His relationships with others are likely to be structured accordingly. Equally important, his successes make available a "public good," one that is of interest to all, unpredictably acquired, readily divisible, and thus likely to be shared widely. . . considerations that draw still more favorable attention his way. That attention might include deference to his wishes, support in disputes, positive dealings with his spouse and children, and more frequent mating opportunities.[16]

Seen from this perspective, swordfish may have been hunted precisely because they were the most challenging species in the Moorehead phase environment, and that successful swordfish hunters earned great prestige. That such is the case among more recent maritime-hunting societies seems clear. Among the Nootkans of Vancouver Island, for example, it was said that "[w]haling was the noblest calling, and the whaler was always a chief."[17] Drucker goes so far as to claim "that the prestige value of whaling outweighed its economic importance is clear."[18]

If we are correct in attributing a similar motivation to Red Paint swordfish hunters, might it help us understand other aspects of their archaeological record? Societies that undertake dangerous or other emotionally charged activities frequently crave support or protection provided by outside sources: the pregame pep talk from the coach or the prayer before battle. Such practices amount to risk-aversion strategies in that they invoke the protective intervention of spiritual forces in the face of danger and uncertainty. Risk aversion is a nearly universal trait of human cultures but is especially well developed in some maritime hunting societies. Among the whale hunters of the northwest coast, for example, hunters from several groups undergo an intense and extensive ritual in preparation for hunting.[19]

In the case of the Red Paint People, we are fortunate to have ethnographic accounts for two swordfish-hunting cultures, the Chumash of southern California and the Ainu of Japan, both of which practiced complex rituals specifically surrounding swordfish hunting. In Chumash legend, the swordfish was a deity, and when swordfish hunting was on their minds, a shaman performed a ritual dance dressed in a swordfish costume constructed of abalone shell "scales" attached to a helmet made from a swordfish head. The deep historic importance of such ritual may be reflected in the fact that fragments of such a costume were recovered from the grave of a prehistoric shaman who was buried around 2,000 years ago.[20] The Ainu did not consider the swordfish a deity, but hunting it was suffused with religion and ritual and when butchered its head was placed on an outdoor altar "so that it might return to the open sea . . . and regain its original shape."[21] The following description of ritual-laden Ainu swordfish hunting may capture the essence of such hunts wherever they occurred and is here quoted at length:

> The pursuit of the great swordfish (shirikap), called hunting and not fishing, still draws some Ainu far out to sea. When I saw it early in the [twentieth] century it excited great enthusiasm, with rivalry between the crews of the dug-out canoes. It was not without danger, for the mighty fish often attacked, sometimes driving its sword through a boat or otherwise overturning it. In such a case the crew knocked on the boat as a signal for help from the other hunters, who were usually not far off.

> As it is a risky venture, religion and magic enter largely into the preparations for it. Prayers are said to Kamui Fuchi, to Rep-un Kamui, chief deity of the deep sea, and a curious one to Penup Kamui. We have already noticed that swallow-wort (penup or ikema [the plant *Cynanchum louiseae*]) is believed to be a powerful repellent of evil spirits; the prayer is said while the harpoon rope is being smeared with the chewed root of this plant. To deceive the evil spirits the rope or cord, made of hemp and about the thickness of a pencil, is not called tush but munin-pe (rotten thing). To emphasize its rottenness, water from the bottom of the boat, supposed to be rotten, is sometimes poured on part of the rope. In this prayer, and indeed while at sea, the word for boat (chip) must not be spoken in case an evil marine spirit might hear it and cause a storm or a fatal attack by the swordfish. The boat is called "wood swimming lady" (ni-mam katkimat ) or "spirit cradle" (Kamui Shinda), the latter occurring also in the epics. The same precaution is taken while fishing and boat-building.[22]

We need not be troubled by the absence of specific similarities in the rituals of swordfish hunters because symbolic behavior dealing with similar matters may be highly variable from one culture to another. The Christian cross, the Star of David, and the Crescent of Islam, for example, though very different, all symbolize religious claims on the same deity. Seen in this light, we can at least ask: Do the slate crescents in figure 27 represent swordfish tails? Do the slate bayonets in figures 29 and 30 represent swordfish rostra?

It is tempting to see the ritual complexity of the Red Paint People as having motivations similar to the Ainu and the Chumash, but can we critically evaluate this speculation?

The symbolism evident in the portable art of the Red Paint People suggests a well-developed and distinct, if not complex, sense of identity. They seem to be a society where, as Rowley-Conwy put it, "style is actively used to express personal and ethnic differences and one's position in society."[23] Ritual intensity can also be seen in the numerous cemeteries, which are uncommon among hunter-gatherers generally. Archaeologists hold varied opinions about the social significance of hunter-gatherer cemeteries.[24] Underlying this variability, however, is a sense that, like distinctive art styles, cemeteries are evidence of group self-awareness and that participation in cemetery rituals signifies group identity.

Though this idea deserves more attention than it has yet received, for many archaeologists cemeteries are regarded as territorial markers indicating claims to important resources, such as anadromous fish, and to social stress, such as that created by potentially encroaching neighbors. Considering the fate of these people, it is worth noting that at the macro level such stress may well have existed between the Red Paint People and others to the south and west of them, where a culture known as the Susquehanna tradition was spreading into the Northeast from the southern Appalachians beginning around 3,800 years ago.[25]

It is beyond doubt that the robustness of Moorehead phase was not derived from either an ancestral culture or from other cultures in the region, but was it complex in the sense that its members were socially differentiated? Agricultural and urban societies usually have leaders whose power is inherited and validated by supernatural authority, but ultimately their power depends on their ability to accumulate wealth through tribute, taxation, or some other mechanism. Most hunter-gatherer societies, on the other hand, have few social distinctions beyond those of gender and age. All adults perform the full range of tasks customary to their gender. There are no specialized arrow makers, net menders, hide workers, or food preparers who provide services to the community. As pointed out above, two exceptions to this general pattern are found among many hunter-gatherers—the shaman and the headman. A shaman, such as the Chumash example discussed above, is a male or female intermediary between the human and spiritual domains who affects physical cures and solves community problems through spiritual means. Such persons often attain their status by personal revelation that is recognized by the group. Although historic accounts often referred to headmen as chiefs, they did not rule and their offspring did not automatically replace them as headmen. Rather, headmen are simply "chiefs among equals" whose personal characteristics as hunters, shamans, or arbitrators attract a following. Should these abilities fail them, their followers are typically free to select another headman.

It seems to me that things are quite different among maritime hunter-gatherers, where there often appears another kind of unusual person—the boat captain. The power of this high-status or powerful chief emerges from hunting dangerous animals in the sea. The cause-and-effect relationship between hunting prowess and wealth is difficult to work out, but there seems to be a link between risk taking and the ability to acquire the wealth, in labor and material, needed to build a boat and maintain it and provide for its crew. On the northwest coast, for example, "only chiefs command the resources to pay for a great canoe."[26] Among the whale-hunting Nootka of Vancouver Island, British Columbia, "[w]haling was the noblest calling, and the whaler was always a chief."[27] And among the Tareumiut, the coastal Inupiat of northern and northwestern Alaska, senior male family heads are called *umialik*, meaning "*umiak* captain," the umiak being a large boat used to hunt whales.[28] While umialik have no chiefly power, the title implies a degree of wealth and enhanced status. Finally, among the Alutiiq people of Kodiak Island, though they hunted from small kayaks and lacked high status, whalers were deemed too powerful and dangerous to live or be buried among normal people.[29] These examples of high-status boat builders, boat captains, and even solitary whale hunters among societies that pursue dangerous marine prey suggest that some similar situation prevailed among the Red Paint People as well.

In many North American maritime cultures, the status of boat captains was further enhanced by the activities they alone could undertake. Thus, in addition to directing hunts, umialik used their watercraft to conduct trade and diplomacy. Through gift giving and wife exchange, they competed to attract and hold onto good boat crews. Umialik can also be glossed "whaling captain." The case of the swordfish-hunting Chumash is similar in that men who could muster the support in labor to buy a plank canoe, called a *tomol*, thus attained relatively great wealth. The builders, too, attained elevated status by belonging to the "brotherhood of the tomol," though the available literature is not clear about whether or how these two high-status groups intersected.[30] In sum, the hunting of dangerous marine animals tends to create status differentials of a sort rarely seen in other hunter-gather societies.

Social distinctions are often archaeologically visible in the treatment of the dead. Can we see this kind of status differential in the grave furnishings of the Red Paint cemeteries? In prehistoric urban societies, members of a hereditary elite routinely received very different mortuary treatment from commoners. Extreme examples are the pyramids erected nearly 5,000 years ago to honor deceased Pharaonic leaders of the Egyptian state. The megalithic tombs of Europe are another example appropriately scaled for the ancient tribal leaders of that region. Is it possible that in certain highly productive maritime environments, elites such as those found among agricultural societies developed to the extent that they became archaeologically visible in their burials?

The richness and complexity of cultural life on the Pacific Northwest coast are well known to us because these societies persisted into the historic period, where written records of their cultures could be produced and examples of their complex material culture could be collected and preserved. From these sources, we know that they had heavy stone woodworking tools with which they manufactured large dugout canoes for the pursuit of large marine animals. Their technology also included ground slate lance tips. They maintained trading connections with distant groups. Chiefs of the northwest coast even owned slaves. The driving force for this complexity seems to have been competition for control of aquatic resources, especially of rivers where salmon spawned, as well as the necessary number of people needed to catch and process the fish. These competitive forces seem to have acted similarly to those that caused elites to develop in larger agricultural societies. Unfortunately, no extensive study of elite northwest coast burials has appeared in the literature, so we cannot evaluate whether they resembled those of the Moorehead phase.

A different approach to the question of social complexity among the Red Paint People would be to ask not whether the graves of powerful boat captains might be distinguishable from those of commoners, but rather whether there are enough graves to account for the likely number of people who lived during the Moorehead phase. In other words, we might ask whether the number of people buried in the cemeteries might represent the whole population or a subset of it. To examine this question, we should begin by recognizing that the existence of the cemeteries is, by itself, unusual for hunter-gatherers. Most prehistoric cemeteries were created by agricultural groups who lived in established year-round villages where they tended and stored their crops; some have argued that this kind of sedentary lifestyle is the prerequisite for establishing a cemetery. Others, however, have pointed out that what actually leads to cemetery building is a dependence on "spatially fixed resources critical to their survival," and that maritime hunter-gatherers, such as the Red Paint People, also meet this criterion.[31]

Assessing the number of people buried in the cemeteries is difficult. Despite their fame, we have no accurate way of estimating the number of individuals buried in them—grave by grave, site by site, or on any larger scale—because the cemeteries were excavated by so many different parties in so many different ways. Many were subject to some amount of uncontrolled digging, leaving us with no information on grave counts. Some ocher-filled pits very likely held no human remains at all, while some held those of more than one individual. Adding to the difficulty, an unknown number of coastal cemeteries must have been totally eroded by the sea.

On the other hand, the Red Paint cemeteries are unusual in one respect. In most prehistoric cultures where cemeteries have been discovered, they are regarded as members of a set of cemeteries the size of which is unknown. No one knows how many there are or over what spatial extent they were distributed. In the case of the Red Paint cemeteries, however, archaeologists have some confidence that all, or nearly all, have now been discovered, meaning that instead of trying to extract information from one grave or one cemetery at a time, we can attempt some degree of quantification of their contents overall.

There remain, of course, considerable uncertainties involved in any such procedure. Look, for example, at the disparity between Warren K. Moorehead's 1922 estimate of 1,440 Red Paint burials and Brian Robinson's confirmed tally of only around 475, depending on how you count.[32] Their estimates divergence by over 300 percent. Uncertain as they are, however, they remain instructive. To get at their possible meaning, let us begin by assuming that Moorehead was closer to the mark, so that we do not underestimate the number of individuals they represent. Then, based on skeletal information available from the Nevin site, we can make some educated guesses about the numbers of disappeared skeletons at the others. The Nevin site tells us that, while many graves may have contained more than one individual, grave size there seems close to those of the other cemeteries. This suggests that none were mass burials likely to badly skew body counts. Then, to introduce an abundance of caution, let us adjust Moorehead's estimate upward to reflect the loss to erosion of some coastal cemeteries and the fact that some graves were multiple burials. Recall that the tally for the Nevin cemetery was twenty-five individuals in twelve graves. Now let's not adjust it back downward to accommodate the strong likelihood that not all red ocher deposits contained human remains.[33] This leaves us with a rough estimate of between 2,500 and 5,000 individuals buried in all the Red Paint cemeteries.

In light of the high population densities that boat technology permits among many maritime hunter-gatherers,[34] it might seem reasonable to estimate that from 2,500 to 5,000 people occupied Moorehead phase territory at a given time, but that is not what the estimate means. Rather, it suggests that these 2,500 to 5,000 individuals were buried over roughly five centuries, which means only 25 to 50 people were buried in the cemeteries per century. This small number must represent only a small percentage of the whole local population.

Moreover, the richness—by hunter-gatherer standards—of the best-furnished graves indicates a considerable expenditure of time and effort in preparing the body for secondary burial, making fine tools and weapons to be buried with the dead and arranging to obtain, through travel and diplomacy, exotic burial furnishings from distant places. If it seems unlikely that such expense could be lavished on the entire deceased population, what then might have been the criteria for admission to a Red Paint cemetery? Could it have been the families of boat captains, their own graves containing the best and most abundant furnishings, with lesser amounts devoted to their wives and children? It may be worth mentioning in this regard that, following a somewhat similar line of reasoning regarding the stone mound burials of the Labrador coast, Hood, Fitzhugh, and Rankin also suggest that these, too, are the graves of boat captains.[35] These studies track the growth of complexity in maritime hunting cultures over time, usually with the benefit of detailed ethnographic analogies, which are available because the activities under study lasted into the historic period. This approach has worked well because most of these maritime societies live in the Arctic and Subarctic, where the intensification of maritime hunting is the best option for survival, given the cold, harsh environment and the high costs of hunting failure.[36] Until recently, I thought they worked well for the Moorehead phase, too. Just as natural selection favored antelopes with longer necks to access high-growing leaves, ultimately leading to giraffes, so, I thought, cultural selection favored some Middle Archaic groups to alter their subsistence patterns to take advantage of new environmental conditions, creating the Moorehead phase in the process.

Some support for the marine productivity argument can be drawn from our NCEAS research into the history of marine productivity. Today, the process of fishing down marine food webs has become widely recognized as affecting the abundance of the world's oceans, and researchers have demonstrated its existence in an increasing number of marine ecosystems.[37] More recently, some researchers have begun to side-step the difficulties of interpreting historical records by focusing on other proxies for the past, such as genetics and isotopic chemistry. This research is exciting because it promises to greatly sharpen our understanding of how marine ecosystems changed over time. The hope is that, like a person who has always lived without corrective lenses, improving the clarity of vision will reveal details that were formerly invisible or seen only as vague shadows.

Genetic analysis is one way of opening our eyes to new levels of detail. A good example is the work of Roman and Palumbi, whose analysis of modern North Atlantic whale DNA led them to conclude that before commercial whaling began there in the eighteenth century, whale populations may have been a full order of magnitude larger than they are today.[38] If there were a lot more whales, did the Red Paint People hunt them? We don't know, but the absence of whalebone in their coastal sites suggests probably not, or not often. Even so, the mere presence of more whales would have impacted their lives, for according to Roman and McCarthy, whales significantly augment tidal upwelling in bringing nutrients from the bottom of the Gulf of Maine to the surface where they nourish plankton blooms.[39] According to their estimates, whales (and seals) still move a lot of nutrients in the gulf, but probably moved three times more before commercial whaling began.

Moving from the largest organisms in the gulf to some of the smallest, if the deep waters of the Gulf of Maine were full of whales, what did the shorelines look like? Bertness examined the impact of the introduced periwinkle *Littorina littorea*, on the intertidal zone.[40] The species was introduced to North America around 1840, arrived in the Gulf of Maine in the 1860s, and is now the dominant periwinkle along the coast there. Bertness found that the foraging habits of this humble snail have caused declines in soft-bottom littoral habitats and fringing salt marsh environments, both of which are important contributors to the gulf's marine productivity.

Both the "whale pump" and the negative impacts of the introduced *Littorina littorea* suggest that prehistoric marine conditions in the gulf may have been extraordinarily more productive than even our NCEAS team's analyses suggested. Imagine how different would be the reconstructions offered for prehistoric northwest Atlantic maritime hunting cultures if the shorelines had more productive mud flats and salt marshes than today and if the seas teemed with thousands of whales, instead of hundreds, and with huge schools of cod that averaged over a meter in length, instead of the few puny survivors of today.

While I find the discovery of the whale pump and recognition of the depredations of *Littorina littorea* exciting, these new discoveries do not boost my confidence that the Moorehead phase can be explained by growing resource abundance. A hugely productive Gulf of Maine certainly may have enabled their flamboyant lifestyle, but to me this line of thinking has two weaknesses. To repeat a point made earlier, the first is that these resource trends were too broad geographically and began too early and continued too long to coincide with the Moorehead phase event. There is nothing we know about their environment, terrestrial or marine, that seems adequate to explain when and where they appeared, nor the sudden cessation of sword fishing for all of prehistory and, indeed, the cessation of the entire lifestyle it supported.

The second is that arguments for adaptation assume, at least implicitly, that there should be a rough equivalence between the magnitude of cause and effect. For example, Kline and Boyd recently demonstrated that islands with small populations generally have simpler, more generalized maritime technologies than islands with large ones.[41] Similarly, we might expect a trend of increasing productivity of the marine ecosystem leading to increased complexity over time. I don't see this kind of proportionality in the emergence of the Moorehead phase. Instead, both its appearance and its disappearance were sudden events, and it is far from clear that environmental conditions either preceding or following its existence would have prohibited or even constrained their lifestyle.

# 8

# Explaining the Moorehead Phase: Part 2

So the two central questions of Moorehead phase robusticity remain: Why did it appear when it did, and why didn't other mid-Holocene cultures in the Gulf of Maine mimic it? My struggle to make sense of this phenomenon has been influenced by recent literature on evolutionary theory that doesn't rely on traditional adaptationalist thinking. By the late twentieth century, some ecologists began to recognize that biological systems don't always behave in ways that are simply adaptive in a reductionist sense.

## Niche Construction

In 2000, Harvard biologist Richard Lewontin suggested that, in such cases, a more complex process of interaction between the species and its environment was at work.[1] He called the process niche construction. Niche construction can be defined as "the process whereby organisms, through their metabolism, their activities and their choices, modify their own and/ or each other's niches."[2] Niche construction points out the weaknesses in the Darwinist idea that cultures are only survival mechanisms.

> The metaphor of adaptation, while once an important heuristic for building evolutionary theory, is now an impediment to a real understanding of the evolutionary process and needs to be replaced by another. Although metaphors are dangerous, the actual process of evolution seems best captured by the process of construction.[3]

Proponents of niche construction argue that conventional reductionist explanations are inadequate in many cases because they ignore the interactive processes by which some species alter their environments even as the environments are altering them through natural selection.[4] In niche construction, ecological feedback between organism and environment becomes part of the evolutionary process. Dam-building beavers are an often-cited example of niche constructors, but there are a multitude of other examples. Indeed, many biologists now regard niche construction as essential to understanding biological evolution. This change in evolutionary thinking amounts to what philosopher Thomas Kuhn called a paradigm shift in scientific thinking, a revolutionary change that greatly improves their ability to understand the phenomena being studied.[5]

Anthropologists are also exploring ways in which niche construction can help them understand human cultures. An example is Lansing's study of water temple networks, centuries-old irrigation systems that are apparently too complex for anyone to have designed consciously but that optimally irrigate the rice terraces of hundreds of Balinese villages.[6] For Lansing, niche construction creates societies organized "from the bottom up, as a result of feedback processes linking social actors to their environments."[7]

According to Laland and O'Brien, because cultural processes typically operate faster than natural selection, cultural niche construction probably has had more profound consequences than gene-based niche construction.[8] Not surprisingly, then, archaeologists, too, see utility in niche construction. For Bruce Smith, it "provides an important evolutionary and behavioral context for understanding . . . the initial domestication of plants and animals," and demonstrates that domestication "was not the product of unusual 'outside the envelope' behavior patterns, but emerged out of coherent preexisting resource management systems."[9]

Archaeologists interested in small-scale, hunter-gatherer societies have often employed the niche concept in the reductionist manner of cultural ecology, often to identify cases of resource depletion. Prehistoric Californians living near what is now San Francisco, for example, depleted local populations of elk, sturgeon, deer, geese, oysters, and mussels.[10] More recently, some have explored the advantages of niche construction theory in explaining prehistoric culture change among terrestrial hunter-gatherers.[11] Hunter-gatherer cultures living in forested environments, for example, almost universally alter patterns of vegetation by extensive burning.

So far, however, these explorations of human-environmental interaction have focused on only the biological not the social environment. None has extended niche construction theory to include behaviors like costly signaling that are likely to have been involved in the emergence of robust cultures such as the Moorehead phase. I suspect that in the case of the Red Paint People, something we might call social niche construction included costly signaling by boat captains and that their sword fishing and maintenance of extensive trade networks across both land and sea were aspects of this costly signaling, as was the construction of Red Paint cemeteries. Alternatively, shamans of the society may have been the ones who acquired exotic goods during long-distance transformative journeys. In either case, social interactions with other distant peoples can probably be considered as aspects of niche construction.

My basic argument in this book is that the Red Paint People should not be seen as incapable of cultural dynamism merely because they were hunter-gatherers. What has drawn me to study them has been my perception not merely of their robustness but of the suddenness with which they burst on the scene and the geographic extent of their social contacts. They occupied well-defined temporal and spatial ranges, undertook the rare practice of swordfish hunting, buried their dead in the ocher-rich cemeteries that gave them their name, manufactured a highly distinctive suite of bone and stone artifacts, and maintained some kind of complex relationships with faraway cultures. They also did many of these things earlier than any other North American society. Any of these traits alone would serve to identify them culturally, and taken together they contribute to a sense of complexity and robustness unequaled among other definable prehistoric cultures of the Northeast and much farther afield.

In sum, cultural adaptation, which has so often been used in archaeological explanations, seems to me incapable of accounting for what we are learning about the Red Paint People. There appears to be no change of sufficient magnitude, in either the natural or the social environment of the Gulf of Maine region, that could account for their ancestors' sudden metamorphosis. Future research will possibly prove me wrong, but I suspect instead it will reveal that something more like rapid social niche construction was in operation.

## A Northern Doppelgänger: Distant Contacts of the Red Paint People

In 1898, F. W. Putnam was the first to assert that the graves Willoughby excavated at Bucksport, Ellsworth, and Orland should be considered ancient in comparison to what he called the "Algonquins" (by which he meant recent, pottery-using speakers of Algonquian languages who occupied Maine when Europeans arrived). He then immediately offered the best ethnographic analogy available to him for comparison:

> [I]t is essential that a burial place in Newfoundland, the known country of the Beothuks, should be explored in order to provide a means of comparison [i.e. ethnographic analogy] with the burial customs of the prehistoric people on the coast of Maine.[12]

Lacking any way to establish even the relative (much less the absolute) ages of the cultures he was referring to, Putnam was drawn to the naïve suggestion that because the indigenous population of Newfoundland, also known as "Red Indians," made ubiquitous use of red ocher, they were the most appropriate comparison to what Willoughby was finding in his excavations. He assumed that if one could examine a burial site of the Red Indians, they would find a close analog to what Willoughby had encountered. Ironically, as naïve as Putnam's suggestion seems today, it is precisely to the far north that we must turn to understand some important cultural dimensions of the Red Paint People.

As we have seen, a salient characteristic of many maritime cultures, past and present, is a complex system of exchange facilitated by the ubiquity of boats, which allowed access to distant places and the carrying of much larger cargos to and from those places than could be transported by humans traveling overland.[13] The Red Paint People were no exceptions to this pattern, and it is clear that their links extended northward, across the Gulf of St. Lawrence. The evidence includes actual artifacts (exotic cert points, gouges, and adzes), some very close parallel artifact forms (barbed and toggling harpoons, seabird effigies, and virtually identical ritual bone tubes), and, of course, Red Paint mortuary ceremonialism. Tuck thought this evidence so strong that he regarded the Red Paint People and his Port au Choix population as belonging to the same culture, or "whole cultural tradition," which he called the Maritime Archaic tradition.[14]

Tuck thought the Maritime Archaic tradition had roots reaching far back into the prehistory of Labrador and Newfoundland, to the arrival of immigrants from south of the St. Lawrence River around 8,000 years ago. This scenario is based largely on the surprising results of a foray northward along the archaeologically unknown Quebec-Labrador coast in 1973 by Tuck and Robert McGhee of the National Museum of Canada.[15] What they found was a great surprise: a sequence of cultures reaching much further back than anyone expected, back at least 8,000 years. Most archaeologists considered that region habitable only by Paleo-Eskimo peoples who were well adapted to life in cold environments; no one had suspected that Indians could have penetrated so far northward in early times. Moreover, these Indian sites seemed to follow at least the general cultural trends extending across the Gulf of St. Lawrence as far southward along the Atlantic coast as the Carolinas.[16]

Based on these discoveries, McGhee and Tuck suggested that, once established along the coasts Newfoundland and Labrador, Indian populations persisted in place for several millennia.[17] Then, around 4000 B.P., evidence of links to the Moorehead phase appeared, and other discoveries on the Labrador coast by Tuck and others caused him to extend the term northward as well so that the Maritime Archaic tradition now covered an incredible distance from the Kennebec River to the mid-Labrador coast.[18] As mentioned earlier, I and others working in the Gulf of Maine were skeptical of this extended scenario because we could see ever more clearly evidence that the Moorehead phase had local ancestry.[19]

Tuck's unwanted orthodoxy, the notion that a unified Maritime Archaic tradition once occupied Newfoundand, Labrador, and as far south as Maine, is now pretty much discredited among Canadians as well. Accord-

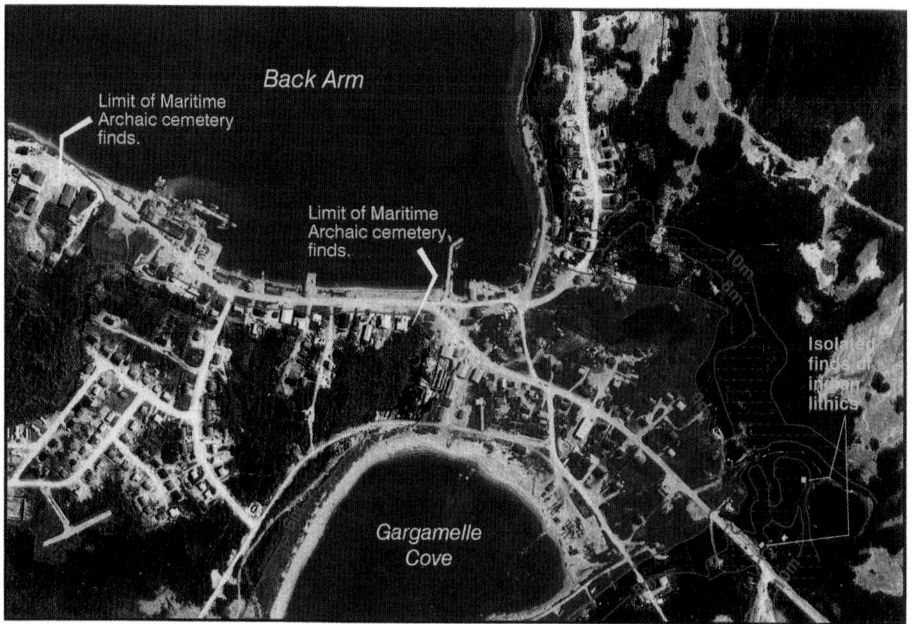


**FIGURE 72.** Aerial view of Port au Choix, Newfoundland.

ing to the Memorial University of Newfoundland research team of Priscilla Renouf (archaeologist) and Trevor Bell (geographer), for example, any general understanding of the Maritime Archaic in Newfoundland "is sketchy at best. It is overgeneralized, based on a small number of sites, one of which, Port au Choix, is clearly non-representative."[20] Instead, there is an emerging consensus among northern archaeologists that the Archaic tradition of Newfoundland was not closely related to that of Labrador. There is also general recognition of a brief pulse of alien projectile points, if not populations, into both Labrador and Newfoundland that originated to the south of the St. Lawrence.[21] Thus, what to Tuck was a large unitary Maritime Archaic tradition now appears to be a qualitatively more complex pattern, the details of which still need to be worked out.

With this more complex view of the Maritime Archaic in mind, it is useful here to underscore the many *differences* between it and the Moorehead phase. These include climate (subarctic versus temperate), subsistence practices (sea mammal and caribou hunting versus swordfish, deer, and moose hunting with mollusk gathering) and many aspects of technology. Most importantly, however, the nearest Maritime Archaic sites in both Labrador and Newfoundland lie roughly four hundred miles from the easternmost Moorehead phase cemetery at Cow Point. Between them lies most of New Brunswick, with, at best, a very light scattering of artifacts that might connect the two, not to mention the Gulf of St. Lawrence. Tuck's original expectation that the void in New Brunswick and Nova Scotia would eventually be filled by future research has not been fulfilled despite forty years of fieldwork.

But setting aside these differences and long distances separating the north and south, a remarkable series of parallels remain. Taking bone technology first, both made similar to nearly identical barbed and toggling harpoons, barbed spears, harpoon foreshafts, daggers, delicate bone needles, beaver incisor tools, animal canine teeth, and identically modified bird wing bones (figure 73). None of these items has parallels anywhere in eastern North America. Both were also fond of marine bird figurines carved from bone, though the styles differ. Both also produced locally, or obtained from elsewhere, pyrite fire kits, stone gouges, adzes, slate bayonets, plummets, unusual rounded beech pebbles, and large books of muscovite mica as grave furnishings. Many of these items, too, have been found only in the two cultures, and the stylistic similarities between north and south are often truly striking.

In a 1968 interview at Port au Choix, Tuck once said that the site was "something we've been looking for a long time."[22] The "we" in his statement includes most archaeologists then working in the Northeast. In fact, the discovery was so exciting that William Ritchie, who had trained both Tuck and me, made the trip to Port au Choix that summer to visit Tuck at the site. The "something" in Tuck's interview is a suspected burial cult thought to be responsible for widely scattered discoveries of red ocher burials from the Great Lakes to Maine to northern Newfoundland. It was perceived as fleeting and hard to pin down. Tuck elsewhere described it as "a similar underlying set of beliefs, which, although they grow more complex with time, may ultimately be related to the beginnings of a burial cult before 3000 B.C.[23]

By that time, however, archaeology was becoming concerned not with linkages connecting the prehistoric Northeast, but with how it should be divided, based on ecological variablility. Tuck, for example, suggested dividing the Northeast into three "widespread cultural patterns" that were coterminous with three forest types.[24] For the coastal Northeast, it was maritime hunting rather than forest type that bound the Red Paint People to the Maritime Archaic tradition.

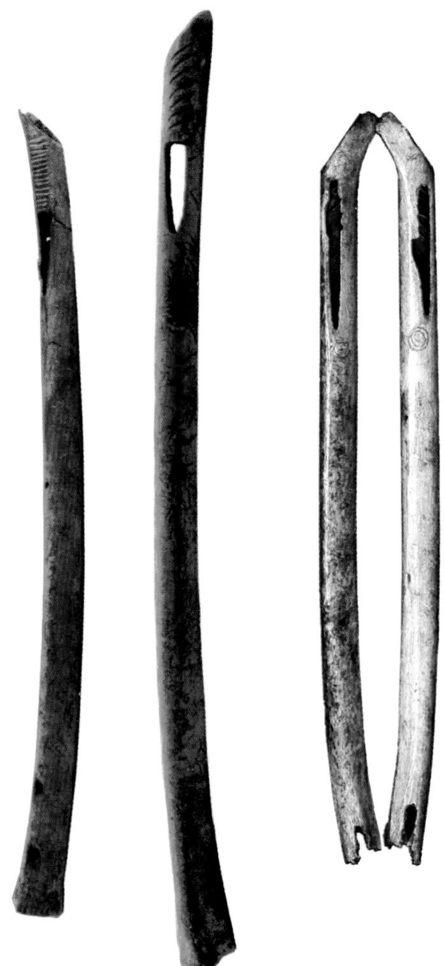

**FIGURE 73.** Modified bird wing bones from the Turner Farm and Port au Choix sites. The paired specimens are Canada goose (*Branta Canadensis*) and are from the Turner Farm site. They are slightly more than 17 cm long. (*Specimens at left courtesy of The Rooms.*)

Whatever the merits of this reorientation, it distracted attention from this sense of far-reaching connectedness around 4000 B.P. that linked people from southern Ontario to Maine to northern Newfoundland. Over the ensuing decades, however, we have learned something more about these connections. The evidence lies mainly in the ground slate bayonets that feature so prominently in the burials of the Red Paint People and the northern cemeteries, especially Port au Choix. Of the four styles typical of the Red Paint cemeteries, only two are local, the narrow hexagonal and small barbed forms. The wide pie-wedge and wide hexagonal forms occur over a much broader region and, moreover, are often made of banded slate that almost certainly originated far to the west, although there appear to be a few local copies of both styles made in local materials. Unfortunately, most of the outliers are isolated finds, so we don't have a clear idea of who made them or why. Moreover, the Great Lakes region at that time lacked the kind of robust, regionally bounded cultural manifestations we see in the Moorehead phase or the late Maritime Archaic tradition(s). Thus, even if well dated, we could only associate them with rather vaguely defined cultural phases that represent apparently unremarkable lifestyles. What is important, however, is that these are also the styles prominent at Port au Choix, very specifically in the case of wide pie-wedge bayonets, though more generally in the case of the wide hexagonal form.

These two bayonet forms, then, were less exchanged between north and south than they were concentrated locally—and independently in both regions—for mortuary use. It is also worth mentioning that the large chert and quartzite projectile points from the Lake Champlain region found in the Maine cemeteries (figure 41) often closely resemble the eared-stem forms that identify that brief intrusion of southern influences across the St. Lawrence around 4000 B.P.[25]

If I am correct in suggesting the existence of a trading partnership between Labrador and Newfoundland in the north with Maine in the south, we should consider what was exchanged for the items we know moved south. One can imagine a one-way flow of items obtained by shamans on a quest, but any less religiously inspired pattern would seem to require some degree of reciprocity, and it seems odd that we cannot identify more southern-originating items in the north. The wide pie-wedge and broad hexagonal bayonets may have arrived at Port au Choix via Maine, but they could equally well have been acquired in the Ohio region by the northerners in the same way the Red Paint People acquired them.

Perhaps a better candidate is dugout canoes. The large white pines I suspect were used to make dugouts in Maine also grew in parts of Newfoundland, and those could possibly have supplied the northerners with all they needed. However, we've seen that the Late Maritime Archaic of Newfoundland seems to have had little to do with that of Labrador. Furthermore, gouges, which probably had everything to do with dugout construction, are rarely found north of the Rattler's Bight burials, even though the culture itself extended as far north as Ramah Bay. This suggests that dugouts may have originated in the south and then traded north.

## AN ALTERNATIVE TO THE UNWANTED ORTHODOXY

In Tuck's original formulation of the Maritime Archaic tradition, which I have called his "unwanted orthodoxy," the Moorehead phase was *part* of the Maritime Archaic tradition. Tuck never specifically said the Maritime Archaic tradition gave rise to the Moorehead phase, but this conclusion follows from his argument. If the Maritime Archaic tradition dates back over 7,500 years in the north, and remained "the dominant (and at times the *only*) cultural manifestation for better than 4,000 years," then the origins of the Moorehead phase must also lie to the north.[26]

This issue matters, because it is one thing to claim that the Moorehead phase was merely the end product, a late southern extension, of a 4,000-year-old cultural tradition and quite another to argue, as I do here, that it arose entirely on its own. It fails for two reasons. The first, based on general patterns of cultural development in subarctic and temperate North America, is that cultural influences generally do not move from north to south. Instead, the general thrust of cultural influence, after Paleo-Indian times, has been from south to north. The second is that the past forty years of research have failed to locate the missing Maritime Archaic sites in the Maritime Provinces, while at the same time it has greatly strengthened the argument that the Moorehead phase has roots firmly planted in earlier cultures in the Gulf of Maine.[27] Moreover, the ground may have shifted concerning temporal primacy, for recent radiocarbon dates suggest that the Late Maritime Archaic tradition fluoresced only around 3800 B.P., about the same time as the Moorehead phase was ending.[28]

I now wish to offer an alternative to Tuck's orthodoxy, one based on social interaction rather than deep cultural ancestry. Archaeologists spend a good deal of time reconstructing exchange networks among prehistoric people from artifact distributions. A common pattern among hunter-gatherers is group-to-group exchange, in which the exchanged artifact type originated at a raw material source or point of manufacture by a specific group, and is then exchanged with a neighboring group that lacks the raw material or the ability to manufacture the artifact. Archaeologists studying such an exchange pattern would find that the artifact was most commonly found at sites near the raw material source or point of manufacture and that this frequency would decline at increasingly distant sites in a pattern. This pattern is called distance decay. Many departures from simple distance decay have been noted among complex prehistoric cultures, but many fewer departures have been noted among prehistoric hunter-gatherers, so the strongly bimodal distribution of exchanged artifacts between the Moorehead phase and the Late Maritime Archaic tradition is a real surprise.

But what social mechanisms connected them? The linear distance from Penobscot Bay to the nearest Late Maritime Archaic sites in either Newfoundland or Labrador is at least four hundred miles, and the actual water routes involved, though unknowable in any detail, must have been much longer. Why did people from these two distant regions find it worthwhile to establish contact? Why was it expressed so dramatically in the exchange of symbolically laden artifacts. Who carried it out? How frequent were the contacts? We have suggested above that they may have been acquired through shamanistic journeys. But there are other mechanisms that may have been operating. Let's look at one from the other side of the world.

An important clue to the exotic items found in the cemeteries may be that most of the traded items were "articles of high value, but of no real use." The quote comes from the opening lines of anthropologist Bronislaw Malonowski's famous paper describing the Kula ring, a pattern of trade involving eighteen islands in the Massim region of Papua, New Guinea.[29] Despite their negligible utilitarian value, ownership of items involved in the Kula ring greatly enhanced the prestige of their owners, and an enormous amount of energy went into maintaining the Kula network. The goods exchanged "carry specific biographies of manufacture, use, and possession that establish the political reputations of influential men and their followers."[30] In this way, perhaps the items traded between the Late Maritime Archaic and the Moorehead phase resemble those of the Kula ring.

Malinowski was perplexed by the fact that, despite its minimal importance in real economic terms, the Kula "looms paramount in the tribal life of all the peoples who participate in it."[31] He goes on to explain:

> The usual a priori notion of savage trade would be that of an exchange of indispensable, or, at least, useful things, done under pressure of need by direct barter, or casual give and take of presents, without much ceremony and regulation. Such a conception would almost reverse all the essential features of the Kula. Thus, first, the objects of exchange . . . are not "utilities" in any sense of the word. . . . Nevertheless, they are extremely highly valued. . . . Secondly, the exchange, far from being casual or surreptitious, is carried on according to very definite and very complex rules. Thus it cannot be performed between members of these tribes taken at random. A firm and lifelong relationship is always established between any participant in the Kula, and a number of other men, some of whom belong to his own community, and others to overseas communities. Such men call one another karayta'u ("partner," as we shall designate them), and they are under mutual obligations to trade with each other, to offer protection, hospitality and assistance whenever needed.[32]

The waterborne Kula ring illustrates how complex and culturally important nonutilitarian patterns of exchange can become among simple maritime societies, and to the extent that it resembles the known details of the Moorehead phase–Maritime Archaic pattern, it should make us aware of that system's potential for social importance.

In sum, granted that recent research has increased the evidence for strong north–south connections, I still do not think it is at all useful to think of the Red Paint People and the Maritime Archaic tradition as part of single unified culture, primarily because they were separated by a vacant quarter, which included most of the Maritime Provinces of Canada, but also because of fairly profound differences in their economies and settlement patterns. If we image scenarios ranging from a single culture at one extreme to geographically distinct but socially connected maritime hunting cultures at the other, the latter seems more in accord with the archaeological data.

The cultural picture in the south is clear. The Red Paint People emerged in place from a preceding culture and developed a distinctive one of their own that included extensive deer and moose hunting as well as fishing and a distinct pattern of mortuary ritual, which flourished for a few centuries and then vanished. The picture in the north is more complex as it includes both a Labrador component and the anomalous Port au Choix cemetery. Faunal preservation is poor at the Labrador sites, but the economy was likely based on caribou and marine mammals. The people of Port au Choix also depended on these resources. Both developed elaborate but quite different funerary rituals, the former likely including only boat captains while the latter was more inclusive, including males and females, possibly the entire population. The Labrador variant was the source of Ramah chert points and heavy woodworking tools. No such direct imports seem to have come from the people of Port au Choix, though their bone technology, which was even more elaborate than that of the Moorehead phase, bore some remarkable parallels to it. We might summarize this picture as a pattern of cultural convergence among three interconnected cultures.

## Disappearance of the Red Paint People

The very beginnings of the Moorehead phase date to around 5,000 years ago when simple, early Red Paint cemeteries began to appear. Thereafter, it grew rapidly, soon becoming a highly successful maritime hunting culture that, for several centuries, led a complex lifestyle that included hunting the formidable swordfish, trading over great distances, and maintaining an elaborate pattern of mortuary rituals. But then, suddenly, around 3,800 years ago, it vanished. Its elaborate technology disappeared, the cemeteries were abandoned, and swordfish hunting ceased for the rest of prehistory. This all happened very quickly, an instant in archaeological terms, and the region was immediately overrun by immigrants from the south, whom archaeology has dubbed the Susquehanna tradition (figure 74).

Archaeologists struggling to understand this event have wrestled with a variety of possible explanations. One is that the disappearance is only apparent and that the Moorehead phase simply morphed into or merged with the Susquehanna tradition. Those favoring this line of thinking have sought archaeological traces that bridge the two groups, so far without success. Almost annually, we hear that someone has found a more recent fragment of swordfish bone, but these have all been misidentifications. Almost as frequently we hear of a gouge, plummet, or some other Moorehead phase tool type occurring in some later archaeological context, but so far these discoveries have turned out to be from disturbed sites where artifacts from different periods have been mixed together. Another explanation is that people of the Susquehanna tradition possessed some advan-

**FIGURE 74.** Artifacts of the Susquehanna tradition from the Turner Farm site. Grooved axe is 9.4 inches (24 cm) long.

tage that allowed them to displace the Moorehead phase, though no one has suggested what this might have been.

The third possible explanation holds that some environmental change made the Moorehead phase lifestyle difficult, and the population died out. Such a perturbation can't be ruled out, but no evidence for one has yet been found. I have often been asked if an outbreak of epidemic disease might have been the cause, but this too is highly unlikely because acute epidemic diseases of the sort that cause mass mortality, such as small pox and epidemic typhus, were only introduced to the New World by Europeans around five hundred years ago.

Somewhat surprisingly, another mechanism that could have placed the Red Paint People under stress has recently came to light, one that may have been generated by themselves.

A 2001 study of declining fisheries (Jackson et al.) proceeded from the assumption that the world's fish stocks were at their original "pristine" levels until European-styled industrial fishing began to degrade them; the investigators assumed that indigenous precolonial people lived in harmony with their natural surroundings, not depleting species important to them.[33] This assumption is an instance of has come to be called the ecological Indian myth, and it has been called into question by anthropologist Shepard Krech.[34] Krech's argument is that the world of prehistoric America was far more complex, including many cases of game depletion and other ecological misdeeds. Krech focuses mainly on terrestrially oriented cultures. More recently, however, archaeologists began to notice cases around the planet where even preindustrial, aboriginal fishers seem to have had a negative impact on fish stocks. We have already noted a case of sturgeon and shellfish depletion by the prehistoric people of San Francisco Bay. We've also taken notice of the disappearance of swordfish from the Moorehead phase shell middens after Moorehead phase times, as well as the onset of a rapid decline in cod. The issue certainly remains debatable, but taken at face value, it appears that, beginning with the Moorehead phase, human populations began systematically to overfish large species. If overfishing pushed cod stocks into decline, and if hunting swordfish was motivated by the quest for prestige rather than for more calories as I've suggested, the resulting stress on the basic economy may have led to the collapse of the social and ceremonial superstructure, or at least have rendered it vulnerable to challenge by arriving immigrants.

Another effect of such stress may have been lower birth rates, resulting in the loss of defining cultural characteristics as the survivors were absorbed by the immigrants. Hunter-gatherer cultures live in small groups of closely related individuals. This means that they are often prohibited from marrying within their group and must instead find mates outside it, through a process called exogamy. When different cultures come into contact, blending through exogamy is a frequent outcome, and even between hostile groups, exogamy may be achieved by wife stealing.

But cultural blending is only one possible outcome of cultures in contact. Others include hostility, particularly where culture differences are marked, as they seem to have been between the Moorehead phase and Susquehanna tradition.[35] In such situations, one group usually gives ground, and if this happened in a Red Paint–Susquehanna confrontation, the archaeological record clearly indicates that the former gave way to the latter through a process called outmigration. But if outmigration occurred in this case, we have no clear idea of where the Red Paint People migrated to. One possibility is that the group disbanded, its members joining other communities and assuming new cultural identities. This is what many anthropologists think happened to groups known as the St. Lawrence Iroquoians, who lived in the region between Montreal and Quebec in the sixteenth century. When French explorer Jacques Cartier visited the region in the 1530s and 1540s, it was occupied by large populations of agriculturalists who spoke Iroquoian languages. The next European to visit the region was Samuel de Champlain in 1603, when he found it abandoned, probably because its inhabitants had been driven out by warfare.[36]

There remains one more possibility worth mentioning, which is that the Red Paint People migrated northeastward to join, or to become part of, the Late Maritime Archaic tradition. This hypothesis has a few arguments in its favor. First, the richest and possibly the most recent Red Paint cemetery at Cow Point, New Brunswick, is also the closest to Newfoundland, which could be interpreted as an expansion of Moorehead phase territory, perhaps in retreat from Susquehanna demographic pressure.[37] Second, wide pie-wedge bayonets, which are rare in other Red Paint cemeteries, closely resemble those from Port au Choix-3, as do its radiocarbon dates.[38] Thirdly, we have seen that as new data have become available, Port au Choix has become an outlier of the Maritime Archaic, one with far more specific ties to the south than any other. I am among those archaeologists who believe it is possible that Cow Point may have been the cemetery of a people on the move, possibly across the Gulf of St. Lawrence to Newfoundland and to the Port au Choix area.

Before we end this discussion about cultural disappearances, we must look at another intriguing north–south parallelism between the Maritime Archaic and the Moorehead phase. At about the same time the Susquehanna tradition was occupying Moorehead phase homelands, the Maritime Archaic too disappeared as its territory was overrun by immigrants. In a recent review of the Labrador data, William Fitzhugh of the Smithsonian Institution suggested a scenario for the north that includes the existence of a dugout-based, maritime-hunting culture organized around high-status boat captains who conducted summer voyages to the north to obtain Ramah chert terrestrial and marine food resources as well as Ramah chert, which they brought south to wintering sites at the end of summer.[39] There is now little doubt that these northerners were well aware of the Red Paint People far to their south, because they are almost certainly the source of Ramah chert points found in cemeteries. Then, like the Red Paint People, they disappeared and their territory was taken over by an alien culture. In this case, the aliens were Paleo-Eskimos who had crossed from Siberia to North America around 4,500 years ago and arrived in the eastern Subarctic around 4,000 years ago and then spread throughout the region, including Labrador and Newfoundland.

Fitzhugh argues that these immigrants had a significant military advantage over the Maritime Archaic population: Asian bow and arrow technology. There is a widespread belief among the public that North American Indians always had the bow and arrow, but this is not the case. Bows developed relatively late in North America, and there is no evidence of their existence during the era of the Maritime Archaic tradition. The Asian bow is a highly sophisticated weapon, recurved in that its tips point away from the archer and also reflex in that, when unstrung, the whole shape of the bow curves away from the archer. It is also a composite bow made from multiple materials in addition to wood, such as bone, horn, sinew, and hide. All these characteristics allow it to fire arrows with great force but still to be quite short, around a meter, compared to the straight wooden self-bow favored by Europeans, which are often as tall as the archer.[40] The Asian bow would thus have given the intruders a great advantage in confrontations with any Archaic Indian group.

# 9

# Conclusion

The goal of this book has been to tell the clearest possible story of the Red Paint People, the vanished culture that has held my interest for four decades. I hope it is a more detailed and accurate story than those told by an earlier generation of archaeologists. If so, that is partly because my discipline now understands that prehistoric people lived in the natural world and were strongly impacted by it. It is also partly because archaeologists have learned to deploy some of the best ideas developed during the same period by our colleagues in the natural sciences. We touched on some of these, such as adaptation and niche construction, as they applied to the archaeology of the Red Paint People.

An interesting question to consider at the close of this book is how will the story be different the next time it is told. I suspect that one difference is that it will be written, not by a single archaeologist, but by a consortium of behavioral and natural scientists accustomed to framing their research questions as historic processes couched in the natural world. At the end of the twentieth century, archaeologists used and benefited form the services of the natural sciences, but in an asymmetric way. The palynologist, ecologist, or geochemist came and went, leaving a contribution that the archaeologist integrated into her story. They might also leave a handy new methodology, such as radiocarbon dating, or isotopic analysis, but they were not invited to collaborate, to sit down with the archaeologist when research questions were being shaped.

During the same period that I have been working on the Red Paint People, the natural sciences have undergone many of their own favorable changes, none more welcome than what I see as a rather profound shift in perspective from what we might call shallow to deep history. As we have seen, that model changed for me during my work at NCEAS in the late 1990s and early 2000s. At first I was flattered that the ecologists wanted my data on the Red Paint People, but as our project went on, I felt the group come alive as we learned how useful this multidisciplinary environment could be in leaning about a difficult problem—the decline of the world's fisheries—and then in communicating our results to the public. The process was infectious as we moved from our assigned task to other related issues that came up in conversation. In the beginning, I had no idea about fishing down marine ecosystems, nor could my natural science colleagues understand how to characterize species declines in terms of human history. In the end, we published a coherent picture about how human cultures had impacted marine ecosystems for much longer than was generally understood, a picture that included ideas about how to reverse this process.

That work led to a second generation of papers that explored spin-off issues covering topics ranging from how humans got to North America in the first place (possibly by boat) to whether small indigenous cultures have the power to fish down marine food webs (They do.). The collaborations continue to ramify, and the National Science Foundation has recognized this trend.

For anthropologists, the trend actually began in the 1980s with Eric Wolf's *Europe and the People without History*. In it, he gives us a wonderful thumbnail sketch of Western academic history, bemoaning the splitting of the social sciences during the nineteenth century into their modern splinter groups—economics, sociology, political science, economy, anthropology—and tries to fashion a resynthesis that gives voice not only to the European colonizers but also to those they colonized. But Wolf's book is really about space and geography rather than history, a fact recently pointed out by Shryock and Smail in *Deep History*.[1] This volume is the collective product of historians, archaeologists, linguists, and primatologists, which broadens Wolf's approach and addresses the "translation problems" that continue to impede cross-disciplinary discussions about it. The terms *long chronology* and *short chronology* used in this book are inspired by *Deep History*, and I think it is a significant contribution to the larger project of reunifying research on the human and natural past.

Archaeology's role in this trend is an interesting one. I believe our anthropological perspective brings valuable ideas to the multidisciplinary table. What archaeologists dig out of the ground, however, is also increasingly valuable to a whole range of scientists who wish to explore a wide variety of questions, ranging from the temperature and salinity of ancient oceans, to the trophic structure of coastal marine ecosystems, to the genetic composition of ancient fish stocks. As we relearn the value of collaborating with other disciplines, we must be prepared to see those materials increasingly valued by our colleagues. As I write this, I am offering materials from the Turner Farm site for analysis to colleagues at several institutions, aware that they need them as much as I do. I can foresee a time when the excavation team may still be led by archaeologists, but staffed by several natural scientists eager to collect from archaeological sites the specimens their research requires. The increasing importance of voucher samples for reconstructing stories about deep time raises to a high level the importance of the material remains of all prehistoric peoples, none more so than those of the ancient swordfish hunters of the Gulf of Maine, the Red Paint People.

# Notes

## Preface

1. Martijn 1979:5.
2. Moorehead 1916.
3. Hamlin 1873, 1884.
4. Moorehead actually borrowed the term from a thesis written by Harvard undergraduates Oric Bates and Herbert E. Winlock in 1912.
5. Moorehead 1913:33.

## 1. The Red Paint People, Archaeology, and Me

1. See, e.g., Bourque 1995:225–41.
2. Doyle 1995.
3. Ritchie 1932.
4. Bourque 2001:46–50; Kidder and Sassaman 2009.
5. Stiner et al. 2011:146–250.
6. Ritchie 1968:218–19; Bourque 1995:234–36.
7. Robinson 2001.
8. Figure 3; Sanger 1973.
9. This argument is well summarized in Snow 1980:202–4.
10. Bushnell 1914.
11. Moorehead 1916:359.
12. Bushnell 1915.
13. Moore 1915.
14. Willoughby 1915.
15. Anderson 1991:204.
16. Willoughby 1898:4.
17. Moorehead 1922:150–51.

18. Byers 1959:242.
19. Morlot 1861: 300–1.
20. Bourque, Bruce J. 1971 *Prehistory of the Central Maine Coast.* PhD dissertation, department of Anthropology, Harvard University.
21. Bourque 1995:290–95.
22. Pastore 1987.
23. Erlandson 2001:291, 300–2.
24. Rouse 1958.
25. Anthony 1993.
26. The reader is excused for becoming confused at the inconsistent application of "tradition." Its accepted definition as a long-lasting cultural phenomenon was published by Willey and Phillips in 1956. But there were other definitions of tradition circulating at the time, and though Willey and Phillips did their best to quash them, they remained current for several years.
27. Tuck 1976:101–12.
28. Figure 3.
29. Tuck 1976:103–8.
30. Pauly 1995.
31. Pauly 1995; Pauly et al. 1998.

## 2. The World 4,000 Years Ago

1. Huntington 1915.
2. Diamond 1998.
3. Ibid., 139–41.
4. The origin of the alpaca remains unclear; one possibility includes hybridization between llamas and the wild vicuña.
5. Kadwell et al. 2001; Flannery 1967; Spotorno et al. 2007; Speller et al. 2010.
6. Finucane 2009.
7. Barker 2002; Harris and Gosden 1996; Price 2000.
8. Rosenswig 2006.
9. Boaretto et al. 2009.
10. Cooper 2000.
11. Pool 2007; Roosevelt 1999:318–19; Bourque 2001:76.
12. Haas, Creamer, and Ruiz 2004; Diehl 2004:9–25.
13. Belknap, Gontz, and Kelley 2005.
14. Ibid.

## 3. Discovering the Turner Farm Site

1. Bates and Winlock 1912:78.
2. Archaeological excavation in the 1960s was shifting to the metric system, which is now universal, but because I had borrowed measuring equipment that used British units that first summer, we conducted the entire Turner Farm project using feet and inches.

3. Spiess and Lewis 1995.
4. Purchas 1906.
5. Around forty-five kilograms; Bigelow and Schroeder 2002:182–209.
6. Hadlock 1939:16; Rowe 1940:viii.
7. About 1,200 pounds; Bigelow and Schroeder 2002:510.
8. Jackson et al. 2001; Bourque, Johnson, and Steneck 2007.
9. Kageyama et al. 2006.
10. See, e.g., Lotze et al. 2006.

## 4. Discovering the Moorehead Phase

1. Moorehead 1916:359.
2. Hamlin 1873, 1884.
3. Its full title is *Primitive Industry: or Illustrations of the Handiwork, in Stone, Bone and Clay, of the Native Races of the Northern Atlantic Seaboard of America.*
4. Robinson 2001:307; figures 3 and 4.
5. Ocher? Robinson 2001.
6. Ritchie 1969:215–24; Dincauze 1971:198.
7. Robinson 1985:40–41, 57–58.
8. Moorehead 1922:53.
9. Sanger 1973:97.
10. Willoughby 1898.
11. Roebroeks et al. 2012.
12. Bonnichsen and Jones 1998.
13. Jackson et al. 1863:16–21.
14. Hanson and Sauchuk 1991.
15. Moorehead 1916:362.
16. Moorehead 1922:222–23.
17. King and Foord 1994:184.
18. Fitzhugh 2006:58; Tuck 1976:142, 177.

## 5. Gleaning Information from the Artifacts

1. Moorehead 1916:360.
2. Knoblock 1939.
3. Nuttall 1891.
4. Robinson 2001:161–80.
5. Bourque 1995:235; Robinson 2001:201.
6. Bourque 1995:250.
7. Ibid., 44–46, 304.
8. Byers 1939:245.
9. Ibid., 249.
10. Bourque 1995:46, 49–50.
11. Petersen 1991:108.

12. Douglas and D'Harnoncourt 1941.
13. Wright 1962:135.
14. Knoblock 1939.
15. See, e.g., Harp 1963; MacNeish 1951; Ritchie 1969; Simonsen 1961; Steffian, Saltonstall, and Kopperl 2006:114; Wright 1966.
16. Crowell and Laktonen 2001:166–69; Crowell 1994.
17. Gjessing 1944, 1948; Bryan 1957; Spaulding 1945.
18. Ritchie 1971:37–38.
19. A recent survey of Ramah chert points from Maine has raised this total to fifty-three.
20. Pintal 2006.
21. Blustain, Levesque, and Robinson 1999.
22. Willoughby 1898:21.
23. Hough 1928:517–77; Ritchie 1944:153, 156, 199, 224, 220.
24. Woodrow Thompson, personal communication 2011.
25. Carr and Case 2005:201; Harner 1980:27–31.
26. Carr and Case2005:202.
27. *Dryocopus pileatus*, Byers 1979:40–42; Robinson 2001:375.
28. Werness 2004:438.
29. Shryock and Smail 2011:220.
30. Ibid., 225.
31. Ibid., 17.
32. Byers 1979:28.
33. Ibid., 52–69; figure 30.
34. Bourque 1995:54.
35. Rowley-Conwy 2001:83.

## 6. Parsing the Moorehead Phase

1. Moorehead 1922:127–33.
2. Robinson 2001:183–93, 189–91, 208–9.
3. Sanger 1973.
4. Bourque 1995:34, 38.
5. Figures 40 and 50; Bourque 1995.
6. Cordain et al. 2000:690.
7. Bourque 1995:92.
8. Spiess and Lewis 2001.
9. Ibid., 11–13.
10. Mead, Spiess, and Sobolik 2000; Wozencraft 2005:619.
11. Bourque 1995:91,349.
12. Personal communication 2004.
13. McGhee 1897:386.
14. Lee and Daly 2004:1–4.
15. Lee, Richard B and Irven DeVore 1968 *Man the Hunter*. Chicago, Aldine Publishing Company.

16. Ross and Biagi 1991:229.
17. Ames 2002; Kelly 1995:125.
18. Jackson et al. 2001:631.
19. Bigelow and Schroeder 2002:351–53.
20. Gudger 1940.
21. Gibson 1998:88; Bigelow and Schroeder 2002:351–58.
22. Rich 1947:58–59.
23. Gibson 1998:7.
24. Watanabe 1972:147.
25. Gibson 1998:91; DiMartini 1999:187; ICCAT 1999:4.
26. Gibson 1998:106–10; DiMartini 1999:165.
27. Goode 1883:68-69.
28. Carey 1990:103
29. Gibson 1998:8; Tibbo, Day, and Doucet 1961:13; Bigelow and Schroeder 2002:512; Francklin D'Entremont, personal communication 2011.
30. Bigelow and Schroeder 2002:354
31. Quoted in Goode 1883:35. See also, e.g., Gudger 1940; Günther 1880:432–33; Rich 1947:44–52; Bigelow and Schroeder 2002:351.
32. Ames 2002 Going by Boat: The Forager-Collector Continuum at Sea. In. *Beyond Foraging and Collecting: Evolutionary Change in Hunter-Gatherer Settlement Systems.* Fitzhugh B. and J. Habu, editors. New York, Kluwer/Plenum Press. p. 17–50
33. Bourque 1995:264.
34. Adney and Chapelle 1964:174–211.
35. Champlain 1929:338–39.
36. Fitzhugh and Kaplan 1982:80–81.
37. McGhee and Tuck 1975:76-94, 232–41.
38. Byers 1979:42.
39. Nichols and LaMonte 1937:2–3; Reitz, Andrus, and Sandweiss 2008; Morales-Muñiz and Roselló-Izquierdo 2008.
40. Van Neer, Zohar, and Lernau 2005:145.
41. Niimi 1994; Fukui 1993; Watanabe 1972:146–47.
42. Kusaka et al. 2010:1972; Bourque 1995:140.
43. Arnold and Bernard 2005:116–17; Bernard 2004:44.
44. Byers 1979:42.

## 7. Explaining the Moorehead Phase: Part 1

1. Rich 1947:58–59.
2. Eldridge 2007; Bourque 1995:242.
3. See, e.g., Ames and Maschner 1999; Rowley-Conwy 1983; Koyama and Thomas 1981; Pearson 2007.
4. Ames 2002.
5. Mayewski et al. 2004.
6. Williams et al. 2004; figure 1.

7. Ibid., 313.
8. Broughton and Bayham 2003:784.
9. See, e.g., Sih and Christensen 2000.
10. Anderson and Ethridge 2009:72.
11. Fried 1967:111.
12. Wimsatt 2007:195.
13. Lansing 2002:288.
14. Smith and Bird 2006.
15. Speth, John D. 2010 *The Paleoanthropology and Archaeology of Big-Game Hunting: Protein, Fat or Politics?* New York: Springer.
16. Bird and O'Connell 2006:164–65.
17. Arima and Dewhirst 1990:395.
18. Drucker 1951:49–50.
19. Arima and Dewhirst 1990:395; Renker and Gunther 1990:423; Powell 1990: 431.
20. Davenport, Johnson, and Timbrook 1993.
21. Watanabe 1972:147.
22. Munro 1963:114.
23. Rowley-Conwy 2001:92.
24. See, e.g., Goldstein 1980; Charles 1995.
25. Bourque 1995:244–54.
26. Ames 2002:32.
27. Arima and Dewhirst 1990:395.
28. Prtizker, Barry 2000 *A Native American Encyclopedia: History Culture and Peoples.* New York: Oxford University Press.
29. Crowell and Laktonen 2001:168.
30. Hudson, Timbrooke, and Rempe 1978:39, 152–67.
31. Milner, Buikstra, and Wiant 2009:121.
32. Moorehead 1922; Robinson 2001:304–8.
33. Byers 1979:24.
34. Ames 2002:19–20.
35. Hood 1995; Fitzhugh 2006; Rankin 2008.
36. Rowley-Conwy 2001:79.
37. Jackson et al. 2001; Steneck, Vavrinec, and Leland 2004; Lotze et al. 2006.
38. Roman and Palumbi 2003.
39. Roman and McCarthy 2010.
40. Bertness 1984; see also Lubchenco 1978.
41. Kline and Boyd 2010.
42. Kline, Michelle and Robert Boyd 2010 Population Size Predicts Technological Complexity in Oceanea. *Proceedings of the Royal Society* 277: 2559-2564.

## 8. Explaining the Moorehead Phase: Part 2

1. Lewontin 2000:48.
2. Odling-Smee, Laland, and Feldman 2003:419.

3. Lewontin 2000:48.
4. Odling-Smee, Laland, and Feldman 2003:1–35.
5. Kuhn 1962.
6. Lansing 2009.
7. Lansing 2002:287.
8. Laland and O'Brien 2010:310.
9. Smith 2007:195–96
10. Broughton 2002:60–70.
11. Rowley-Conwy and Layton 2011.
12. Willoughby 1898:4.
13. Ames 2002.
14. Tuck 1978:29.
15. McGhee and Tuck 1975.
16. Ibid.
17. Ibid.
18. Tuck 1976:103–6.
19. Bourque 1995: 234–37.
20. Renouf, M. A. P. and Trevor Bell 2006 Maritime Archaic Site Locations on the Island of Newfoundland. In *The Atlantic of the Far Northeast*, 1-19. Edited by David Sanger and M. A. P. Renouf. Orono: University of Maine Press.
21. See also Pintal 2006:105–38.
22. Nova 1987.
23. Tuck 1978:41–42.
24. Tuck 1978; see also Snow 1980:187–233.
25. Pintal 2006:134; figure 9.
26. Tuck 1982:203.
27. Bourque 1995:225–37; Robinson 2001: 253–71.
28. Bourque 1995:231–34; Renouf and Bell 2011:50.
29. Malinowski 1920.
30. Smail, Stiner, and Earle 2011:224.
31. Malinowski 1920:98.
32. Ibid., 97–98.
33. Jackson et al. 2001.
34. Krech 1999.
35. Bourque 1995:244–52.
36. Trigger 1976, vol. 2:214–18, 220–24.
37. Sanger 1973:136; Robinson 2001:272.
38. Robinson 2001:193–95; Jelsma 2000:30–31.
39. Fitzhugh 2006: 63-65.
40. Nieminen 2010.

## 9. Conclusion

1. Shryock and Smail 2011:7–8.

# Glossary

**B.P.:** stands for before present; a time scale used in archaeology, geology, and other scientific disciplines to specify when events occurred in the past, with 1950 A.D. designated as the origin of the scale.

**CHERT:** a very fine-grained form of microcrystalline quartz that tends to form in massive beds of marine sediment; similar to flint, it is relatively rare and was eagerly sought by some cultures because it flakes easily and possesses a sharp edge; its highly variable coloring is mainly the result of different iron compounds.

**ETHNOGRAPHIC ANALOGY:** a method of interpreting archaeological remains by comparing them to those of historic cultures.

**EXOTIC:** in archaeology, something that originated outside the area under investigation, where it was brought by human activity, such as trade.

**FISHING DOWN MARINE FOOD WEBS:** the result of overfishing where the largest species, such as cod, swordfish, and tuna, are depleted first, resulting in a sequence of targeting ever-smaller species; this process damages the marine ecosystem by reducing its number of trophic levels.

**HUNTER-GATHERER:** a society (or individual) that obtains its livelihood from wild plants and animals, as opposed to agricultural societies, which rely on domesticated species.

**PALEO-ESKIMO:** the peoples who inhabited the coastal Arctic region from eastern Siberia to Greenland between 4500 B.P. and 1500 A.D., when they were replaced by modern Inuit, Eskimo, and other related peoples.

**PARADIGM SHIFT:** a scientific revolution in which older interpretations of the data are replaced by different, more accurate ones.

**PEGMATITE:** an exceptionally coarse-grained igneous rock with large interlocking crystals, often including mica.

**PHASE:** in archaeology, a unit of archaeological analysis used to distinguish what a cultural anthropologist might call a culture; phases are internally similar and differentiable from other phases in time and space.

**PRESTATE:** in archaeology, a society that has not developed the size and social complexity of states.

**PROJECTILE POINT:** an artifact, usually made of stone, that armed a weapon such as an arrow, spear, or lance, or served as the blade of a knife.

**QUARTZITE:** a granular form of quartz formed when water-deposited sand grains have been cemented together by geological heat and pressure; quartzites are often visually appealing and can be flaked more easily than rhyolite.

**RED INDIAN:** also known as the Beothuk, indigenous inhabitants of Newfoundland; hostile relations with Europeans, who arrived in the sixteenth century, caused their extinction as an ethnic group in the early nineteenth century

**RED PAINT CEMETERY:** a term used occasionally to refer to cemeteries in other times and places, but for the purposes of this book, a Red Paint cemetery is a mortuary site of the Moorehead phase containing between one and seventy ocher-filled graves. (See figure 2 for locations of known Red Paint cemeteries.)

**SCALAR CHANGE:** in anthropology, a qualitative change in the size or complexity of a society.

**SHAMAN:** someone with special gifts who can communicate with the spirit world; shamans are especially common and influential in hunter-gatherer societies that lack other kinds of religious specialists.

**SHELL MIDDEN:** large scatters of refuse left behind by prehistoric coastal villages made up mostly of shell, but also charcoal, rock hearths, and a scattering of artifacts, such as spear tips, pottery fragments, and animal bones (*midden* is an ancient Scandinavian and Middle English word for trash heap).

**STRATIGRAPHY:** in geology and archaeology, the study of layers that were laid down sequentially over time such that the older strata lie beneath the younger.

**TROPHIC LEVEL:** a species' position in a food chain, where primary producers such as plants support herbivores, which in turn support carnivores, which in turn support large apex predators.

**TYPOLOGY:** in archaeology, typology is the attempt to classify archaeological objects into clearly defined categories that denote cultural or functional differences.

**UMBO:** in bivalves, the portion of the shell formed when the animal was a juvenile.

**VOUCHER SPECIMEN:** a biological sample with detailed collection data that serves as a record of an individual in time and space.

**ZOOARCHAEOLOGY:** the study of faunal remains from archaeological sites.

# References

Abbott, Charles C. 1881. *Primitive Industry*. Salem, Mass.: Salem Press.

Adney, Edwin Tappan, and Howard I. Chapelle. 1964. *The Bark and Skin Boats of North America*. Bulletin no. 230. Washington, D.C.: Smithsonian Institution Press.

Ames, Kenneth M. 1994. The Northwest Coast: Complex Hunter-Gatherers, Ecology, and Social Evolution. *Annual Review of Anthropology* 23:209–29.

———. 2002. Going by Boat: The Forager-Collector Continuum at Sea. In *Beyond Foraging and Collecting: Evolutionary Change in Hunter-Gatherer Settlement Systems*, 19–52. Edited by Ben Fitzhugh and Junko Habu. New York: Kluwer Academic/Plenum Publishers.

Ames, Kenneth M., and Herbert D. G. Maschner. 1999. *Peoples of the Northwest Coast: Their Archaeology and Prehistory*. New York: Thames and Hudson.

Anderson, Benedict. 1991. *Imagined Communities: Reflections on the Origin and Spread of Nationalism*. London: Verso Press.

Anderson, David G. 1990. The Paleoindian Colonization of Eastern North America: A View from the Southeastern United States. In *Early Paleoindian Economies of Eastern North America*, 163–216. Research in Economic Anthropology, Supplement 5. Edited by Kenneth. B. Tankersley and Barry L. Isaac. Greenwich, Conn.: JAI Press.

Anderson, David G., and Robbie Ethridge. 2009. On Chiefdoms and Other Archaeological Delusions. *Native South* 2:69–73.

Anthony, David. 1993. Migration in Archaeology: The Baby and the Bathwater. *American Anthropologist* 92(4):895–14.

Arima, Eugene, and John Dewhirst. 1990. Nootkans of Vancouver Island. In *Northwest Coast*, 391–11. Edited by Wayne Suttles. Vol. 7 of *Handbook of the North American Indians*. Washington, D.C.: Smithsonian Institution Press.

Arnold, Jeanne E., and Julienne Bernard. 2005. Negotiating the Coasts: Status and the Evolution of Boat Technology in California. *World Archaeology* 37(1):109–31.

Barker, G. 2002. Transitions to Pastoralism and Farming in North Africa. In *Examining the Farming/Language Dispersal Hypothesis*, 151–62. Edited by P. Bellwood and C. Renfrew. Cambridge, Mass.: McDonald Institute Monographs.

Barrett, William K., and John W. Hoopes, eds. 1995. *The Emergence of Pottery: Technology and Innovation in Societies*. Washington, D.C.: Smithsonian Institution Press.

Bates, Oric. 1917. The African Department of the Peabody Museum. *Harvard Graduate Magazine* 25(100):479–85.

Bates, Oric, and Herbert Eustis Winlock. 1912. Archaeological Material from the Maine Littoral, with a Special Reference to the Bates Collection. Typewritten thesis. Department of Anthropology. Cambridge, Mass.: Harvard University Press.

Belknap, Daniel F., Allen M. Gontz, and Joseph T. Kelley. 2005. Calibrating and Updating the Maine Relative Sea-level Curve in a Search for Regional Variations in Crustal Response. *Geological Society of America Abstracts with Programs* 37(1): 6.

Bellwood, Peter. 2005. *First Farmers*. London: Blackwell Publishing.

Bernard, Julienne. 2004. Status and Swordfish: The Origins of Large-Species Fishing among the Chumash. In *Foundations of Chumash Complexity: Perspectives in California Archaeology*, vol. 7, 25–51. Edited by Jeanne E. Arnold. Los Angeles: Cotsen Institute Press.

Bertness, Mark D. 1984. Habitat and Community Modification by an Introduced Herbivorous Snail. *Ecology* 65(2):370–81.

Bigelow, Henry B., and William C. Schroeder. 2002. *Fishes of the Gulf of Maine*. 3rd ed. Edited by Bruce B. Colette and Grace Klein-MacPhee. Washington, D.C.: Smithsonian Institution Press.

Bird, D. W., and J. F. O'Connell. 2006. Behavioral Ecology and Archaeology. *Journal of Archaeological Research*. 14(2):143–88.

Blustain, Malinda S., Margaret A. Lavesque, and Brian S. Robinson. 1999. Two Fossilized Late Archaic Textiles from Maine: Pyrite Pseudomorphs from the Hartford Cemetery Site. *Archaeology of Eastern North America* 27:185–96.

Boaretto, Elizabeth, et al. 2009. Radiocarbon Dating of Charcoal and Bone Collagen Associated with Early Pottery at Yuchanyan Cave, Hunan Province, China. *Proceedings of the National Academy of Sciences*, June 1, 2009.

Bonnichsen, Robson, and Scott Jones. 1998.Anzick Clovis Burial. In *Archaeology of Prehistoric Native America: An Encyclopedia*, 22–23. Edited by Guy Gibbon with Kenneth M. Ames. New York: Garland Publishing.

Borden, Charles E. 1962. West Coast Crossties with Alaska. In Prehistoric Cultural Relations Relations Between the Arctic and Temperate Zones of North America, 9–19. *Arctic Institute of North America Technical Paper*, no. 11. Edited by John M. Campbell. Montreal: Arctic Institute of North America.

Bourque, Bruce J. 1994. Evidence for Prehistoric Exchange on the Maritime Peninsula. In *Prehistoric Exchange Systems in North America*, 23–46. Edited by J. E. Ericson and T. G. Baugh. New York: Plenum Press.

———. 1995.*Diversity and Complexity in Prehistoric Maritime Societies: A Gulf of Maine Perspective*. New York: Plenum Press.

———. 2001 *Twelve Thousand Years: American Indians in Maine*. Lincoln: University of Nebraska Press.

———. 2002Maine Shell Midden Archaeology (1860–1910) and the Influence of Adolphe von Morlot. In *New Perspectives on the Origins of Americanist Archaeology*, 148–63.

Edited by David L. Browman and Stephen Williams. Tuscaloosa: University of Alabama Press.

Bourque, Bruce J., Daniel F. Belknap, and Detmar Schnitker. 1996. Prehistoric Responses to Changes in the Gulf of Maine. Poster session at Gulf of Maine Ecosystem Dynamics: A Symposium and Workshop. September 16–20, 1996. St. Andrews, New Brunswick.

Bourque, Bruce J., Beverly Johnson, and Robert Steneck. 2007. Possible Prehistoric Hunter-Gatherer Impacts on Food Web Structure in the Gulf of Maine. In *Prehistoric Impacts on Marine Ecosystems*, 165–85. Edited by Jon Erlandson and Torbin Rick. Berkeley: University of California Press.

Brew, John O. 1966. *Early Days of the Peabody Museum at Harvard University*. Cambridge, Mass.: Peabody Museum.

Brooks, David A. 1987. The Influence of Warm-core Rings on Slope Water Entering the Gulf of Maine. *Journal of Geophysical Research* 92(C8):81–83.

Brooks, David A., and Wendell S. Brown. 1985. An Overview of the Physical Oceanography of the Gulf of Maine. Summaries of Plennary Session Talks by Invited Speakers, Gulf of Maine Workshop. August 20–22, 1985, Portland.

Broughton, Jack M. 2002. Prey Spatial Structure and Behavior Affect Archaeological Tests of Optimal Foraging Models: Examples from the Emeryville Shellmound Vertebrate Fauna. *World Archaeology* 34 (1):60–83.

Broughton, Jack M., and Frank E. Bayham. 2003. Showing off, Foraging Models, and the Ascendance of Large-Game Hunting in the California Middle Archaic. *American Antiquity* 68(4):783–89.

Browman, David L. 2002a. Frederic Ward Putnam. In *New Perspectives on the Origins of Americanist Archaeology*, 209–41. Edited by David L. Browman and Stephen Williams. Tuscaloosa: University of Alabama Press.

———. 2002b. Origins of Stratigraphic Excavation. In *New Perspectives on the Origins of Americanist Archaeology*, 242–64. Edited by David L. Browman and Stephen Williams. Tuscaloosa: University of Alabama Press.

Bryan, Alan Lyle. 1957. Results and Interpretations of Recent Archaeological Research in Western Washington with Circum-Boreal Implications. *Davidson Journal of Anthropology* 3(1):1–16.

———. 1963. *An Archaeological Survey of Northern Puger Sound*. Idaho State University Museum Occasional Papers, no. 11. Pocatello, Id.: Idaho State University Museum.

Bushnell, David I. Jr. 1914. The "Red-paint People." *American Anthropologist* 15(4): 707–10.

———. 1915. The "Red-paint People"—II. *American Anthropologist* 17(1):207–9.

Byers, Douglas S. 1939. Warren King Moorehead. *American Anthropologist* 41:286–94.

———. 1959. The Eastern Archaic: Some Problems and Hypotheses. *American Antiquity* 42(3):233–56.

———. 1979. *The Nevin Shellheap: Burials and Observations*. Papers of the Robert S. Peabody Foundation for Archaeology. Andover, Mass.: Phillips Academy.

Carey, F. G. 1990. Further Acoustic Telemetry Observations of swordfish. In *Planning the Future of Billfishes: Research and Management in the 90s and Beyond*, Part 2: Contributed Papers, vol. 13, 103–22. Edited by Richard H. Stroud. Savannah, Ga.: National Coalition for Marine Conservation.

Carr, Christopher, and D. Troy Case. 2005. *Gathering Hopewell: Society, Ritual, and Ritual Interaction*. New York: Kluwer Academic/Plenum Publishers.

Champlain, Samuel de. 1929. *The Works of Samuel de Champlain*. Vol. 1 of 6 volumes. Edited by H.P. Biggar. Toronto: The Champlain Society.

Charles, Douglas. 1995. Diaonic Regional Social Dynamics: Mortuary Sites in the Illinois Valley/American Bottom Region. In *Regional Approaches to Mortuary Analysis*, 77–99. Edited by Lane Anderson Beck. New York: Plenum Press.

Charles, Douglas, and Jane E. Buikstra. 1983. Archaic Mortuary Sites in the Central Mississippi Drainage: Distribution, Structure, and Behavioral Implications. In *Archaic Hunters and Gatherers in the American Midwest*, 117–45. Edited by James L. Phillips and James A. Brown. New York: Academic Press.

Clark, Donald. 1980. Relationships of North Pacific and American Arctic Centres of Slate Grinding. *Canadian Journal of Archaeology* 4:27–38.

———. 1982. An Example of Technological Change in Prehistory: The Origin of Regional Ground Slate Industry in South-Central Alaska. *Arctic Anthropology* 19(1):103–25.

Cobb, Charles R., and Michael S. Nasanney. 2002. Domestication Self and Society in the Woodland Southeast. In *The Woodland Southeast*, 525–39. Edited by David G. Anderson and Robert C. Mainfort Jr. Tuscaloosa: University of Alabama Press.

Cooper, Emanuel. 2000. *Ten Thousand Years of Pottery*. Philadelphia: University of Pennsylvania Press.

Cordain, L. et al. 2000. Plant to Animal Subsistence Ratios and Macronutrient Energy Estimations in Worldwide Hunter-Gatherer Diets. *American Journal of Clinical Nutrition* 71:682–92.

Corning, Peter A. 2002. The Re-emergence of "Emergence": A Venerable Concept in Search of a Theory. *Complexity* 7(6):18–30.

Cox, Steven L. 2001. The Paleo-Indian Period. In *Twelve Thousand Years: American Indians in Maine*, 13–36. By Bruce J. Bourque. Lincoln: University of Nebraska Press.

Crowell, Aron. 1994. Koniag Eskimo Poisoned-Dart Whaling. In *Anthropology of the North Pacific Rim*, 217–42. Edited by William W. Fitzhugh and V. Chausssonnet. Washington, D.C.: Smithsonian Institution Press.

Crowell, Aron, and April Laktonen. 2001. Sugucihpet—Our Way of Living. In *Looking Both Ways: Heritage and Identity of the Alutiiq People*, 37–88. Edited by Aron Crowell, Amy F. Steffian, and Gordon L. Pullar. Fairbanks: University of Alaska Press.

Davenport, Demorest, John R. Johnson, and Jan Timbrook. 1993. Chumash and the Swordfish. *Antiquity* 67(255):257–72.

Diamond, Jared. 1998. *Guns, Germs and Steel: The Fates of Human Societies*. New York: W. W. Norton.

DeMartini, Edward. 1999. Stock Structure. In *Proceedings of the Second International Pacific Swordfish Symposium*, 185–95. Edited by Gerard T. DiNardo. NOAA Technical Memorandum NMFS. Honolulu, Hawaii: U.S. Department of Commerce.

Diehl, Richard A. 2004. *The Olmecs: America's First Civilization*. London: Thames and Hudson.

Dincauze, Dina F. 1971. An Archaic Sequence for Southern New England. *American Antiquity* 36(2):194–98.

Douglas, Frederic H., and Rene D'Harnoncourt. 1941. *Indian Art of the United States*. New York: Museum of Modern Art.

Doyle, Robert G. 1995. Appendix 6. In *Diversity and Complexity in Prehistoric Maritime Societies: A Gulf of Maine Prespective*, 317–35. By Bruce J. Bourque. New York: Plenum Press.

Drucker, Philip. 1951. Nootka Whaling. In *The Northern and Central Nootkan Tribes*, 49–53. Smithsonian Institution, Bureau of American Ethnology, Bulletin no. 144. Washington, D.C.: Smithsonian Institution Press.

Durah, William C. 1951. *Powell of the Colorado*. Princeton, N.J.: Princeton University Press.

Eldridge, Stewart. 2007. Archaeology at the Stanley Site, Monhegan Island, Maine: Implications for Modeling Late Archaic Coastal Adaptations. *The Maine Archaeological Society Bulletin* 47(2):1–20.

Emerson, T. E., Dale L. McElrath, and Andrew C. Fortier, eds. 2009. *Archaic Societies: Diversity and Complexity Across the Mid-Continent*. Albany: State University of New York Press.

Erlandson, Jon M. 2001. The Archaeology of Aquatic Adaptations: Paradigms for a New Millennium. *Journal of Archaeological Research* 9(4): 287–350.

Fagan, Brian. 2000. *The Little Ice Age: How Climate Made History*. New York: Basic Books.

Fewkes, Jesse W. 1896. A Prehistoric Shell Heap on Prince Edward Island. *American Antiquarian and Oriental Journal* 18(1):31–34.

Finucane, Brian C. 2009. Maize and Sociopolitical Complexity in the Ayacucho Valley, Peru. *Current Anthropology* 50(4):535–45.

Fitzhugh, William W. 1972. *Environmental Archaeology and Cultural Systems in Hamilton Inlet, Labrador*. Smithsonian Contributions to Anthropology, vol. 16. Washington, D.C.: Smithsonian Institution Scholarly Press.

———. 2006. Settlement, Social and Ceremonial Change in the Labrador Maritime Archaic. In *The Archaic of the Far Northeast*, 47–81. Edited by David Sanger and M. A. P. Renouf. Orono: University of Maine Press.

Fitzhugh, William W., and Susan Kaplan. 1982. *Inua: Spirit World of the Bering Sea Eskimo*. Washington, D.C.: Smithsonian Institution Press, 1982.

Flannery, Kent V. 1967. Vertebrate fauna and hunting practices. *Environment and Subsistence*, 132–77. Edited by Douglas S. Byers. Vol. 1 of *Prehistory of the Tehuacan Valley*. Austin: University of Texas Press.

Fried, Morton. 1967. *The Evolution of Political Society*. New York: Random House.

Fukui, Junichi. 1993. Swordfish Fishing in the Jomon Period on the Pacific Coast in Fukushima Prefecture. *Rissho Koko* 32:77–90.

Gibson, Charles Dana. 1998. *The Broadbill Swordfishery of the Northwest Atlantic: An Economic and Natural History*. Camden, Maine: Ensign Press.

Gimbutas, Marija. 1956. *The Prehistory of Eastern Europe. Part I: Mesolithic, Neolithic and Copper Age Cultures in Russia and the Baltic Area*. American School of Prehistoric Research, Bulletin no. 20. Cambridge, Mass.: Peabody Museum.

———. 1959. Post-Paleolithic Asia in the Territories of the USSR. *Encyclopedia Britannica*, vol. 2:259/O–259/Q.

Gjessing, Gutorm. 1944. The Circumpolar Stone Age. *Acta Artica* 2. Copenhagen.

Goldstein, Lynne Gail. 1980. *Mississippian Mortuary Practices: A Case Study of Two Cemeteries in the Lower Illinois Valley*. Scientific Papers No. 4. Evanston, Ill.: Northwestern University Archaeology Program.

Goode, G. Brown. 1883. Appendix E. In *Materials for a History of the Swordfishes*, 289–367. Extracted from the Annual Report of the Commissioner of Fish and Fisheries for 1880. Washington, D.C.: Government Printing Office.

Green, Jesse, Sharon Weiner Green, and Frank Hamilton Cushing. 1990. *Cushing at Zuni: The Correspondence and Journals of Frank Hamilton Cushing, 1879–1884*. Albuquerque: University of New Mexico Press.

Griesmer, James. 2006. Genetics from an Evolutionary Process Perspective. In *Genes in Development*, 199–237. Edited by Eva M Neumann-Held and Christoph Rehmann-Sutter. Durham, N.C.: Duke University Press.

Gudger, Eugene W. 1940. The Alleged Pugnacity of the Swordfish and the Spearfishes as Shown by Their Attacks of Vessels. *Memoirs of the Royal Asiatic Society of Bengal* 12(2): 215–315.

Günther, Albert. 1880. *An Introduction to the Study of Fishes*. Edinburgh: Adam and Charles Black.

Haas, Jonathan, Winifred Creamer, and Alvaro Ruiz. 2004. Dating the Late Archaic Occupation of the Norte Chico Region in Peru. *Nature* 432(7020):1020–23.

Habu, Junku. 2002. Jomon Collectors and Foragers: Regional Interactions and Long-term Changes in Settlement Systems among Prehistoric Hunter-gatherers in Japan. In *Beyond Foraging and Collecting*, 53–72. Edited by B. Fitzhugh and J. Habu. New York: Kluwer Academic/Plenum Publishers.

Hadlock, Wendell S. 1939. *The Taft's Point Shell Mound at West Gouldsboro, Maine*. Robert Abbe Museum, Bulletin no. 5. Bar Harbor, Maine.

Hamlin, Augustus C. 1873. *The Tourmaline: Its Relation as a Gem*. Boston: James R. Osgood & Co.

———. 1884. *Leisure Hours Among the Gems*. Boston: James R. Osgood & Co.

Hanson, Lindley S., and Scott A. Sauchuk. 1991. *Field guide to the geology and geomorphology of the Carrabassett Formation and economic deposits in central Maine*. Fieldtrip guide for the summer meeting of the Geological Society of Maine. Augusta: Maine Geological Survey.

Harner, Michael. 1980. *The Way of the Shaman: A Guide to Power and Healing*. New York: Harper and Row.

Harp, Elmer Jr. 1963. Evidence of Burial Archaic Culture in Southern Labrador and Newfoundland. *National Museum of Canada Bulletin* 193:184–261.

Harp, Elmer Jr., and David R. Hughes. 1968. Five Prehistoric Burials from Port au Choix, Newfoundland. *Polar Notes* 8:1–47.

Harper, J. Russell. 1956. *Portland Point, Crossroads of New Brunswick History: Preliminary Report of the 1955 Excavations*. Historical Studies no. 9. St. John, New Brunswick: New Brunswick Museum.

Harris, David R., and Chris Gosden. 1996. The beginnings of agriculture in western Central Asia. In *The Origins and Spread in Agriculture and Pastoralism in Eurasia*, 370–89. Edited by David R. Harris. London: UCL Press.

Hobson, R. L., Edward S. Morse, and Rose Sickler Williams. 1914. *Chinese, Corean, and Japanese Potteries: Descriptive Catalogue of Loan Exhibition of Selected Examples*. New York: Japan Society.

Holmes, William H. 1919. *Handbook of Aboriginal American Antiquities. Part 1: Introductory, The Lithic Industries*. Smithsonian Institution Bureau of Ethnology, Bulletin no. 60. Washington, D.C.: Government Printing Office.

Hood, Brian C. 1995. Circumpolar Comparison Revisited: Hunter-Gatherer Complexity in the North Norwegian Stone Age and the Labrador Maritime Archaic. *Arctic Anthropology* 32(2):75–105.

Hough, Walter. 1928. *Fire-making Apparatus in the United States National Museum*. Washington, D.C.: Government Printing Office.

Hovers, E., et al. 2003. An Early Case of Color Symbolism: Ochre Use by Modern Humans in Qafzeh Cave. *Current Anthropology* 44:491.

Hudson, Travid, Janice Timbrook, and Melissa Rempe, eds. 1978. *Tomol: Chumash Watercraft as Described in the Ethnographic Notes of John P. Harrington*. Santa Barbara: Ballena Press.

Huntington, Ellsworth. 1915. *Civilization and Climate*. New Haven, Conn.: Yale University Press.

ICCAT. 1999. *Detailed Report for Swordfish*. ICCAT SCRS Swordfish Stock Assessment Session, Madrid, Spain. September 27 to October 4, 1999.

Ingold, Tim. 1990. An Anthropologist Looks at Biology. *Man* 25(2):208–29.

Jackson, Charles T., et al. 1863. *Katahdin Iron Works, Katahdin, Maine*. Boston: T. R. Holland.

Jackson, Jeremy B. C., et al. 2001. Historical Over fishing and the Recent Collapse of Coastal Ecosystems. *Science* 293:561–748.

Jelsma, Johan. 2000. *A Bed of Ocher: Mortuary Practices and Social Structure of a Maritime Archaic Indian Society at Port au Choix, Newfoundland*. The Netherlands: Rijksuniversitet Groningen.

Kadwell, Miranda, et al. 2001. Genetic Analysis Reveals the Wild Ancestors of the Llama and the Alpaca. *Proceedings of the Royal Society of London, Biology* 268:2575–84.

Kageyama, Mariko, et al. 2006. The Changing Significance and Definition of the Biological Voucher. In *Museum Studies: Perspectives and Innovation*, 257–64. Edited by Stephen L. Williams and Catherine A. Hawks. Washington, D.C.: Society for the Preservation of Natural History Collections.

Kahneman, Daniel, and Amos Tversky. 1979. Prospect Theory: An Analysis of Decision under Risk. *Econometrica* 47:263–91.

Kelly, Robert L. 1995. *The Foraging Spectrum*. Washington, D.C.: Smithsonian Institution Press.

Kidder, Alfred V. 1960. Reminiscences of Southwestern Archaeology. *Kiva* 25(4):1–32.

Kidder, Tristram R., and Kenneth Sassaman. 2009. The View from the Southeast. In *Archaic Societies: Diversity and Complexity Across the Midcontinent*, 667–94. Edited by T. Emerson, D. McElrath, and A. Fortier. Albany: State University of New York Press.

King, Vandall T., and Eugene E. Foord. 1994. *Mineralogy of Maine, Volume 1: Descriptive Mineralogy*. Augusta: Maine Geological Survey.

Knoblock, Byron W. 1939. *Banner-stones of the North American Indian*. LaGrange, Ill.: Published by author.

Koyama, S., and D. H. Thomas, eds. 1981. *Affluent Foragers*. Senri Ethnological Studies 9. Osaka: National Museum of Ethnology.

Krech, Shepard. 1999. *The Ecological Indian: Myth and History*. New York: W. W. Norton.

Kuhn, Thomas. 1962. *The Structure of Scientific Revolutions*. Chicago: University of Chicago Press.

Kusaka, Soichiro, et al. 2010. Carbon and Nitrogen Stable Isotope Analysis on the Diet of Jomon Populations from Two Coastal Regions of Japan. *Journal of Archaeological Science* 37:1968–77.

Laland, Kevin N., and Michael J. O'Brien. 2010. Niche Construction Theory and Archaeology. *Journal of Archaeological Method and Theory* 17:303–22.

Lansing, J. Steven. 2002. "Artificial Societies" and the Social Sciences. *Artificial Life* 8: 279–92.

Lansing, J. Stephen., J. N. Kremer, and B. B. Smuts. 1998. System-Dependent Selection, Ecological Feedback, and the Emergence of Functional Structure in Ecosystems. *Journal of Theoretical Biology* 19:337–91.

Lansing, J. Stephen, et al. 2009. A Robust Budding Model of Balinese Water Temple Networks. *World Archaeology* 41(1):112–33.

Lapham, Increase A. 1855. *The Antiquities of Wisconsin*. Smithsonian Contributions to Knowledge. Washington, D.C.: Smithsonian Institution Press.

Leach, Foss, et al. 1988. Prehistoric Fishing at Mochong, Rota, Mariana Islands. *Man and Culture in Oceania* 4:31–62.

Lee, Richard B., and Richard Daly, eds. 2004. *The Cambridge Encyclopedia of Hunters and Gatherers*. Cambridge, Mass.: Cambridge University Press.

Lee, Richard B., and Irven DeVore, eds. 1976. *Kalahari Hunter-Gatherers: Studies of the !Kung San and their Neighbors*. Cambridge, Mass.: Harvard University Press.

Leighton, Alexander H. 1937. Twilight of the Indian Porpoise Hunters. *Natural History* 40: 410–58.

Lewontin, Richard C. 2000. *The Triple Helix*. Cambridge, Mass.: Harvard University Press.

Lotze, Hieke K., et al. 2006. Depletion, Degradation, and Recovery Potential of Estuaries and Coastal Seas. *Science* 312:1806–09.

Lubchenco, J. 1978. Plant Species Diversity in a Marine Intertidal Community: Importance of Herbivore Food Preference and Competitive Abilities. *American Naturalist* 112:23–29.

Lurie, Edward. 1960. *Louis Agassiz: A Life in Science*. Chicago: University of Chicago Press.

MacArthur, R. H., and E. R. Pianka. 1966. On Optimal Use of a Patchy Environment. *American Naturalist* 100:603–9.

MacNeish, Richard S. 1951. An Archaeological Reconnaisance in the Northwest Territories. *National Museum of Canada Bulletin* 123:24–41.

Malinowski, Bronislaw. 1920. Kula: The Circulating Exchange of Valuables in the Archipelagoes of Eastern New Guinea. *Man* 20:97–105.

Martijn, Charles. 1979 Archaeological Research in Quebec: An Historical Overview. *Man in the Northeast* 18:3–13.

Mayewski, Paul A., et al. 2004. Holocene Climate Variability. *Quaternary Research* 62(3):243–55.

McGhee, Robert, and James A. Tuck. 1975. *An Archaic Sequence from the Strait of Belle Isle, Labrador*. Archaeological Survey of Canada, Mercury Series, No. 34. Ottawa: National Museums of Canada.

McGhee, William J. 1897. Bureau of American Ethnology. In *The Smithsonian Institution, 1846–1896: The History of its First Half Century*, 367–96. Edited by George Brown Goode. City of Washington.

Mead, James, A. E. Spiess, and K. D. Sobolik. 2000. Skeleton of Extinct North American Sea Mink (*Mustela macrodon*). *Quaternary Research* 53:247–26.

Milner, George R., Jane E. Buikstra, and Michael D. Wiant. 2009. Archaic Burial Sites in the American Midcontinent. In *Archaic Societies: Diversity and Complexity Arcoss the Midcontinent,* 115–36. Edited by Thomas E. Emerson, Dale L. McElrath, and Andrew C. Fortier. Albany: State University of New York Press.

Mohr, Albert, and L. L. Sample. 1955. The Religious Importance of the Swordfish in the Santa Barbara Channel Area and Its Possible Implications. *Masterkey* 29(2):62–68.

Moore, Clarence B. 1914. The Red Paint People of Maine. *American Anthropologist* 16:137–39.

———. 1915. The "Red Paint People" II. *American Anthropologist* 17:209.

Moorehead, Warren K. 1913. The Red Paint People of Maine. *American Anthropologist* 15:33–47.

———. 1916. The Problem of the Red-Paint People. In *Holmes Anniversary Volume: Anthropological Essays*, 359–65. Washington, D.C.: J. W. Brian Press.

———. 1920. *Prehistoric Implements: A Reference Book; A Description of Ornaments, Utensils, and Implements of Pre-Columbian Man in America*. Cincinnati: Robert Clarke Co.

———. 1922. *A Report on the Archaeology of Maine*. Andover, Mass.: Andover Press.

Morales-Muñiz, A., and E. Roselló-Izquierdo. 2008. Twenty Thousand Years of Fishing in the Strait: Archaeological Fish and Shellfish Assemblages from Southern Iberia. In *Prehistoric Impacts on Marine Ecosystems*, 245–77. Edited by Jon Erlandson and Torbin Rick. Berkeley: University of California Press.

Morlot, Adolphe von. 1861. General Views on Archaeology. *Annual Report of the Smithsonian Institution for 1860*, 284–43. Washington, D.C.: Government Printing Office.

———. 1863. An Introductory Lecture to the Study of High Antiquity Delivered at the Academy of Lausanne, Switzerland, on the 29th of November, 1860. In *Annual Report of the Smithsonian Institution for 1862*, 303–17. Washington, D.C.: Government Printing Office.

Morse, Edward S. 1879. *Shell Mounds of Omori*. Tokyo: University of Tokio.

———. 1901. *Catalogue of the Morse Collection of Japanese Pottery*. Museum of Fine Arts, Boston. Cambridge, Mass.: Riverside Press.

———. 1925. Shell-mounds and Changes in the Shells Composing Them. *Scientific Monthly* 21:429–40.

Munro, Neal G. 1963. *Ainu Creed and Cult*. New York: Columbia University Press.

Nichols, John T., and Francesca R. LaMonte. 1937. *Notes on Swordfish at Cape Breton, Nova*

*Scotia*. American Museum Novitates No. 901. New York: American Museum of Natural History.

Nieminen, Timo A. 2010. *The Asian War Bow*. In 19th Australian Institute of Physics Congress. ACOFTAOS. Edited by E. Barbiero, P. Hannaford, and D. Moss. Unpaginated. Conference proceedings.

Niimi, Michiko. 1994. Sea Mammal Hunting in Northern Japan During the Jomon Period. *Archaeozoology* 6(2):37–56.

Nova. 1987. *Secrets of the Lost Red Paint People*. Season 15, episode 10.

Nuttall, Zelia. 1891. *The Atlatl or Spear-Thrower of the Ancient Mexicans*. Archaeological and Ethnological Papers of the Peabody Museum, Harvard University, Vol. 1, No. 3. Cambridge, Mass.: Peabody Museum.

Odling-Smee, F. John, Kevin N. Laland, and Marcus W. Feldman. 2003. *Niche Construction: The Neglected Process in Evolution*. Cambridge, Mass.: MIT Press

Ozker, Doreen. 1982. *An Early Woodland Community at the Schultz Site 20SA2 in the Saginaw Valley and the Nature of the Early Woodland Adaptation in the Great Lakes Region*. Museum of Anthropology, Anthropological Papers 70. Ann Arbor: University of Michigan.

Pastore, Ralph T. 1987. Fishermen, Furriers, and Beothuks: The Economy of Extinction. *Man in the Northeast* 33:47–62.

Pauly, Daniel. 1995. Anecdotes and the Shifting Baseline Syndrome of Fisheries. *Trends in Ecology and Evolution* 10(10):430.

Pauly, Daniel, et al. 1998. Fishing Down Marine Food Webs. *Science* 279:860–63.

Pearson, Richard. 2007. Debating Jomon Complexity. *Asian Perspectives* 46(2):361–88.

Petersen, Erik Brinch, and Christopher Meiklejon. 2007. Historical Context of the Term "Complexity" in the South Scandanavian Mesolithic. *Acta Archaeologica* 78(2):181–92.

Petersen, James B. 1991. *Archeological Testing at the Sharrow Site: A Deeply Stratified Early to Late Holocene Cultural Sequence in Central Maine*. Occasional Publications in Maine Archaeology, No. 8. Maine Archaeological Society and Maine Historic Preservation Commission, Augusta.

Phillips, Phillip, James Ford, and James Griffin. 2003. *Archaeological Survey in the Lower Mississippi Alluvial Valley, 1940–1947*. Edited and with an introduction by Stephen Williams. Tuscaloosa: University of Alabama Press.

Pintal, Jean-Yves. 2006. The Archaic Sequence of the St. Lawrence Lower North Shore. In *The Archaic of the Far Northeast*, 105–38. Edited by David Sanger and M. A. P. Renouf. Orono: University of Maine Press.

Pool, Christopher A. 2007. *Olmec Archaeology and Early Mesoamerica*. Cambridge World Archaeology. New York: Cambridge University Press.

Powell, James V. 1990. Quileute. In *Northwest Coast*, 431–37. Edited by Wayne Suttles. Vol. 7 of *Handbook of the North American Indians*. Washington, D.C.: Smithsonian Institution Press.

Price, T. D. 2000. *Europe's First Farmers*. Cambridge, Mass.: Cambridge University Press.

Pringle, Heather. 2008. Did Humans Colonize the World by Boat? *Discover* (June).

Pritzker, Barry. 1999. *A Native American Encyclopedia*. New York: Oxford University Press.

Purchas, Samuel. 1906. English Discoveries and Plantations in New England and Newfoundland. *Hakluytus Posthumus or Purchase His Pilgrimes: Contayning a History of the World in Sea Voyages and Land Travells by Englishmen and others.* Glasgow: James MacLehose and Sons.

Pyke, Graham H. 1984. Optimal Foraging Theory: A Critical Review. *Annual Review of Ecology, Evolution and Systematics* 15: 523–75.

Rankin, Lisa. 2008. Uncaching Hunter-Gatherer Culture in Labrador: From Daily Life to Long-Term History. *North Atlantic Archaeology* 1:117–56.

Reitz, Elizabeth J., C. Fred T. Andrus, and Daniel H. Sandweiss. 2008. Ancient Fisheries and Marine Ecology of Ancient Peru. In *Human Impacts on Ancient Marine Ecosystems: A Globla Perspective*, 125–46. Edited by Torben C. Rick and Jon M. Erlandson. Berkeley: University of California Press.

Renfrew, Colin. 1975. Trade as Action at a Distance: Questions of Integration and Communication. In *Ancient Civilizations and Trade*, 3–59. School of American Research Advances Seminar Series. Edited by Jeremy Sabloff and Carl C. Lamberg-Karlovsky. Albuquerque: University of New Mexico Press.

Renker, Ann M., and Erna Gunther. 1990. Makaah. In *Northwest Coast*, 422–30. Edited by Wayne Suttles. Vol. 7 of *Handbook of the North American Indians.* Washington, D.C.: Smithsonian Institution Press.

Renouf, M. A. P., and Trevor Bell. 2011. Across the Tickle: The Gould Site, Port au Choix-3 and the Maritime Archaic Indian Mortuary Landscape. Chap. 3 in *The Cultural Landscapes of Port au Choix: Precontact Hunter-Gatherers of Northwestern Newfoundland*, 43–63. Edited by M. A. P. Renouf. New York: Springer Science+Business Media.

Rich, Walter H. 1947. *The Swordfish and the Swordfishery of New England.* Portland: Maine Portland Society of Natural History.

Rick, C. Torben, and Jon M. Erlandson. 2008. *Prehistoric Impacts on Marine Ecosystems.* Berkeley: University of California Press.

Ritchie, William A. 1932. *The Lamoka Lake Site: Researches and Transactions of the New York State Archeological Association.* Rochester, N.Y.: Lewis H. Morgan Chapter.

———. 1944. *The Pre-Iroquoian Occupations of New York State.* Rochester, N.Y.: Rochester Museum of Arts and Sciences.

———. 1951. Ground Slates: East and West. *American Antiquity* 43(4): 385–91.

———. 1961. *The Archaeology of New York State.* Harrison, N.Y.: Harbor Hill Books.

_____. 1968. *The Archaeology of Martha's Vineyard: A framework for the prehistory of southern New England.* Garden City, N.Y.: Natural History Press.

———. 1969. *The Archaeology of New York State.* Garden City, N.Y.: Natural History Press.

———. 1971. *New York Projectile Points: A Typology and Nomenclature.* New York State Museum and Science Service Bulletin no. 384. Albany: University of the State of New York.

Ritzenthaler, Robert E., and George I. Quimby. 1962. *The Red Ocher Culture of the Upper Great Lakes and Adjacent Areas.* Fieldiana Anthropology series, vol. 36, no. 11. Chicago: Chicago Natural History Museum.

Robinson, Brian. 1985. The Nelson Island and Seabrook Marsh Sites: Late Archaic, Marine-Oriented People on the Central New England Coast. *Occasional Publications in Northeastern Anthropology* 9:1–104.

———. 2001. *Burial Ritual, Groups and Boundaries on the Gulf of Maine: 8600–3800 B.P.* Ph.D. dissertation, Department of Anthropology, Brown University.

Roebroeks, Will, et al. 2012. Use of Red Ochre by Early Neandertals. *Proceedings of the National Academy of Sciences*. Edited by Richard G. Klein. Published online January 23, 2012.

Rogers, Edward S., and Murray H. Rogers. 1948. Archaeological Reconnaissance of Lakes Mistassini and Albanel, Province of Quebec, 1947. *American Antiquity* 14(2):81–90.

———. 1952. Archaeological Investigations in the Region about Lakes Mistassini and Albanel, Province of Quebec, 1948. *American Antiquity* 15(4):322–37.

Roman, Joe, and James J. McCarthy. 2010. The Whale Pump: Marine Mammals Enhance Productivity in a Coastal Basin. *PLoS ONE* 5(10):e13255. Online: doi:10.1371/journal.pone.0013255.

Roman, Joe, and S. R. Palumbi. 2003. Whales before Whaling in the North Atlantic. *Science* 301:508–10.

Roosevelt, Anna C. 1999. The Maritime, Highland, Forest Dynamic and the Origins of Complex Culture. In *South America*, 264–349. Edited by Frank Salomon and Stuart B. Schwartz. Vol. 3, part 1 of *The Cambridge History of the Native Peoples of America*. Cambridge, Mass.: Cambridge University Press.

Rosenswig, Robert M. 2006. Sedentism and Food Production in Early Complex Societies of the Soconusco, Mexico. *World Archaeology* 38(2):330–55.

Ross, Michael R., and Robert C. Biagi. 1991. *Recreational Fisheries of Coastal New England*. Amherst: University of Massachusetts Press.

Rouse, Irving. 1958. The Inference of Migration from Anthropological Evidence. In *Migrations in New World Culture History*, 63–68. Edited by Raymond H. Thompson. University of Arizona Social Science Bulletin vol. 29, no. 2; Social Science Bulletin. Tucson: University of Arizona Press.

Rowe, John H. 1940. Excavations at the Waterside Shell Heap, Frenchman's Bay, Maine. In *Papers of the Excavators Club*, vol. 1, no. 3. Cambridge, Mass.: Harvard University Press.

Rowley-Conwy, P. 1983. Sedentary Hunters: The Ertebølle Example. In *Hunter-Gatherer Economy in Prehistory*, 111–25. Edited by G. Bailey. Cambridge, Mass.: Cambridge University Press.

———. 2001. Time, Change and the Archaeology of Hunter-Gatherers: How Original Is the "Original Affluent Society"? In *Hunter-gatherers: An Interdisciplinary Perspective*, 39–72. Edited by Catherine Panter-Brick, Robert H. Layton, and Peter Rowley-Conwy. Cambridge, Mass.: Cambridge University Press.

———. 2006. The Concept of Prehistory and the Invention of the Terms "Prehistoric" and "Prehistorian": The Scandinavian Origin, 1833–1850. *European Journal of Archaeology* 9:103–30.

Rowley-Conwy, Peter, and Robert Layton. 2011. Foraging and Farming as Niche Construction: Stable and Unstable Adaptations. *Philosophical Transactions of the Royal Society* (Biology) 366(1566):849–62.

Sahlins, Marshall. 1968. Notes on the Original Affluent Society. In *Man the Hunter*, 85–89. Edited by Richard B. Lee and I. DeVore. New York: Aldine Publishing Company.

Sanger, David. 1973. *Cow Point: An Archaic Cemetery in New Brunswick*. National Museum of Man, Mercury Series Paper No. 12. Ottawa: National Museums of Canada.

Sargent, Winthrop, and Benjamin B. Smith. 1796. *Papers Relative to Certain American Antiquities*. Philadelphia: American Philosophical Society.

Schiffer, Michael B. 1978. Taking the Pulse of Method and Theory in American Archaeology. *American Antiquity* 43(2):153–58.

Schortman, E. M. 1989. Interregional Interaction in Prehistory: The Need for a New Perspective. *American Antiquity* 54:52–66.

Schultz, Emily. 2009. Resolving the Anti-Antievolutionism Dilemma: A Brief for Relational Evolutionary Thinking in Anthropology. *American Anthropologist* 111(3):224–37.

Seeman, Mark F. 1979. *The Hopewell Interaction Sphere: The Evidence for Interregional Trade and Structural Complexity*. Indianapolis: Indiana Historical Society.

Shryrock, Andrew, and Daniel Lord Smail. 2011. Introduction. In *Deep History: The Architecture of Past and Present*, 1–20. Edited by Andrew Shryrock and Daniel Lord Smail. Berkeley: University of California Press.

Sih, Andrew, and Bent Christensen. 2000. Optimal Diet Theory: When Does It Work, and When Does It Fail? *Animal Behaviour* 61:379–90.

Simenstad, Charles A., James A. Estes, and K. W. Kenyon. Aleuts, Sea Otters and Alternate Stable-State Communities. *Science* 200:430–11.

Simonsen, Povl. 1961. *Varanger-Funnene II* (vol. 2.). Tromsø Museums Skrifter series, vol. 7, no. 2. Tromsø; Oslo; Bergen: Universitetsforlaget.

Smail, Daniel L., Mary C. Stiner, and Timothy Earle. 2011. Goods. In *Deep History*, 219–41. Edited by Andrew Shryrock and Daniel L. Smail. Berkeley: University of California Press.

Smith, Bruce D. 2002. *Rivers of Change, Essays on Early Agriculture in Eastern North America*. Washington, D.C.: Smithsonian Institution Press.

________. 2007. Niche Construction and the Behavioral Context of Plant and Animal Domestication. *Evolutionary Anthropology* 16:188–99.

Smith, Bruce D., and Richard A. Yarnell. 2009. Initial Formation of an Indigenous Crop Complex in Eastern North America at 3800 B.P. *Proceedings of the National Academy of Sciences* 11(16):6561–66.

Smith, Eric A., and Rebecca Bleige Bird. 2006. Costly Signaling and Cooperative Behavior. In *Moral Sentiments and Material Interests: The Foundations of Cooperation in Economic Life*, 115–48. Edited by Herbert Gintis, Samuel Bowles, and Robert T. Boyd. Cambridge, Mass.: MIT Press.

Snow, Dean R. 1980. *The Archaeology of New England*. New York: Academic Press.

Spaulding, Albert C. 1945. Northeastern Archaeology and General Trends in the Northern Forest Zone. In *Man in Northeastern North America*, 143–67. Edited by Frederick Johnson. Papers of the Robert S. Peabody Foundation for Archaeology, vol. 3. Andover, Mass.: Phillips Academy.

Speller, Camilla F., et al. 2010. Ancient Mitochondrial DNA Analysis Reveals Complexity of Indigenous North American Turkey Domestication. *Proceedings of the National Academy of Sciences* 107(7):2807–12.

Spiess, Arthur E., and Robert A. Lewis. 1995. Appendix 8: Features and Activity Areas; The

Spatial Analysis of Faunal Remains. In *Diversity and Complexity in Prehistoric Maritime Societies*. By Bruce J. Bourque. New York: Plenum Press.

Spiess, Arthur E., and Robert A. Lewis. 2001. *The Turner Farm Fauna: 5000 Years of Hunting and Fishing in Penobscot Bay*. Maine State Museum and Maine Historic Preservation Commission Occasional Publication in Maine Archaeology No. 11.

Spotorno, Angel E., et al. 2007. Domestication of Guinea Pigs from a Southern Peru: Northern Chile Wild Species and Their Middle Pre-Columbian Mummies. In *The Quintessential Naturalist: Honoring the Life and Legacy of Oliver P. Pearson*, 367–88. Edited by Douglas A. Kelt, et al. Berkeley: University of California Press.

Squier, Ephriam G., and Edwin H. Davis. 1848. *Ancient Monuments of the Mississippi Valley*. Smithsonian Contributions to Knowledge, vol. 1. Washington, D.C.: Smithsonian Institution Press.

Steffian, Amy F., Patrick G. Saltonstall, and Robert E. Kopperl. 2006. Expanding the Kachemak: Surplus Production and the Development of Multi-Season Storage in Alaska's Kodiak Archipelago. *Arctic Anthropology* 43(2):93–129.

Steneck, Robert S. 1998. Human Influences on Coastal Ecosystems: Does Overfishing Create Trophic Cascades? *Trends in Ecology and Evolution* 18:429–30.

Steneck, Robert S., et al. 2002. Kelp Forest Ecosystems, Biodiversity, Stability, Resilience and Future. *Environmental Conservation* 29(4):436–59.

Steneck, Robert S., John Vavrinec, and Amanda V. Leland. 2004. Trophic-level Disfunction in Kelp Forest Ecosystems of the Western North Atlantic. *Ecosystems* 7:523–52.

Steward, Julian H. 1955. *The Theory of Culture Change: the Methodology of Multilinear Evolution*. Urbana: University of Illinois Press.

Stiner, Mary C., et al. 2011. Scale. In *Deep History: The Architecture of Past and Present*, 242–72. Berkeley: University of California Press.

Strauss, Alan E. 1979. *A Study of Prehistoric Swordfishing by Members of the Moorehead Burial Tradition between 4500 and 3700 B.P.: The Exploitation of a Dangerous Resource and its Effects on Social Status and Religion*. Masters thesis, Department of Anthropology, State University of New York at Binghamton.

Stuiver, Minze, and Paula J. Reimer. 1985. A Computer Program for Radiocarbon Age Calculation. *Radiocarbon* 28(2B):1022–30.

Tibbo, S. N., L. R. Day, and W. F. Doucet. 1961. *The Swordfish (Xiphias gladius L.): Its Life History and Economic Importance in the Northwest Atlantic*. Bulletin of the Fisheries Research Board of Canada, no. 130. Ottawa: Fisheries Research Board of Canada.

Trigger, Bruce G. 1976. *The Children of Aataenstic: A History of the Huron People to 1660*. 2 vols. Montreal and London: McGill-Queen's University Press.

———. 1989. *A History of Archaeological Thought*. Cambridge, Mass.: Cambridge University Press.

Tuck, James A. 1970. Port au Choix. *Scientific American* 223(1):112–21

———. 1975. The Northeast Continuum: 8000 Years of Cultural Development in the Far Northeast. *Arctic Anthropology* 12(2):139–47.

———. 1976. An Archaic Cemetery at Port au Choix, Newfoundland. *American Antiquity* 36(3):343–58.

———. 1978. Regional Cultural Development, 3000 to 300 B.C. In *Northeast*, 28-43. Edited by Bruce G. Trigger. Vol. 15 of *Handbook of the North American Indians*. Washington, D.C.: Smithsonian Institution Press.

———. 1982. Prehistoric Archaeology in Atlantic Canada Since 1975. *Canadian Journal of Archaeology* 6:201–18.

Van Neer, W., I. Zohar, and O. Lernau. 2005. The Emergence of Fishing Communities in the Eastern Mediterranean Region: A Survey of Evidence from Pre- and Protohistoric Periods. *Paléorient* 31(1):131–57.

Watanabe, Hitoshi. 1972. *The Ainu Ecosystem: Environment and Group Structure*. Seattle: University of Washington Press.

Werness, Hope B. 2004. *The Continuum Encyclopedia of Animal Symbolism in Art*. New York: Continuum International Publishing Group.

Willey, Gordon R., and Philip Phillips. 1958. *Method and Theory in American Archaeology*. Chicago: University of Chicago Press.

Willey, Gordon R., and Jeremy A. Sabloff. 1993. *A History of American Archaeology*, 3rd ed. New York: W.H. Freeman.

Williams, John W., et al. 2004. Late-Quaternary Vegetation Dynamics in North America: Scaling from Taxa to Biomes. *Ecological Monographs* 74(2):309–44.

Willoughby, Charles C. 1898. *Prehistoric Burial Places in Maine*. Editorial note by F. W. Putnam. Archaeological and Ethnological Papers of the Peabody Museum, Harvard University, vol. 1, no. 6. Cambridge, Mass.: Peabody Museum.

———. 1915. The "Red Paint People" of Maine. *American Anthropologist*, 17:406–9.

Wilson, Daniel. 1865. *Prehistoric Man: Researches into the Origin of Civilisation in the Old and the New World*. 2nd ed. London: MacMillan.

Wimsatt, William C. 2007. *Re-engineering Philosophy for Limited Beings: Piecewise Approximations to Reality*. Cambridge, Mass.: Harvard University Press.

Wolff, Christopher, Robert J. Speakman, and William W. Fitzhugh. 2012. *Assessment of Portable X-ray Fluorescence Analysis for the Evaluation of Slate Procurement and Exchange: A Maritime Archaic Case Study from Newfoundland and Labrador. In press.*

Worm, Boris M., and Ransom A. Myers. 2003. Meta Analysis of Cod-Shrimp Interactions Reveals Top-down Control in Oceanic Food Webs. *Ecology* 84(1):162–73.

Wozencraft, W. C. 2005. Order Carnivora. In *Mammal Species of the World: A Taxonomic and Geographic Reference*, 532–628. 3rd ed. Edited by D. E. Wilson and D. M. Reeder. Washington, D.C.: Smithsonian Institution Press.

Wright, James V. 1962. *A Distributional Study of Some Archaic Traits in Southern Ontario*, Bulletin no. 80. Ottawa: National Museum of Canada.

———. 1966. *Prehistory of Hudson Bay, Boreal Forest*. Ottawa: National Museum of Canada.

# Index

**W**



**X**



**Z**